JUST LIKE YESTERDAY

Some other books by León Ó Broin

Parnell
Emmet
Miss Crookshank agus coirp eile
An Maidíneach

The Unfortunate Mr Robert Emmet
Dublin Castle and the 1916 Rising
Charles Gavan Duffy
The Chief Secretary
Fenian Fever
The Prime Informer
No Man's Man
Revolutionary Underground
Michael Collins
Frank Duff
In Great Haste
Protestant Nationalists in Revolutionary Ireland

Just Like Yesterday

an autobiography

León Ó Broin

Gill and Macmillan

Published in Ireland by
Gill and Macmillan Ltd
Goldenbridge
Dublin 8
with associated companies in
Auckland, Dallas, Delhi, Hong Kong,
Johannesburg, Lagos, London, Manzini,
Melbourne, Nairobi, New York, Singapore,
Tokyo, Washington

5 4 3 2 1
0 7171 1431 7
Print origination in Ireland by Galaxy Reproductions Ltd
Printed in Great Britain by
Richard Clay (The Chaucer Press) Ltd, Bungay, Suffolk.

CONTENTS

ONE

IT WAS just like yesterday. I was in Stephen's Green and Lily, the girl who was supposed to be looking after me, was sitting on a bench engrossed in a yellow back romance. It must have been very good, for she did not notice me toddling out of the Green, up Harcourt Street and on to Portobello Bridge where, finding nobody I knew in the crowd around me, I yelled my head off. That night my anxious parents found me in Lad Lane police station. I was asleep with a slate and cutter to write with before me. I had had biscuits to eat and sips of porter to drink; and I can hardly have been more than two years old. A year later perhaps I was sitting on a gallery in a school room wearing something like a turban made of bandages with nuns fussing about me. The day before, in a laneway on my way home, an Italian fellow had picked up a pig's cheekbone and skeeted it in my direction. By ill-luck rather than skill, I imagine, he hit me across the forehead and sent me home in a welter of blood. But there was recompense afterwards in his father's ice cream saloon. What about a cut forehead when one is a celebrity?

I stayed with the nuns until I was thirteen. It was a happy school in which the important things in our little lives were kept before our eyes. The Sisters led us into our first Confession and first Holy Communion and saw to it that we were confirmed by the great if physically undistinguished figure, Willie Walsh. I remember that occasion so clearly: the packed vastness of the church, the monotony of the long wait for the archbishop to reach me, which was broken when my mother's sister Katty Anne somehow worked her way through the crowd to place a bag of cream buns on my lap. The school had a rough edge to it, however. One day in the tiny yard during the lunch break I saw two fellows stripped to the waist knocking skelps out of each other. It took a world war to civilise fellows like that, but meanwhile little Sister Mary de Ricci did her best with her leather strap. By the middle of 1913, when I was in a class half-way up the school, the shadow of Jim Larkin fell across us. The boy sitting beside me, Hopkins, was the son of a Larkinite member of the Dublin Corporation; there were others affected as he was by the great strike in the city and together some of them decided to stage a walk out. This form of striking did not last long. Sister de Ricci went out after them and drove them back to their classes. The odds seemed to me to be so unequal. Some of the bruisers I have been describing, had they been so disposed, could have lifted this veiled black and white figure on their shoulders and carried her a mile without feeling her weight; but to them I suppose Sister de Ricci represented something untouchable. I was not involved in the demonstration anyhow, and hardly knew of it before it was over; but outside the school one day I struck a blow for Larkin none the less.

I saw a police inspector using his walking stick to break up a crowd of tramwaymen who were marching towards Liberty Hall in what I considered was an orderly fashion. He struck a man in the front row and was about to strike another when something came over me. I bent down and, picking up a stone that lay handy in the gutter, I threw it at the inspector. I was always a rotten shot, but some devil or other directed this one, and it hit him on the shoulder. I started to run, shouting 'I didn't do it' as two plain-clothes bobbies chased after me. When I had done about half a mile I looked back; they were still after me; I did not dare to look back again until I was exhausted. They were gone by then. I did not go home until late evening and actually crossed to the north wall of the river by ferry before making a long and leisurely detour homewards. From that performance you can judge that we had a very healthy respect for the Dublin police who were more than able to look after themselves in tough situations. That remained the case until Michael Collins came on the scene.

Some of the fellows I knew had a sort of natural dislike for the Dublin police, the D.M.P. They inveigled them into dark halls to fall over dustbins that had been piled up ready for them. And when a company of R.I.C. men made their first appearance at the end of the street during the labour troubles, and foolishly stood with their backs to sunlit shops the lads shattered the windows behind them with a hail of stones. In those days the Dublin police had a section on horseback, and my recollection of the first Bloody Sunday was not of Larkin's appearance in disguise on a balcony of the Imperial Hotel – I only heard of that – but of the slops that were poured down on the mounted police from back street tenements.

It was inevitable, I suppose, that sooner or later somebody like Larkin would arise to confront the appalling industrial conditions in the city. Workers were grossly underpaid and on all sides – even among the families of men who were regularly employed – there were signs of poverty and deprivation: ugly tenements, barefooted children, and a trek every Monday morning to the pawn shops. Nevertheless, people divided over Larkin. Nothing was too bad to say of him; he was even accused of being a son of Carey, the man who betrayed the Invincibles. My mother and I, however, took delight in his wild speeches and flaying arms, and from his burning of the proclamations of Dublin Castle; but we enjoyed rather less the baton charges that nearly always seemed to follow. Our family were not directly caught up in the strike; my father had a steady job as a bookkeeper with a potato factor; but my mother's mother and a nephew who lived with her were involved because the nephew was on strike and, as I used to run messages for them, I found myself one day taking a jug of soup back to where they lived from a soup kitchen in Liberty Hall, and on another day collecting a sack full of foodstuffs from a warehouse on the quays. This was being stacked from a ship alongside that had been sent over by the English trade unions.

The strike disturbed the nuns greatly. And they became particularly unhappy when word went round that Larkin was sending children to England, where they would be housed and fed but where the nuns believed their Catholic faith would be at risk. The nuns could see the hunger in the faces of some of their pupils, and tried to cope with it by giving the whole school a meal every day of lovely fresh currant buns and hot cocoa.

Larkin was a great man to start strikes but not so good at settling them. And he lost friends faster than he made them. By February 1914 the strike, which had developed into an employers' lock-out, was over, and people's minds turned once more to the old subject of home rule and the Ulster opposition to it. Then the gun-running began and on a Sunday afternoon my older brother, Paddy, arrived home with a couple of Mauser rifles he had got that day at Howth. They were huge things, and so heavy that I had to prop one of them up on the back of a chair to look down the barrel. I followed Paddy into the Fianna and attended gatherings in a hall in Camden Street for a time. I also went out on a route march to the Dublin hills. But I tired of forming fours and all that sort of nonsense, and never returned to it. What I did like was to read a story by a man called Pearse, about a Fianna man or Fenian of another time who was known as the Wandering Hawk.

Wars seemed to be never far off. The newspapers that came into our house spoke unceasingly of tumult in the Balkans which I tried desperately but unsuccessfully to understand. Then the World War came and Ireland, a small island in the western seas, was caught up in it. I stood at the bottom of a densely crowded Grafton Street which was festooned with Union Jacks and witnessed a seemingly endless stream of soldiers on their way to the battlefields where so many of them would face disillusion. A sort of madness spread among young men. This was something they felt they should be in before it was over, because it might not last until Christmas. The fellows I had seen boxing in the school yard went off, but others I knew who seemed to be more balanced went off, too. One evening, in response to a knock, I opened the door to a young fellow in the glittering uniform of the 5th Hussars. He came from a family with close Fenian ties and was related to my mother somehow. He was now in all his innocence on his way to the front to fight for little Belgium. He was a Dundalk boy, and did not know the city. I, then eleven, took him over. We walked to Nelson Pillar, up Henry Street, and into the Waxworks, a house of entertainment. I have no recollection of what the show was like. When it was over I walked him back to the Pillar, put him on a tram to Portobello Barracks, and bid him good-bye. No one ever saw him again. He went into the battle of Mons, where the British Expeditionary Force fired its first shots, and died. He became just a digit in the list of dead, wounded, and missing that got longer and longer every day. That Christmas passed, and others, and the war went on.

I remember the preparation for the periodical religious examinations, the nuns insisting, presumably because the diocesan examiners did, that we should get the answers in the penny catechism and some other things off by heart. On examination day we were marched in single file into the heart of the convent, up flights of stairs, and then led, one by one, into the room where the priest, the examiner, sat. He was by no means the ogre that had been presented to us; and from a colleague of his I received the first prize I ever won, not that there were to be many of those. It was a huge turnip of a watch he had offered to the school for an essay on the Mass. I am sure that the watch did not cost very much, but Father MacMahon – I think that was his name – praised it at such length that I was very proud of it the day I took it home and showed it to the family. Unfortunately, I took Father McMahon's commendation of it too seriously. He had said that it was waterproof: if I dropped it into the Liffey no harm would befall it. I did not drop it into the Liffey; I knew how difficult it would be to fish it out again, but I did introduce it to a basin of water which did it no good at all.

As I reached the top class I found myself spending a great deal of my time singing. I must have had a moderately good voice, was in the Church choir, and whenever benediction was to follow the 11 o'clock Mass, I was sent down to the Church where, usually alone, I sang the service hymns, but with no feelings that corresponded to the majestic words I was uttering. There was music in the school itself on Friday afternoons and occasionally I was asked by Sister Mary Catherine, a formidable member of the community who could use the pointer when some vagabond had her strap, to sing the song that she herself had taught me, 'The Little Shirt my Mother Made For Me'. Looking back I can hardly give Sister Mary Catherine a high mark for taste; she thought the piece very good and funny, and so apparently did the school. In time I was to achieve greater musical prominence. There was a public concert in the local hall and I was to sing the Bach-Gounod 'Ave Maria' with Leonard Shanahan, the church organist, at the piano and a distinguished violinist to play an obligato. The intention was excellent, but my performance was dismal. I had been standing round in the wings all the afternoon waiting to go on, and when I did, tired, parched, and a bag of nerves, I sang without feeling and made a screeching mess of the final high note. I was never put in that sort of situation again.

We were, I suppose, a united family, but we seemed to act very independently of each other. We took our meals more or less together – or roughly at the same time – but of conversation there was little or none. My father, soon after he took his tea, went over to the church building to work there until within an hour or so of going to bed. He was there on Saturday afternoons too, writing letters and making entries in the huge ledgers of the Confraternity of which he was the Secretary.

On Sunday mornings some old cronies would drop in to my father's office for a chat and I often joined them there, mainly to listen. My godfather, James Devlin, would come sometimes, and, though I barely remember him, I knew that politically he was an Irish Party man and worked as an agent for James Brady, the local M.P. who many years later I would come to know fairly intimately through the St Vincent de Paul Society. My father did not share Devlin's political opinions but how they differed had to be gauged or surmised. Father did not say very much anyhow. He was at heart a Griffithite Sinn Féiner, bought Griffith's papers, was accepted as one of their own by men like Tom Shine Cuffe, Sean Fitzgibbon, and Paidin O'Keeffe, and sent us to Irish language classes that were held under Sinn Féin auspices. I believe a man who sat near me at a class I attended just once in a room over a shop in O'Connell Street was Griffith himself; and I remember, only too well, another occasion when a class in a backroom off Dame Street was interrupted while the teacher ejected a number of young fellows, somewhat older than myself, whose laughter and jeers had got out of control. This was a Dublin reaction to hearing those funny guttural Irish sounds and being asked to reproduce them.

A man I frequently saw in my father's office was a Schools Attendance Officer. He, without learning more than a few words of Irish, was an enthusiastic Gaelic Leaguer, and insisted on using them on me on every occasion. He even tried to teach me Irish step-dancing. He was well-intentioned, of course, but a man to keep away from. Like my father, he was a member of the Confraternity and for some special occasion would 'dress' in the Confraternity habit and scapular and join the community of priests on the high altar in the church. He was among the very first male members of what in time became the Legion of Mary and went out with the women in a protecting capacity when they made their first sorties among the prostitutes of the city.

I put together having my hair done by the nuns and my first contacts with the Irish language. I had a quiff, a stray piece of hair over my forehead that was always out of control. Its appearance must have provoked the nuns, and one of them decided to do something about it. She kept a brush and comb specially for me and in the afternoon, before the school broke up, she would take me into the hall outside the main schoolroom and 'operate' on me. This, I'm afraid, became something of a joke in the community. One day, while the cosmetic exercise was in progress, a nun I had not seen before came on the scene and was introduced to me as being from the West of Ireland. She knew Irish, I was told, and was what I would know later to be a native speaker. It was probably then that I understood that there was an area of the country which produced people with the strange-sounding language that left the Dublin Jackeens in stitches when they heard it.

My mother rarely left the house save to go to church. With a husband and four children she had plenty to do, and did it with no fuss whatever. She was a good provider, and out of my father's salary, which was never great, she even managed to save a little money. She paid her nursing expenses when she was old and ill, and after her death there was something left over. She followed my father's thinking, I imagine, in most things. She dressed us in clothes she bought at a Sinn Féin centre in South William Street that was run by Alderman Tom Kelly, who, with Willie Cosgrave, led for Sinn Féin in the Dublin Corporation; and I remember being brought by my father to Winstanley's in Back Lane when I needed a new pair of boots. They would be Irish-made, of course. The principle, taken from Dean Swift, was: burn everything English except her coal. That, of course, could not always be applied. More than once on a Saturday night my mother sent me to Lipton's in Dame Street to buy a piece of the slab cake we all enjoyed at tea on Sundays, and I was not to tell where it came from.

She also differed from my father in what he would have regarded as an important respect. He wore the pin, that is to say he was a teetotaller: she was not, until well into her middle years. I remember being surprised to notice that whenever Mary O'Brien, her bridesmaid, came to visit her – it was not very often – she prepared a coddle of bacon and potatoes which set up a smell that filled the house with delight, and drank a glass of stout.

There was some little estrangement between my mother and her own mother. At any rate she rarely went to see her, though through Lily, the young lady who had allowed me as a child to wander out of the Green, she maintained a daily link. And it was most unusual for me not to see my grandmother every Saturday. I have often wondered what kept my mother from going to see her mother who, because of some ailment, never left her room. Neither of them ever spoke to me about the subject; and perhaps I, in my old age, am making too much of it. A marriage had broken up. My mother remembered tearfully meeting her father, by arrangement, somewhere in the town, of being entertained by him, and then a sad parting. A seaman, he had ceased coming home; and Granny for some reason did not want to see him. After his death – when and where, I don't know – a message was said to have come from the Custom House inviting her to come about something affecting him, but she ignored it.

In our family, in which I saw my father infrequently and where my mother was always around, there were beside myself, my three brothers. The eldest of these who was two or three years older than me, I saw very rarely. He was attending a vocational school in Ringsend and to get there had to leave early in the morning; and, especially if the bridge over the basin was closed, he would get home quite late. He was doing something that must have been quite unusual for that time: completing the study of subjects, notably mathematics, he had done in the convent school. On finishing at Ringsend he became apprenticed for five years as an electrician but when his time was up there were no jobs in that field and the army was the only alternative to continuous unemployment. So he, potentially the best mind in the family and in a sense the best educated, was a failure. As I say, I did not see much of him. Most of his spare time interests were not mine. He drifted towards the Fianna, was known to us to go to Madame Markievicz's house occasionally, brought home a picture she had painted and put it up over the fireplace in the 'boys' bedroom.

The great war continued through 1915, and more and more men were needed to fill the gaps caused by the enormous casualties. As a region of disaster the Dardanelles was added to France and Flanders. Allowances were, of course, paid to soldiers' wives, which enabled some women to have what might later on be called 'a good war'. I saw a couple of them one afternoon lying in the gutter in Golden Lane tearing each other to pieces, an awesome sight. While their men risked their lives in the trenches, they drank their heads off in the Dublin pubs. Simultaneously the Volunteers, both those who would be called Sinn Féiners and the Redmondites, came together to do honour to the old Fenian, O'Donovan Rossa, before parting company for ever. My father, who was not a soldiering man, turned out in his hard hat for the funeral of Rossa, and wore an arm band which my mother kept and gave to a grandchild. Apart from getting into the crowded City Hall to sell flags for the Fianna at Rossa's bier I remember nothing affecting myself from that year or from the early months of 1916. On a night in that Holy Week, however, I took a message from my father to a Volunteer meeting in No. 2 Dawson Street, the headquarters of the Volunteer Executive, and on another day became aware that he was flush with money and bought a lot of military hardware from Lawlor's of Fownes Street which was to be stored in a dump in Long Lane. This pointed to something bigger than the general mobilisation and march-out that was announced for Easter Sunday. On that day there appeared in the *Sunday Independent* a notice in bold type from Eoin MacNeill, the President and Chief of Staff of the Volunteers, which was intended to scotch plans for a Rising that had been made behind his back. My father accepted the countermand, and I could feel a sense of relief spreading through the house. On Easter Monday morning early the relief continued, but was suddenly replaced by confusion and gloom. A young man had arrived and spoken to my father as he lay in bed. I gathered from what my brother Paddy and I were told to do that somebody had decided that the earlier arrangements for the Sunday were to be enforced. Paddy was to hurry to the northside and call out a horse and cart my father had engaged to remove stuff from the dump; I was to go to an address on the southside and speak to a man who had promised the use of his new Ford van. Paddy was successful; I was not. My man was very nice, but he needed the van himself that day to take the family to the races at Fairyhouse. That was that. I brought back the story which added to the confusion and, later, saw my father and Paddy going off together. I did not see either of them for many days.

By that Monday afternoon a rebellion – that was the word everybody used – was under way and I saw the first results of it as a queue of men, women and children came into the street carrying various objects home that they had looted downtown. Next morning my mother was anxious about my brother James, who was two or three years younger than me. He had gone camping to Killiney with school friends, the Martins, for the weekend. Was he safe? Could not I go and find him? I made my way by the back streets to where the Martins lived; they were caretakers of an Insurance Office in Trinity Street at the intersection with St Andrew Street and had a flat at the top of a tall building. The campers had just arrived before me, when an unmerciful burst of gunfire erupted around us. The firing came from Trinity College which was only a few yards away and was aimed in the direction of the City Hall at the other end of Dame Street, which was occupied by the rebels. Things got so bad that we all moved into a corridor and sat down on the floor. Even then we were not safe. Some bullets came through the walls, one just avoiding the Martins' grandmother who was in bed in a room near us. We remained there until the firing ceased; then James and I made our way to the street. We were immediately called upon by a couple of soldiers in khaki to halt and to put our hands up. These were Dublin Fusiliers and as they covered us with their rifles, they wanted to know who we were and what we'd been doing in that building. We told them; they let us go; and James and I went home, again using the back streets. Needless to say, my mother and Lily were greatly relieved to see us. They had heard the firing and were understandably worried. When Lily heard our account of the bullets coming into the Martins' flat, she immediately thought of a sideboard of her own. She was going to be married and was keeping this sideboard with a glass back to it in our drawing room. It was intended to be the centrepiece of her new home, and she feared dreadfully for its welfare. She left us, and when she returned she had a plank which she placed across the glass back of her sideboard, fancifully hoping it would save the glass from a stray bullet. That, and drawn shutters, left us in a condition of siege.

Next day I made another sortie – this time in search of food. Keeping to the back streets again, I managed to get a couple of chops, some bread, and a stone of potatoes. That would keep us going for a while I thought. Meanwhile my mother had been called to help a neighbour whose time to deliver a baby had come. It was a difficult business apparently and, as neither a nurse nor a doctor could be got, my mother had to leave us to our own devices for long stretches over the next few days. The woman's husband, an army sergeant, had been given compassionate leave for the event and was in and out of his home in civvies. I didn't know why, but he had a revolver which he produced towards the end of the week to deal with a threatening mob.

So it was until Saturday. Confined to the house, we were increasingly alarmed by occasional shots from the soldiers who had taken up a position at the end of the street. The British Army was obviously in total command of the situation; and at night we could see from an upper back window a reddening sky which could only mean that buildings occupied by Volunteers in the city centre were in flames. Mother must have started to think of the likelihood that the house would be searched by the police and military when the end came, and plotted how to get rid of telltale evidence. Some associates of my father came one night and took away some trench tools that had been bought the previous week; and, on the Saturday morning, just after daybreak, she put on an apron, filled it with cartridges which some of her mother's friends had brought home as souvenirs of the Boer War, and went with me into the street. We sneaked down to a nearby laneway in our bare feet to avoid being heard, lifted the shore and she spilled the cartridges down into the drain. We sneaked back unobserved, and I can't remember that then or ever after we talked about what we had done.

The nuns made it known to my parents that year that I had out-grown my stay with them and that they should begin to think of my future. They did so, and no other alternative appearing possible, I went with my father to the nearest Brothers' school and, after a brief interview with the Superior, I was introduced to the Fifth, a preparatory stage in the Intermediate system. I was ill-mannered enough to leave the nuns without saying 'thank you' or bidding them good-bye.

The Brothers' regime was markedly different from what I had hitherto known. The teachers were, of course, all men, two out of three of them Brothers. There were three classes in the Fifth, and I suppose it was either a tribute to what I had picked up from the nuns or a pointer to the fact that I should have left them earlier that I was put into the first class. I adjusted quickly to the change of environment, and had no trouble at all with Irish and French, subjects I had not done before. Like everything else on the curriculum these were well taught. I took to Irish with genuine avidity – perhaps the developing national spirit had something to do with it – and I have the kindliest recollection of how an old brother we called the Golly introduced us to French. His insistence that we should pronounce it properly produced some suppressed snivelling but the point of what he was up to was obvious, and I carried everything he told us into all my subsequent efforts with languages generally.

The lay teacher was quietly impressive too, though he had an ugly habit, as he stood at the blackboard, of picking at a sore on his face, a touch perhaps of what was called the King's Evil. The Brother in charge of the school was a splendid specimen of manhood. He must have been inches over 6 feet tall, was built proportionately, and was good looking.

A kind man, too, he moved about the room quietly when he was not teaching, and yet had only to glance to impress his authority. This was particularly noticeable on Friday afternoons when we had singing for an hour. The lay teacher who came in to do this with us took us through the tonic solfa scales, and taught us a few operatic choruses, one of which had a motto that has stuck in my mind: 'Happy are those who in each other's faith repose.' For an hour or so each week we went across the yard to a carpentry or woodworking class. The teacher, a Mr O'Callaghan, was a charmer, and the class, with a couple of exceptions, made great progress under him. I was one of the exceptions as Mr O'Callaghan made known at the end of the year. In a little farewell speech he thanked us for our attention and achievements. But 'in fairness to you and myself,' he thought he had to mark how far another boy and I had fallen below the standard and had carelessly blunted some of his instruments: so he gave us both a couple of slaps with his steel rule. The physical pain was nothing to my sense of disappointment with Mr O'Callaghan. I had not failed to pay attention: I just had not got what it takes to make an elementary woodworker, or elementary anything that might be useful in the home. Afterwards, whenever anything practical had to be done, it was made clear to me that it would be just as well if I made myself scarce.

The first year with the Brothers passed quickly; and when the summer came I went for a fortnight to the Connacht Summer College of Irish in Spiddal. A fortnight was a very short time in which to acquire much of the language, but it was all my father could afford. Indeed I don't know how he managed even that. With the war still running, railway fares were high, and my father was never over-paid in his clerking job. However, he saw that the Irish language was taking a hold on me, and somehow put together a few pounds while I studied the prospectuses of the summer colleges which were all located in what nowadays would be recognised as tourist areas. Would I go to Ballingeary or Ballinskelligs or Carigaholt – with my Brothers background and their *Aids to Irish Composition* I should have gone to one of these – but I was drawn to the West, and there it was a choice between Spiddal in Galway or Tourmakeady in Mayo, and I chose Spiddal. It was a good choice for, in the years since, Irish has survived better there than it has done in most other Gaeltacht areas. In 1917 it appeared to be fantastically strong; though of course I was by no means a competent judge. My knowledge of the language was minimal. Before I boarded the train to Galway at the old Broadstone it was confined to about a third of the *Aids* which in a sense was an odd book in that you could work quite a distance through it before encountering one of the verbs to be, the *is* verb. On the train I looked at a phrase book I had found in the local public library; but, really, neither *Aids* nor the phrase book seemed to bear any relationship to the language I heard when I got to Spiddal.

The journey to the West was an intriguing experience for a Dublin lad. The train was packed with excursionists, and from Ballinasloe onwards I could see I was entering a new world. The stone-wall landscape was so utterly new to me; but so were the men and women who began to join the train. They wore homespuns and shawls, and many of them spoke what I assumed to be Irish. Some of it might have been English, but I simply could not distinguish the accents. At Galway, a very noisy station, I got a seat on a jaunting car alongside a pious publican from the northside of Dublin who had come down to the West for the day, and paid five shillings as I did for the run out to Spiddal, a matter of ten miles or so. The driver knew Irish but showed no enthusiasm to speak it; I don't blame him, for, if anything, the publican knew less Irish than I did, but insisted on trying to converse in it.

Night was falling by the time I was installed in a thatched cottage in the townland of Sheeaun, high up on the hillside, with views on Galway Bay, the hills of Clare and the Aran Islands. The islands were not always visible: it was said of them, as no doubt of many other places, that when you could see them it was going to rain, and when you couldn't it was raining. After a meal, I sat by the open turf fire in the kitchen to listen, without at all understanding, to what the family and the neighbours who drifted in were talking about. The family consisted of Peadar Clancy and his wife Maire Mhichil, both of them in their eighties, a couple of sons, Pete and John, and a daughter Mag; Pete and Mag were on in years. I was plied with question which I could not even begin to answer; but I don't think I deprived them of any information they had not already received from the lady from the College who had brought me to the house and introduced me. Everything that night was so strange: I had not expected anything like it. The features of the persons around me, the bare-footed women, the homespun clothes, the fire on the hearth, the half-light, and above all the incomprehensible language. It made me think at times that I was somewhere in the Iberian Peninsula.

Next morning in the College I entered another world that was outside my experience. Here were grown men and women, grouping themselves round blackboards in the open air. Among them a few young people like myself, and some clerics, notably Fr MacAlinney, the active parish priest of Spiddal. Most of the students were schoolteachers who had come to learn Irish in order to teach it themselves, for at that time Irish could be taught in the government-financed 'national' schools. These pioneering teacher-students were no less enthusiastic than non-teachers like myself. We had no interest in acquiring a certificate of competency to teach Irish, we just wanted to learn Irish for its own sake while simultaneously enjoying ourselves. A few students from the midlands who may have been Volunteers camped out in the college park and poked fun at the peelers in the village. On the night de Valera was elected across the bay in Clare they lit a bonfire. I found the atmosphere totally diverting and was especially happy in the company of the college professors who, with hardly an exception, were splendid teachers and good sorts. Most of them were native speakers; and they formed a bridge for me with the people of Sheeaun, but they also made clearer the gap I had begun to discern between the vernacular and the Irish of the books.

In those couple of weeks in that summer college I made the acquaintance of one of P. H. Pearse's collection of short stories – *Iosagán* – and don't mind confessing that it exercised a spell over me. Pearse had died before a firing squad recently, and that may have had something to do with it. That the stories were drawn out of Pearse's idealised concept of that fringe of Connemara added a charm to which I easily succumbed. I did not see then, as later I did, that they were over-sentimental, and even effeminate; and of course, there were other aspects of life in that part of the world of stone walls beside the western sea that Pearse did not touch upon, if he had noticed them at all. Women, for instance, lived lives of extraordinary drudgery; if they were married they produced a child every year, while toiling inside and around the house and working on the fragmented holdings. That, no doubt, was common enough elsewhere but, in the area of which I am speaking, women had to suffer other enormities as well. Two pictures stand out in my mind: one from springtime, of a sensitive mother of a large family I knew well coming up from the beach barefooted and soaked to the skin, carrying on her back a load of seaweed to manure the ground for that year's potatoes; the other of something that happened as regularly as the clock every Saturday: women setting out in their heavy shawls and petticoats in the early morning with baskets containing eggs, butter, potatoes, and vegetables to be disposed of in Galway ten miles away. They would walk in their bare feet as far as the suburb of Salthill, and there, as a concession to the need to appear respectable as they entered the town, they would put on their boots and stockings. In the late afternoon they would face home, this time in an empty turf cart, but none the less tired and weary. I saw Mag Clancy once as she arrived home. She plomped down into the nearest chair to the kitchen door, took off her boots and hurled them across the floor and under the dresser. She then pulled off her coarse woollen stockings and scratched and scratched her legs. The satisfaction that gave her was apparent on her face; it would be another week before she had to face the agony again.

Next for me came Junior Grade, and, until recently, the most painful year of my life. The pain was caused by the psychopathic head of the sixth form, a Brother we called the Gilly. He was quite mad, and should never have been allowed near a school, particularly one where a 'payment by results' system operated. He was a strange brutal-looking fellow, and seemed to be always beating the boys in his charge. Detecting somebody idling down the room, perhaps in the third of the classes into which the school was divided, the commercial class, he would take the strap from his desk and charge, wildly, in the direction of the unfortunate individual. When something, in his opinion, went seriously wrong he would put the whole school out to the line with the intention of beating them all. I suffered more perhaps than any boy because, being at the head of the school, I encountered him at his fiercest and strongest on these occasions.

We were hard pressed with our studies. In the ordinary way we had to pass in five subjects, and to be sure that we all did – since it had a bearing on what the school earned from the Education Board – the Gilly made us do extra subjects, which increased the probability of further slapping. The Friday afternoon library session, which should have been a pleasant occasion, became a time of terror. We stood in a semi-circle before the Gilly. You were drilled into accepting a book from the fellow on your right and passing your book to the fellow on the left. But I did not dare to tell the Gilly that this was the third time I had paid a penny for the loan of the same book; for I need hardly say that there was no question of selecting a book or getting one on a subject that was not strictly linked to the curriculum.

I can't remember learning anything from the Gilly. He certainly was not a good teacher. He took us into the science laboratory occasionally for a lesson and I was one of those he punished on one occasion when he burned himself by taking up the hot end of some instrument or other; naturally, we found the whole thing hugely diverting, even if some of us were made to pay for it. I also remember when an experiment he was demonstrating did not work out, and he was compelled with flushing face, to call on one of the lay teachers to finish it for him. There were three such lay teachers in the school and one of them, a monitor, I saw being slapped across the face one day for nothing for which he was responsible. Another of the lay teachers, Paddy Caffrey, became a good friend of mine, even in that terrible year. We used to walk home together after school hours chatting in Irish, but strangely we never mentioned the Gilly. During the schoolday Caffrey would sometimes get me to write on the back of the movable blackboard the answers to questions he had set the class. I had made strides, especially in Irish and French.

I told them at home about the Gilly but got no satisfaction. What was happening in my school was altogether outside my mother's experience and my father did no more than hint that this was something that had to be gone through. He certainly made no protest to the Brothers, not even when the Gilly punished me on my return to school after a week's unavoidable absence. My mother had gone to hospital haemorrhaging badly, and I had to take over while she was away, cleaning up, making the beds, going out to buy food and cooking it. I was delighted, of course, not to be going to school, and rather elated because I was standing in for my mother. The Gilly saw no virtue in this. His concern was the coming exams, and their effect on the school's finances. So, he slapped me as he invariably did and left me full of pity for myself. I had started to knock off the days in my diary as they passed, and count what was left to be endured.

At long and painful last the exams came, and as the first paper was being handed out I looked around me. Quite near me was one of my pals, MacBride, a chap I used run with at lunch time. He had been out ill for some days and a messenger had been sent to his house to make sure that he would attend for the exam. He looked pale and grim. When I lifted my head again, I could see that his nose was bleeding. Again, in between my efforts to answer the questions on the paper before me, I could see that his handkerchief was wet with blood and that drops had fallen on the paper before him. He went home immediately after the morning session and did not return. I was on holidays when I was startled to read an announcement of his death in the *Independent*. I went to his home and was brought by his sobbing mother to his bedroom. It was a bright day and the sun shone through the partly opened window. He had died of a thing called meningitis. It was the first time I had heard the word. I could hardly do more than look at the body on the bed. I got out of the room and the house quickly. I was frankly frightened.

As I returned from my second visit to Cois Fharraige that summer on a crowded train I saw the Gilly waiting to board it at one of the stations. I lowered my head and hoped to God he would not come into my carriage. I was not looking forward to meeting him; he had told us that all of us would fail the exam. So it was still with trepidation that at the beginning of the next school year I faced him to be told, with a mean grin, that I had done well, passing in all subjects. I could proceed to Middle Grade.

All that summer I had applied myself with ever-growing enthusiasm to the study of Irish, and in Sheeaun, getting to know the people better, I went from house to house, and copied into my notebook everything I heard that interested me. I got to know the College teachers more intimately, and, with three or four of them, this led to friendships that lasted for most of my life, and all of theirs. There were minor flaws in this idyllic existence. There were no toilets in the houses, and only made-up words to describe them, so that every time nature called I had to roam the fields or find a corner in the cow byre we called the Teachín Bán. That was not pleasant, but others suffered as I did, or so I assumed, and I heard no complaining voice. Sunday mornings were delightful. We joined the stream of bawneen-clad men and women in their varied-coloured shawls walking to Mass at the Celto-Romanesque Church in the village with which the Killanins were associated and of whose erection I had read about in a Stephen Gwynn book. In the church the men and women occupied different sides, and followed the Mass said in Irish by Father MacAlinney with attention. At that Sunday Mass Father MacAlinney used to lay down the law on every kind of issue that affected the parish and particularly anything he found reprehensible. He did not appear to like Sinn Féin or the Volunteers and was soon making trouble for some of my friends. He was a fine priest, however – let that be said – and untiringly zealous on behalf of his people. There could be no question about his anxiety to promote the Irish language; and he was realistic enough to see that the growth of students at the college helped the local economy.

In Middle Grade I lived the life of a soul released from hell. The Brother Roche in charge of the school was an admirable man, open, bright, and fair, and, though he never taught my particular class, I could see, looking up the room, that his relations with the boys there were irreproachable. We were mainly looked after by three lay men, one of whom, Michael Hayes, was to become in time a friend of mine and actually presented me to the National University for my honorary degree.

He taught Irish and French, and I rated him highly as a teacher. He created an atmosphere about him as he taught, and I can still recall the opening words of the folk song he sang quietly as the seated class took something down from the blackboard: 'Gentle woman of the house give a helping hand to the blind man.' Hayes went into politics in the twenties and became the first Speaker of the Free State Dáil. The other men, Harkness and Crowley, were equally good, and both of them gentlemen. With Brother Roche, they constituted an excellent team which took us to the end of the year and successful examinations with ease. That summer I got away to the West, and, resuming where I had left off the previous year, continued to follow as closely as I could the speech of the people of Sheeaun. It was now 1918. I had started to write – in Irish – which was a ridiculous thing to do; and, yet, in the atmosphere of that time, I could do nothing else. The *Connacht Tribune*, a paper I saw in Galway whenever I was there, published my first piece, an effort to describe the view from Sheeaun looking towards the sea.

I was well into Senior Grade when rather suddenly, as it now appears, I decided to quit school altogether and to go and get a job. It was a strange decision. A number of my schoolmates won scholarships of one kind or another and went on to the university. I suppose I could have done the same but of that area of higher education I knew nothing whatever, nor had I the wit to seek advice; and there was nobody at home or in the school to guide me. Off my own bat I answered a couple of advertisements in the *Independent* and got a couple of indifferent jobs. I was first taken on by the Dublin agent of a firm that supplied monotype machines to newspapers and publishing houses. He was a nice fellow, who spent most of his time travelling, so that he required somebody to write an occasional acknowledgement and deal with demands for spare parts. That was where I came in. I had almost nothing to do, and wasted time doing it. My pay was ten shillings a week, and it came to me on a Saturday morning, a brand new note, by registered post. As I say, I rarely saw my boss. Once, when we did meet, our conversation somehow turned to religion. He was English and a Protestant, the first Protestant I had ever spoken to. I had spent all my days till then in the shadow of two church buildings that were only a few yards from each other. So I had always been aware of a religious separation that had been caused by something in the remote past. But the only Protestant that I was hitherto aware of was a poor old lady, a neighbour that my mother from her limited means used look after. The fact that she was poor surprised me because I had the conviction that Protestants as a class were well off, and that Catholics by and large were not, a state of affairs that also had something to do with history. Here now was a prosperous English Protestant telling me that the Bible was supremely important but that Catholics were not allowed to read it. I said that that was not true, that we had studied the Bible at school, and I promised to bring my copy in to show it to him. I did, but he quickly pointed out that it was not a Bible at all, but a book of Bible stories. The lesson of that encounter was not lost on me.

I left that job for one in a dental factory laboratory where I was occupied most of the time taking customers' orders and preparing their accounts. The first dentures I saw were revolting. They had come straight out of dirty viscous mouths and the dentist had not even put them under the tap before putting them in a box and sending them to the factory. Ugh! I saw something of the workrooms, and on the day following the 1918 General Election I heard a mechanic complaining that when he went to vote the previous day he found that somebody had been there before him. I was by now a member of the local Sinn Féin club, and had heard something about personation from two seasoned ex-Redmondites who, at a meeting over a tailor's shop, instructed us in the mechanics of conducting an election. On election day itself I was positioned outside the Court of Conscience in William Street where there was a polling booth, and where I suspect the 'righteous men' of Sinn Féin voted 'early and often'. Their work was facilitated by the absence of the policeman who had been assigned for duty at the booth. He was partaking of Sinn Féin's hospitality, I understood, in a public house across the way. Next day in the laboratory, a man who was known not to favour Sinn Féin was complaining loudly that his mother found she had been voted for when she arrived at the polling booth. And there was talk of a lady who advertised in the trams as having 'left-off clothes of all descriptions' having been busy supplying disguises for the personators. In the event, that sort of behaviour was hardly necessary, for it seemed to me that there was only one candidate in the field, ours, and he was Honest Tom Kelly. We got him in without difficulty; and outside Ulster, Sinn Féin likewise won the majority of seats. In the following month, January 1919, these Sinn Féin deputies held the first public meeting of Dáil Éireann in the Dublin Mansion House. I was there. I don't remember who gave me a ticket of admission. It was a well staged occasion in which the Irish language was supreme, where the Republic proclaimed in Easter 1916 was ratified, a democratic programme adopted, delegates appointed to a World Peace Conference, and an address issued to the world declaring that the existing state of war between Ireland and England could never be ended until Ireland was definitely evacuated by the armed forces of England.

I was by now also a member of the Central Branch of the Gaelic League. I had joined simply to continue my study of Irish but I was soon immersed in the full warm life of the Branch. You could not get a drink there or a meal but otherwise it was a good club and it cost only a few shillings a year to be a member of it. It shared a fine three-storey building at 39 Parnell Square with the Leinster College of Irish and among its teachers was a Mícheál Breathnach, from whom I learned a lot. He was a Connemara man, and to find him teaching in the Central Branch was not surprising to me because I understood that that branch was a custodian of western Irish generally, whereas the Keating Branch, seven houses down, was a Munster stronghold. Actually a fair amount of Munster Irish had trickled into the Central Branch and in time I became aware that between my original *Aids to Irish Composition*, and what I was now hearing around me in Dublin gave me a mixture of dialects which, while useful to know, did little for the Cois Fharraige strain to which I would have liked to adhere. However, that is by the way. The passion with which the war of dialects had been fought within the Gaelic

League was now largely spent, and interest was beginning to concentrate on the need to adopt the Roman instead of the so-called Gaelic script, and to unify spelling and grammar. The leaders in this contention were Colm Ó Murchú, Piaras Béaslaí, and Liam Ó Rinn. I made many friends in the Branch, among them some men who only dropped in occasionally. One of these was Pearse's gardener from St Enda's in Rathfarnham, Michael MacRory; another, Seán Farrelly, was said to be the last native speaker of Irish from the Co. Meath; a third was the writer Pádraic Ó Conaire; a fourth was the painter Sean Keating; and a fifth was Myles Dillon, one of the splendid sons of John Dillon who, not long before, had been ousted from parliamentary politics by the up-and-coming Eamon de Valera, the president of the Branch. Sean Keating I remember as a nice person and a fine artist whose views on life tended to make me feel uncomfortable. He was a sceptic. He did not believe in the talk, common in the Gaelic League and other circles, of the Irish and Irish things being the best in the world; that we all in fact carried in us something of the saints and scholars of old. On the contrary he believed that the cardinal sin of the Irish was mediocrity, that the individual Irishman might, at best, be a failed perfectionist who was always going to be better next week, or who had already given up the ghost with the excuse that perfection was not achievable anyway in a rotten world. But, paradoxically, Sean also detected in the Irish a large dose of a slave mind.

With Myles Dillon, who was about my own age but a vastly superior scholar, I became particularly friendly. I visited him in North Great George's Street. I stayed with him over a wet weekend in the family abode in Ballaghadereen and travelled across the Co. Mayo with him to Lough Mask along the shores of which, and particularly in Tourmakeady, he imbibed most of what he knew of spoken Irish. Myles's father was in the house that weekend but was unwell, so I had not the pleasure of meeting a man for whom, despite my Sinn Féin leanings, I had a high regard. I remember something that was entirely new to me, a maid in her cap and apron coming into my bedroom in the morning to light a fire and offer me a cup of tea. The library, in which there were fine editions of the English poets, opened my eyes. But no one spoke about politics.

Myles certainly did not. Indeed I never heard any politics in Gaelic League circles or among friends I had made there until the division on the Treaty.

Among the people I met regularly in the Branch was a Keeper in the Dublin Zoo who introduced me to the chimpanzees, and to friends of his who worked at the Kingsbridge headquarters of the Great Southern Railway. I moved easily into that group. We went on weekend outings together, and at holiday-time, at least once, we all travelled down to Cois Fharraige, making the journey out from Galway on our bikes, and devouring everything that was put before us to eat. In their company it dawned on me that I should be doing better for myself than invoicing those dental charges and when they told me of a forthcoming examination for railway clerks I decided to sit for it. I was not at all prepared for, Irish apart, I had got stale on my school subjects. However, I scraped home and was called for interview to the Company Secretary's office at Kingsbridge. There I met a young fellow with flashing teeth, a mop of hair and a fierce West Cork accent, and as he came from Schull he came to be known as Schull in the District Superintendent's office to which we were both assigned. He assisted the senior clerk who dealt with establishment matters and the issue of free passes, while I worked for Tom MacAveney, a pal of mine from the Central Branch whose job was to keep an eye on the running of trains. I was specifically given the job of calculating wagon mileages with a view to claiming a government subsidy. There were four other people in the room: a good-looking chap who had returned gassed from the war; a lady typist in her middle years; an elderly chief clerk; and his next-in-command. The atmosphere was uniformly friendly. The national situation was not discussed; we all refrained from anything like a political comment on what was happening literally outside the room. There was a fair sprinkling of activists at Kingsbridge. Schull, I knew, was a Volunteer; and a few yards away up the platform in the Station Master's office was Sean O'Connell, one of Michael Collins's aides. It was never surprising to me when trains carrying troops were ambushed.

I joined the Railway Clerks' Union, an English body, and settled in to a career which for all I knew would last until sometime in the dim and distant future when I would retire on a pension. I had a complaint, however, and voiced it right away in a letter to the editor of the Union magazine which was published from London. Why should I be paid less, I wanted to know, because I happened to be somewhat younger than fellows in my grade, who were doing the same work as I was doing? My letter appeared in the next issue with a note from the editor hoping that Irish readers would be able to read it; because it was in Irish. Did he call it Gaelic? It was, of course, a bit much for a man who was wet behind the ears to be writing to a paper in any language; but I was raw. The business of writing in Irish had certainly entered my blood. By the end of 1919 I was doing articles for the Gaelic League weekly, though saying nothing of consequence in any of them, and was 'the best writer of Irish' at the Dublin Feis of 1920. The competition may not have been severe, and I can vouch that the content of what I was writing was not very profound either. What I was really doing was giving myself practice in a language I was still learning. Since the middle of October 1919 the League had become an illegal body, but nobody bothered about that. When the official organ, *An Claidheamh Soluis* (the Sword of Light) was suppressed, it appeared immediately in the same form as before with a new name, *Fainne an Lae* (The Dawning of the Day), and when my name began to appear it was in the same paper again but now called *Misneach* (Courage).

Looking back on all that I have since learned about the shape and detail of the Anglo-Irish war, I suppose I was not as impressed as I should have been at what was happening around me. I crossed the city backwards and forwards practically every night, and had to observe the hours of curfew. I was stopped and searched. But until a particular event occured which I shall presently describe, I was not conscious of being unduly restricted. Nevertheless, unknown to us who frequented the Central Branch, real drama was very close. The west side of Parnell Square where the Branch was situated was only a few steps away from 25 Parnell Square North, the Gaelic League headquarters, where my business often took me, and even fewer from Vaughan's Hotel. These two buildings were in constant use by members of the G.H.Q. staff of the I.R.A., and how the British failed to make them and the surrounding area unuseable baffles me. They were aware that these premises were being used for illegal purposes, and often raided them, but to little or no effect. One night, I thought they were about to clean up the whole district. I was in the Branch office on the ground floor at a committee meeting when I heard a sound at the street door and, going out, I found a tin-hatted Tommy with rifle at the ready standing in the doorway. He told me to get back: they were searching the whole area, he said. The search was not as full or as complete as it should have been, however. Anybody at our meeting who had anything to dispose of had ample time to do so; and a thorough search of that house alone would have led to a flat on the top floor which belonged to Dr Paddy Brown of Maynooth College and his sister Margaret and which was one of the many places where Michael Collins stayed from time to time. He was actually in the flat on the night preceding 'Bloody Sunday', and watched from a window a raid on Vaughan's Hotel from which he had fled in time.

The story of that hotel is quite incredible. It was largely run by the proprietor, a Mr McGuire, and by his general factotum Christy Harte who kept a large room with four beds in it for Collins and his close associates. I knew Christy, both in Vaughan's and in Portobello Barracks where he served in the officers' mess in 1922 and later. McGuire was offered £40,000 to betray Collins; Christy was arrested and brought to Dublin Castle where he was interrogated by a masked man who told him he knew all about his dealings with Collins, and could have him shot, but wished to give him a chance. He told Christy he was a poor man but he could become wealthy for life if he would only do one little thing. He would be released; but next time Collins came to the hotel he was to ring a certain number and simply say that Mr X had arrived.

The name of Collins was increasingly being mentioned among the people, and those who knew his work swore by him. I can't put a date on it but sometime in 1920 or early 1921 my father met Paudeen O'Keeffe, the secretary of Sinn Féin, coming from Mass and brought home to us the news that Collins had been caught. 'That's the end of the whole bloody business', Paudeen had said. Collins undoubtedly had become the mainspring of the movement, and not only on the military side. As Minister for Finance he had raised a national loan to which everybody seemed to contribute. I saw something of the organising of this, and later I got to know a fair amount of how his department fitted into the general organisation of Dáil Éireann services. The fighting men recognised his worth. He was their Director of Intelligence, which might seem a relatively secondary portfolio, but with Mulcahy's, the Chief of Staff's approval, he functioned like the top commander. He largely negatived the British intelligence system, which had held Ireland in thrall for centuries, neutralising the G (Detective) Division of the Dublin Metropolitan Police by shooting the most active of its political members and creating such a state of near panic among the remainder that they rarely left Dublin Castle: they just wanted to stay alive. He demoralised the Royal Irish Constabulary, encouraged a mutiny in its ranks, and saw to it that a divisional commander who proposed a shoot-on-sight policy was assassinated. Resignations and the decline in recruitment forced the government to introduce the new divisions that came to be known as the Black and Tans and Auxiliaries and simultaneously to send over secret service agents in fair numbers from Britain. It was the accumulation of intelligence about these men that led to the Bloody Sunday operation which, so well organised, so unexpected, and so ruthlessly executed, had a paralysing effect on the British campaign.

That Bloody Sunday morning, I was getting ready to go to Mass when Mickey Ronan, a young fellow about my own age who lived down the street, came panting and pale-faced to the door. 'Take these and keep them for me', he said. Out of one pocket he drew a revolver and out of another a crude looking grenade. 'There's been a big job on this morning, and a lot of killing.' I took them from him – it never occured to me to refuse him – and he hurried away. I went to Mass, and returned within the half-hour to consider what to do with the revolver and grenade. Living in three rooms with my father, mother and brothers, the possible hiding places were extremely limited. That I knew only too well. I finally wrapped them up in a sock and put them under a pile of letters and odds and ends in a chest of drawers that stood against a wall in the living room. I hardly left the house that day: when I did venture out I was offered tickets for the big football match to be held that afternoon in Croke Park. I refused them on the ground that I had something else on, but as I did it puzzled me a bit that the owner of the tickets should be disposing of them. I sensed, however, that his mind was also on the events of the morning and that there might well be a painful British reaction. How right we both were!

Next morning, with the parcelled sock under my arm, I set off for the office in Kingsbridge with the intention of hiding it there. At Capel Street Bridge, I bought an *Independent* and boarded a tram. There was a fair load of passengers on it, mostly young country fellows in caps who had been up at the match, making for the mid-morning Cork train; but there was a free seat downstairs in the curtained area behind the driver and, putting my parcel behind me, I settled into it and started to read the tremendously exciting news. I can see it still. The tram had not gone very far along the quays when it stopped suddenly: it was not a usual stopping place, so I pulled back the curtain and looked out. There was a tram halted before us, and I could see in a glance that armed soldiers were carrying out a search. We would be the next. Like a flash, I was out of my seat and made for the door with the parcel. As I did, I realised what a stupid thing I had done to bring it out of the house at all, and on that of all mornings, with the British set on taking revenge for what had been done to their intelligence officers the day before. However, I had to go through with it. So I cut up a side street near the Four Courts and worked my way along streets that ran parallel to the quays until I came out at Kingsbridge.

I stood on the Phoenix Park side of the bridge looking over at the station area which appeared to be black with people, mostly those country fellows with the caps who had been at Croke Park, and the more responsible looking commercial travellers, it being a Monday morning. They were being 'stuck up' by Auxiliaries and Black and Tans, and many of the caps and hats that had been taken from them were to be seen floating down the Liffey. I saw enough to convince me that this was no place for me, and that to go forward across the bridge would be utter madness.

At that moment, I saw Miss Twomey, our typist, walking nonchalantly down from the direction of Parkgate, and wearing as usual a regimental cap badge or something of the sort. On the spur of the moment I went straight across to her and asked her if she would be so good as to leave the parcel on my desk and tell the chief clerk that I had to go on some urgent business. It may have been the proverbial aunt who had to be buried! She most kindly took the parcel from me, and it was only when I had done that that I saw how stupidly, not to say unchivalrously, I had acted. What if Miss Twomey was stopped and the parcel taken from her? Would not she, naturally, tell who had given it to her? I could see a trail of circumstances leading back to me, and even to Mickey Ronan. However, for the moment I could only take myself away and for the next couple of hours or so, as I walked the streets, I pondered my possible fate.

I might not have worried. When I came back to the station later, all was quiet, and when, trembling, I opened the door into the office, there on my desk was the parcel. I nodded my thanks to Miss Twomey who was hammering away on her typewriter, whispered something to the chief clerk, and sat down in my own place. Relief! Oh God, what relief!

When I had composed myself, and could do it without drawing attention, I took the parcel down to 'the gorey hole' under the office where we stored our files, and there it rested until Mickey Ronan wanted what was in it again.

A few days afterwards the funeral of the officers who had been assassinated on Bloody Sunday morning took place. The blinds were down in the office and a cessation of work had been ordered while the large military cortege passed. Miss Twomey went out to see the procession; the rest of us stayed within in the relative gloom. It was then that the plump Harry Bergin, the chief clerk, showed a rebel side to him that he had hitherto kept concealed from us. Strolling over to my desk he picked up a library book I happened to be consulting. It was a bound volume, the *Penny Journal*, a periodical of the past. He opened it at a speech delivered in the House of Commons by some Irish parliamentarian or other who had a reputation for oratory.

'I know that speech,' he said, and turning his backside to the fire – outside it was a bright but sharp November day – he started to declaim it, ably and with some passion. It was perhaps his finest hour. We were all astonished at the performance and in such a setting, for we understood he had a copy of a code by which the British and military communicated their needs to the railway company, which meant presumably that his dissociation from anything rebelly was beyond question. He was married, incidentally, to the owner of Finn's Hotel in Leinster Street where Nora Barnacle had worked as a maid before James Joyce found her.

As Christmas came in sight, word went round the office that the stationmaster at Templemore would be selling geese and turkeys cheap. I put my name down for a goose and one morning in the week before the festival I was told the birds had arrived. They were in the goods, and would I collect mine. I was a bit surprised when it was not brought to the office; I had expected to receive it trussed up and parcelled, but then I was told that the goose was alive, and would have to be taken away in that condition. Somehow I took the advantage of having a young brother to get him to bring the bird home. It was an exciting journey for him, on the top of one of the old open-topped trams, and quite a job to save the bird from having its inquisitive head chopped off by the trams passing in the opposite direction. When I got home, I found the goose reclining on a newspaper before an open fire. I was greeted by my parents with no enthusiasm; they rightly thought I could have arranged things better. They had taken time by the forelock, however, and arranged that Amby Doyle, a chicken butcher of their acquaintance, would do what was necessary. He arrived, had a couple of bottles of stout which made the transaction dearer than I had promised, and talked a lot before finally leaving the goose fit for the oven. That very night there were visitors – the military – and afterwards it was noticed that the bird had gone, together with the other comestibles my mother had laid in for the Christmas. It was a night sweep, the soldiers doubtless hoping to pick up some of the men responsible for the November massacre. We were used to being disturbed at night-time, with lorries and Lancia cars travelling noisely up and down the street, and sometimes grinding to a halt followed by a hammering at a door and the sound of voices. But this night it was not a case of a limited raid in pursuit of an individual or in a search for arms, but something like a comb-out of a whole district.

The noise, as house after house was knocked at, broken into and searched from top to bottom, was horrific, and to enable the soldiers to see what they were doing, they turned the night into high-noon with enormous searchlights. It was these searchlights that first alarmed me and my brothers in our little bedroom. The light they shed was intense; it played over us in our beds for so long and so carefully that I, for one, thought that through walls and every other kind of obstacle, they could identify us. Lying on in bed became quite intolerable. We had to get up and dress ourselves and move over to the drawing room where we were not surprised to find father and mother up, too, and the gas lit. There we talked intermittently, listened, and waited. Our turn to be raided would come.

It came as it had come that night to hundreds of other families. A banging on the door. An entry. Shouting near at hand, and then up the stairs there came to us a young army lieutenant, a sergeant, some other tin-hatted soldiers, and with them a single policeman, a young silent D.M.P. man. His presence, no doubt, was to sustain the old pretence that the military were there in support of the police. But that policeman knew as little of the place as the soldiers did, and he took no part whatever in the proceedings. The lieutenant sat down near the fireplace under the gaslight.

'Why are you all up dressed?' he asked, as if he did not know jolly well the answer to the stupid question. The policeman dropped into the background while the sergeant proceeded to search us. In the pocket of my jacket he found a letter in Irish. He knew he had a find.

'Erse, sir,' he said. I knew the word but had never heard it spoken before. He handed the letter to the lieutenant who, hardly looking at it, asked me from his chair, 'Are you a Sinn Féiner?'

'I am,' I said, both bluntly and stupidly, leaving my father aghast. He tried to explain what I suppose one would call the philosophical basis of Sinn Féin. What he really wanted to say was that I was not a gunman, but the lieutenant ended that possibility by just ordering the sergeant to take us all away. My father, two of my brothers and myself. I am sure the others would have liked to strangle me at that moment. However, we put on our overcoats, and our brave little mother saw us out into the cold night.

We were led to a street-corner where other men who had been arrested were standing under a guard beside some military lorries. From there we had a good view of the long main street and of the side streets that ran from it. The searchlights had been lowered – the raiding was obviously coming to an end for the night – but most of the soldiers were carrying lighted Christmas candles which they had taken from some of the shops and this form of illumination could be seen in the windows of houses where the searching was still going on.

The soldiers who formed the guard around us were friendly. They told us who they were – the Lancashire Fusiliers – and warned us about a lance-corporal they pointed out. 'E was no good, E was'. He was a spy, set among them.

I was interested in what was going on in a lodging house a few doors down a side street which I could see clearly from where we stood. I had seen a search party going in and wondered would they have the writer Pádraic Ó Conaire with them when they came out. I knew Ó Conaire stayed there and I had seen him, rather tipsy as usual, moving in that direction just before curfew. But when the party emerged Ó Conaire was not with them. He told me later that he had been sleeping soundly – I can well imagine it – when someone woke him up and started to question him at the point of a revolver. Pádraic, because of his English experience, could speak the soldiers' lingo as good as any of them; so he answered the questions in a put-on English accent. 'Where do Sinn Féiners go when they die', he was asked. ''Ell', said Pádraic; and there they left him. He may have made all that up. He was, after all, a writer of fiction, a story teller. I had read his *Seven Virtues of the Rising* in the National Library with the help of Father Dinneen's dictionary, and met Pádraic himself on one of his rare visits to the Central Branch. The story was going the rounds that he had entered a department of the British Civil Service in London under one form of his name largely on the strength of having passed an examination in Irish – or was it Erse? – which he had himself set under another. But he had left that job, or was sacked, and had come back to Ireland to lead what was effectively the life of an itinerant.

We were finally put into a lorry and driven to Wellington Barracks on the South Circular Road. After a pause in the guardroom we were taken to the first floor of a large building. There we were shown into a lighted room at each end of which were armed guards sitting at fires behind barbed wire. Their charges were the sleeping prisoners in the room. In time we would be given beds too, but for that night we would have to be satisfied to be on the floor in army blankets. I suppose I should have kept awake with worry over our plight, but I slept as soon as I lay down. It was morning when tea – or cha, as the soldiers called it – was being brought round before I opened my eyes.

Next to me where I had been lying, and sitting at the end of his bunk, was a man I knew from pictures of him that had been published after the Rebellion. He was Dick Hayes – Dr Richard F. Hayes – who had been sentenced to twenty years penal servitude for his part in the fight at Ashbourne in 1916. He had been elected an M.P. in the 1918 general election, but he had given his allegiance to Dáil Éireann and had attended its public and private meetings. He was, in other words, a Teachta Dála, a T.D. While my father and brothers were chatting to other prisoners I was engaged with Dr Hayes. He, of course, was the man among us who had the most experience of prison life and appeared to me to be extremely unperturbed by his plight. He was actually putting his enforced idleness to good purpose, studying Irish and getting a page of *Seadna*, an Irish language classic, off by heart every day. Indeed, the first thing I did as a prisoner was to hold the book for him as he rattled off the passage he had acquired the day before. I learned something from his demonstration of composure in the midst of anxiety.

Dr Hayes was with us for about a week before being moved to some other place of confinement, but long enough to show that his status as an M.P. was respected by the military. It happened that one night, late, a prisoner was brought in in a fainting condition. He had been wounded in Croke Park on Bloody Sunday, but his captors, Auxiliaries or Black and Tans, had tried to make out that the wound had been inflicted as he escaped from one of the houses where secret service officers had been murdered that morning. This he strenuously denied, but they persisted, and pulled his poor arm about in the process. When he was brought into our room his condition was so bad that he pitched down on a bed and obviously required medical attention. Dr Hayes hurried to him and did what he could for him. What was more to the point he insisted that the colonel of the regiment should come immediately and see what the situation was, and he made use of his parliamentary status to emphasise the urgency of the matter. The colonel came, and we understood that thereafter these Auxiliaries or Tans were not allowed to come into that part of the barracks where military prisoners were housed.

That episode, and what we heard of five prisoners being charged and executed for their connexion with Bloody Sunday, began to worry me. I feared that under pressure I would tell the story of Mickey Ronan's involvement. That possibility came nearer one day when some of us, including Dr Hayes, were driven over to Kilmainham Gaol. We were left standing for a while in the hall and then our guard took us into a yard where, the rumour went, the leaders of the 1916 business had been shot. Was an attempt being made to frighten us into thinking that a similar fate was in store for us? The younger among us probably saw that as quite likely, but the experienced Dr Hayes whispered to us to take out our cigarettes and smoke them. After a short while we were taken out in pairs and brought through various passages all round the prison. Whoever was with me – I can't remember who – told me to break step, so as not to give the impression that we had had some military training. When we reached a largish yard, I was thrust in and forced to stand before a tin shack which had a slit along its length and there, as I stood, with two police with cocked revolvers on either side I saw a number of sets of eyes looking at me and passing on. They seemed to be the eyes of women for the most part. It was an appalling experience. I was shaking with fright. I was afraid that the owners of those eyes, and particularly as they seemed to return to have a second look, would say that I was like a man they had seen that terrible Sunday morning. And, of course, those police revolvers frightened me, too.

Anyhow no one recognised any of us, and we returned that afternoon to Wellington Barracks much relieved.

For the rest of the time we spent there, there was interest but little excitement. On the day the soldiers got their pay the regimental band became our warders. They brought their instruments into the long room and played for us. They were a superior lot, while among the others every second word spoken was the four-letter one that allegedly won the war. Two brothers among the prisoners squabbled; one of them, who was obviously not the full shilling, had told the soldiers when they called where they could find a gun. The man who was acting as a sort of camp commandant for us gave a clip over the ear to a prisoner whom he found at a window making a plan of the barracks which he thought might be useful to the boys outside. Two Tommies offered to take us out provided we took care of them afterwards, but we knew, even by looking at them, that they were thoroughly unreliable, and we discovered, too, that they had a bad record of drunkeness. We played soccer with a rag ball in the yard below at exercise time and were watched closely from surrounding windows. I was introduced by an old fellow to the game of bezique, and played draughts on a board made out of a woodbine box with orange peel as blacks and whites! And I had elevated talks with Dr Hayes.

Food was bad at first, but improved. We were able to get parcels sent in, and in one of these was a book I had asked for, the short stories in French of Alphonse Daudet. I had done his *Belle Nivernaise* with the Brothers and here were his shorter pieces, his *contes*, which I wanted to translate into Irish. One of them was very apposite to my own confined condition at that time, the story of Monsieur Seguin's goat. The goat had longed to be free, to escape from where she was tied up so that she would roam on the mountains she could see in the distance, as I could see the Dublin hills. '*Lassez moi aller dans les montagnes*.' Ultimately, she managed to get loose only to fall prey to the wolf she had been warned about. My concern to lay hands on that particular story inspired a friend in the Central Branch to compose 'a lay of a nanny goat'. She didn't say, as she might have done, that I fared better than Daudet's animal. I was brought down to a room near the barrack gate one afternoon where the Intelligence Officer, a Mr House, intended to question me. But hardly had I entered the room when he was called somewhere, leaving me to my own devices. I sat for a while, then stood up and went to look at some things on the mantlepiece. Some of them were from St Enda's where the Pearse Brothers had had a school but among them was a picture of a 1918 anti-conscription group. I recognised among the men in the picture a colleague of mine at Kingsbridge, and as soon as I could I sent word to him to make himself scarce. But he had already been arrested. Mr House did not return to examine me, and shortly afterwards my father and two of us were let go. It was late January or early February 1921. My eldest brother, Paddy, whom the authorities had evidence against going back as far as the Howth gun running, was transferred to Arbour Hill and from there to one of the internment camps at Ballykinlar.

When I could get away from the house that evening I went across town to the Branch. There was nobody yet in the office, and I turned into the library. There was no one there I really knew, but two young women were arranging books. One of these was a girl I had not seen before. She was standing high up on a ladder. I heard afterwards that she enquired of her companion who I was. 'Oh, that's the secretary León Ó Broin' she was told. 'He must have got out of jail'. Was it on the next Sunday afternoon that I met the young enquirer on a *turas* in the hills above Rathfarnham? I think it was. She – petite and wearing a scarf or band across her forehead – had broken away from the company and was walking on the top of a wall. I went over and looked up at her. There was something about her, something that drew me to her. 'I'll race you to the top of the hill', I said. Smiling, she came down, and started to run. I let her beat me, she said later.

When we got to the Hell Fire Club, which was our destination, we climbed to the highest point, ran another race or two, danced after tea and walked the four miles back to the tram which took us into the city. By that time she had told me a little about herself. At intervals thereafter I heard some more. I remember particularly a ceili in the D.B.C. rooms in Stephen's Green which brought us excitingly close together. We danced into the early hours and met again for another walk in the hills that afternoon. A 60-year saga had begun.

She was an O'Reilly, a Kathleen O'Reilly, her people hailing from Cavan town, where her grandfather, 'the Governor', once owned the Glebe Hotel, as well as a farm at the Crosswater near Virginia. But involvement in Parnellite politics and unwise entertainment of friends had dispossessed him of the hotel interest. He had a number of sons, and as there had always been a priest in the family, it was accepted that one of them, Henry or Harry, was to go to the diocesan seminary and that an ordination would follow in due course. After some months, however, Harry told an uncle, who was a priest – not daring to break the bad news himself to the Governor – that he had no vocation. The uncle told the Governor, whose reaction is quite unbelievable in modern times. 'If my son Harry leaves the seminary,' he said, 'he will never darken the door of this house again.' Nor did he apparently. He left the seminary, married Jennie McCabe, became the father of three children, and died in Leeds a pharmaceutical chemist. At his death, Kathleen was only four, her sister Eileen some years older, and her brother, Harry, a few years younger. Jane or Jennie, left badly off, had to return to Ireland to rear her children as best she could. She got some training, and secured an appointment from a Board of Guardians as a district nurse or midwife in the Co. Wicklow, in Baltinglass. The salary was £40 a year and for that sum, and travelling usually on her bicycle, she was constantly on the move bringing children into the world. Some of the better off families would give her a pound or two but that did not happen very often; and others would give her gifts of eggs and vegetables. Having to be out so often at night-time, she was glad to have Mrs Ward, an old widow from the Kiltegan countryside, who had nothing to live on but a pension of five shillings a week, to come to live with her for the sake of having a roof over her head and a share of the family meals. 'Wardie' became a most devoted nanny and the children greatly loved her. It was an intensely hard life for Jennie but it was only in later years that the children came to see how hard it had been.

They had a happy childhood and were particularly blessed in having quite near them an excellent convent school. They spent the holiday breaks with relations, not those in Cavan, but with other O'Reillys who lived in Kingstown on Dublin Bay or in the Glens of Antrim. It was in Cushendall and the nearby Waterfoot that, in a house full of children, she heard her uncle, Father Danny Toal, talking about the Irish language and the need to rescue it from extinction. Her Kingstown cousins were all much older than she, so much so that she always spoke of them as aunties, Auntie Madge, Auntie Jennie and so on. They were a long family in which in time ill-health and emigration forced a decline, but not before the women members of it had been educated to the point at which they could, as governesses, educate others. They all spoke exceptionally well. Kathleen's sister Eileen, as she passed out of her teens, went to live with an aunt in the States and also became a governess, which was one of the few avenues open at that time for a young woman. She found employment with well-to-do families in India and Burma, and on coming to England was trained as a nurse in the Middlesex Hospital. She specialised in midwifery and lived a long and happy life in that profession following, as it were, in her mother's footsteps, but in the better class Dublin nursing homes.

While Eileen was in foreign parts, Kathleen and her brother, Harry, were drawn together more than otherwise they would have been. They loved the life of the little town, climbed over the hills behind their house in summer and burned the furze when autumn came. The strong flowing Slaney was only a few fields away; the two of them would run through fields of cattle to swim in it, or fish. Carr's Rock on a hill top was a favourite objective, and Kathleen often spoke of walks through Shrufaun. A butcher's son, showing perhaps a romantic interest in her, would take her up beside him on his cart as he went on his deliveries into the countryside.

Kathleen was happiest perhaps at school and may have stayed on with the Presentation nuns longer than was usual. It was suggested to her to do the King's Scholarship examination and become a national teacher, but her mother could not afford the extra expense involved so she opted for a clerical job in Dublin when one offered. Harry's case was different. I don't know how he did at school in Baltinglass, probably well enough, but when it was time for him to leave, his mother managed to send him away to a secondary boarding school, with help no doubt from her sister in America whose husband Giovanni Short was a couturier. Harry hated the school, and one day, without warning, he arrived home to present his mother with the problem of what else could be done with him. She consulted the relations, no doubt, and succeeded in getting him apprenticed in the engineering branch of the Dublin Tramways. He did not like that either for some reason, and left. The Great War was under its tremendous way; and without, as far as we know, any strong feelings about the issues for which it was being fought, he joined up in a Signals Corps and duly found himself in the trenches in France. I need hardly say that that experience was far from his liking either; and when he got not too seriously wounded, he was pleased to enjoy the comfort and companionship of a hospital in England, before being sent home. When he got as far as Dublin he ran into some fellows who were only too glad to relieve him of his rifle and uniform and to give another turn to his wheel of fortune. One of these fellows was a Houlihan who, in a room at the back of a shop in Amiens Street, told him that the fight that had begun in Dublin in 1916 and which had led to executions and internments was about to be renewed, and maybe Harry would like to play a part in it.

Neither Harry nor his sisters appear to have been moved by the 1916 story: if anything, the fact that Harry had joined the British Army rather late in the War would indicate that any sympathies they had, if they thought about it at all, were for the maintenance of the link with Britain. But they were aware, or were soon to be aware, that another branch of the family were all ferocious Sinn Féiners. Their father's brother, J. K. O'Reilly, a member of the Fenian I.R.B., and author of *Wrap the Green Flag Round Me*, had led three sons into the Rising, and was now, like the Houlihans, planning further disorder.

Harry's immediate problem was how best to hide himself.

We don't know all the steps he took to do so, but one took him to Belfast where under the alias Austin McDermott he – believe it or not – got a clerical job in a government department. He lived for a time in the Glens of Antrim. He may have been helped by his cousins, the Fathers Danny and Ted Toal who were priests in the diocese: he certainly sheltered for a time with Mrs Delargy who ran a hotel in the Glens, and became a close friend of her sons Hamilton and Jack, especially Jack. The problem of avoiding arrest and returning to the British army was one his mother had to share with him. One day, a local police sergeant called on her: 'Where is your son'? he asked. She was ready for him. What did he mean, where was her son? The last she had heard was that he had been wounded. Were they telling her that they did not know where the son she had given to king and country now was? She certainly did not. Perhaps when they had found him, they would be so good as to let her know. She was, as the Sergeant could see, deeply moved and worried. When the policeman left, saying he would report what he had been told, Wardie, not a bit surprised, turned quickly and said: 'So Terry's run away.' She always called him Terry. Jennie grabbed hold of her and shook her. 'Don't let me hear that word from you again,' she hissed, 'or woe betide you.'

By the time this little episode was played out, Kathleen had a job in the Yorkshire Insurance Company whose Dublin office was in Dame Street almost alongside the Bank of Ireland's headquarters in the old parliament building. With little training she became a 'life clerk' and acted for the cashier when he was away. As it was, he was rarely away for more than a day or two, for he was afraid to take holidays, having been fiddling the cash for years. For these really onerous duties Kathleen was paid at first thirty shillings and later £2 a week. She worked every Saturday, but could have got off one Saturday a month had her early attendance record not been against her. The English manager, who knew her worth and commended her to head office, would say to her: 'Reilly, I'll let you off next Saturday, if you promise to come in in time in the morning.' He was a nice old fellow and she never complained about how she was treated. She had female company in the office, too, a few girls in the menial jobs, and a mixed crowd of others, among whom were some women who spoke increasingly of the need to sustain the war effort and who professed not to understand when Kathleen, never flush with money, as you can imagine, refused to contribute to some collection or other. With Harry's problem before her, she pitied one poor fellow whom these women tried to shame into military service by leaving a white feather on his desk.

One autumn day Sheila Maloney, a typist with whom she had made friends, asked her what she was going to do for the winter. Kathleen had no plans. 'Well, you ought to join the Gaelic League,' Sheila suggested, 'and learn Irish; you'd have a fainne in no time.' Kathleen did not know what a fainne was, and Sheila had to explain. Kathleen was convinced that to become a member of the Gaelic League was a good idea. When she got that month's pay, she went with Sheila to the building on Parnell Square which the Central Branch had just agreed to share with the Leinster College of Irish, and paid five shillings which gave her for a twelvemonth the entree to something like a club life as well as to all the classes in the Irish language she could stand.

My membership of that Branch began a little later. Irish had become an obsession with me; I was absorbing it through every pore of my skin. A four-page leaflet had been distributed among the members and Kathleen and I may well have received copies. If I did it made no impression on me at the time. It spoke of 'recent stirring events in Ireland that had convinced the world that Ireland was determined to be a Nation in the real sense, without pretence or humbug' and it explained that 'the present temper of Irish men and women would not allow them to stand idly by while their Nation was losing its language through neglect.' Neither Kathleen nor I would have recognised in these phrases the triumphalism of the new Sinn Féin and the implication that under its political predecessors nothing worthwhile had been done to promote the language revival. We both knew nothing about the historical background of the Gaelic League. We did not know, no more than most people did, that a crisis, provoked by the underground Irish Republican Brotherhood, had forced the resignation of Douglas Hyde, the President, as well as the Secretary of the League, at the 1915 Ard Fheis, and had made it difficult for persons who disapproved of Sinn Féin to continue to be members. At that Ard Fheis, I gather from a minute book I saw recently, the Central Branch was represented by Eamon de Valera, Eamon Price, Sean MacCaoilte and Risteard MacCoitir, all four of them IRB men, probably, at that time and therefore in some measure responsible for the crisis. Kathleen and I were unaware of this, and perhaps indifferent. We just started to enjoy the facilities of the Branch, the library and conversation room, the céilís after the classes, the weekend hikes – they called them *turasanna* then – so that, in the matter of Irish, from being 'a beginner' she speedily became what was distinguished in the Branch as an 'experienced learner,' while I became a writer. I had five articles in the early numbers of *Misneach*, which replaced the League paper that had been suppressed by the government, and maybe it was this facility that caused the Central Branch's committee to make me their secretary.

Being the secretary of the Central Branch of the Gaelic League meant that when I wanted to I could see an awful lot of Cáit, the name I preferred to call her by. I used to take a senior class too, and Cáit, when she felt proficient enough, became one of my pupils. Her awakened keeness to learn Irish had a link with the summers she had spent in the Glens of Antrim with her cousin Father Danny Toal who by now was a noted revivalist. He pioneered the Phrase Method of teaching the language rather than the Direct Method, and had some success with it. This was the method employed in the Ard-Scoil in Dublin and Cáit attended classes there on such nights in the week that were free from her studies in the Central Branch. She was there during the Black and Tan period, and told me of a mutual friend of ours who sat beside her in class while probably carrying something lethal in his pocket. With such enthusiasm for the language, it was not surprising that within one year Sheila Maloney's prediction was fulfilled. Cáit was able to present herself for the Fainne and passed the test. I must say that though I was probably proud of her achievement I feared that a language both of us had learned did not equip either of us sufficiently for love-making.

TWO

I WAS quite happy in the railway job and, if I had stayed on, I might in the normal way have ended up as a station-master. I did in fact dream that one day I might be in charge of a station in the West of Ireland, not too far from Cois Fharraige. Going down there as often as I could, on free passes, my temperature always rose as I came into the stone-wall country and heard Irish being spoken by men in bainin suits and women in shawls. However, my work in the Central Branch, my writing, and friendships I had made decided otherwise. I left the railway service to take up a job in Dáil Éireann's agricultural department. That looks important as I write it, but the department in fact occupied only a couple of rooms over a tailor's shop in North Earl Steet, a few yards from Nelson Pillar, and the staff was correspondingly tiny. When I joined, there was the minister or director of Agriculture, the chubby, good-looking and good-humoured T.D., Art O'Connor, who dealt personally with the strictly agricultural correspondence that had to be done, aided surreptitously, I suspect, by Dan Twomey of the government Department of Agriculture's inspectorate, but there was precious little correspondence of that character. The principal work of the department was that of a Land Settlement Commission, and for that there were two legal commissioners, a registrar, two typists – one of them a sister of Kevin Barry – and a messenger whose father had died in the Rising. My £3 a week job was not defined. I assumed I was to act as a private clerk or secretary to the minister/director as well as being a general dogsbody. And that was how I functioned anyway. My predecessor, Gearoid McGann, had gone to work for de Valera and Collins who were now attempting to reach a political settlement with the British. McGann was kept busy, while I had little or nothing to do. I met him one day in Dawson Street near the Mansion House where his office was, and asked him what sort of a man de Valera was to work with. The relationship was none too happy, I gathered. 'He's an extraordinary man', McGann said. 'If he was only ordering a bag of coal he'd write the letter three times.' I knew what he meant, though I could not see anyone ordering a bag of coal by letter, or Dev particularly being reduced to that condition.

The Land Settlement Commission had been set up to deal with disputes over land which threatened to disturb the national programme. A system of courts had been set up and the commissioners, Kevin O'Shiel and Alec Maguire, as well as some part-time judges, sat in judgment on specific cases. They had help from Martin Heavey and other professional surveyors. The registrar of the Commission was an internee in Ballykinlar when I was appointed, and in his place a tall young Protestant barrister named Henry Conner was acting. Henry came of an historic family. His great-great-grandfather was a brother of Arthur O'Connor, a leader of the United Irishmen, while another kinsman was Fergus O'Connor, the leader of the English Chartists. Henry had served in the Royal Flying Corps during the Great War but, according to himself, he broke the under-carriage of so many planes on landing that it was thought he would be less of a liability in some other branch of the service. I am sure he would have been an excellent decoy if British agents came knocking on the door of the Land Settlement Commission. His general appearance and accent, his spats, and the cigar he usually smoked would have disarmed them. But even if they had managed to enter the office they were not likely to suspect the kind of underground set-up it really was. It looked just like what the brass plate on the door said it was: the office of Carton and Sons, Surveyors and Valuers. There were set-squares and compasses, maps and estate plans. The files, however, would have raised suspicions, for all names on them had been obliterated.

We had an idea, but only that, of where the other Dáil departments were located. Diarmuid O'Hegarty's secretariat was over a shoe-shop in O'Connell Street; Michael Collins's Finance Department was in Mary Street; Austin Stack's

Department of Justice was on the South Quays. We had no bank account of our own. The money we needed for salaries and running expenses came to us from the Finance Department through a man we knew as the Bannc Ar Siúl, which was doubtful Irish for travelling bank. He came to us regularly, and exchanged a white slip I gave him for cash. He knew where all the offices were and would have been a valuable capture for the British. I remember him well. He looked like a D.M.P. man and wore a long black overcoat in the deep pockets of which he kept the money. I never knew his name, and only heard an unpleasant rumour as to how his service ended. I got a reminder recently of the system in a letter from Collins to the Trustees of a Commission of Enquiry, written in January 1921. 'Will you please note', the letter runs, 'that a sum of £2000 (TWO THOUSAND POUNDS) has been passed by the Dáil Ministry. This amount will be made available at once, and a representative of this Department will attend to pay it over at your bank, upon giving me one day's notice of the appointment. As the amount will be paid in cash I am anxious that the appointment should be at your bank, and as I am anxious to get the matter concluded I should like you to make the appointment at once.'

Sometime in November, I think, we had a note from Diarmuid O'Hegarty, saying that there was a real possibility of a breakdown in the London talks, that we should be ready for a resumption of hostilities, and that, as it was likely the British had been spying out during the Truce where our departments were located, we should consider making a change. We did, moving to two floors over Bewley's tea rooms in Westmoreland Street, and above the offices of R. F. O'Connor, an accountant, which were on the first floor. The caretaker, who had a flat on the top floor and who called me Mr Carton, was surprised and disappointed when I did not let her in to clean our rooms. We naturally made our own arrangements for that service as we had done in North Earl Street. We had now more accommodation than we needed, and were able to give a room to the Department of Fisheries which consisted of a minister and one head of staff, Dick King, who was described as an inspector of fisheries. That was probably the smallest Dáil department of all. King, whom I got to know well, had a good sense of humour and a rough tongue. I never saw his minister, Sean Etchingham, in the office but I did see a rather dour Liam Mellowes there more than once.

At that time I am sure I had anything but a competent understanding of what was happening politically. I doubt, for example, if I realised the significance of recent events in the North where, in consequence of a British Act, a separate state had been established and the parliament of that state opened by the king. It was a strange and unexpected development that the part of Ireland which had strongly opposed home rule should be the first to achieve it, and, having achieved it, should resolve to have as little to do as possible with the entity to be created in the South. The creation of that southern entity had been the outcome of preliminary conversations in London between de Valera and Lloyd George and the subsequent formal negotiations between British and Irish delegations. These negotiators came to the table to discuss the Irish reaction to Lloyd George's offer of dominion home rule. The original Irish response was that they did not seek dominion status; neither did they say anything about a republic. What they aimed at was an external association with the dominions then evolving into a Commonwealth. An agreement was reached, but not on the basis of external association. We were to enter the Commonwealth as a dominion, an Irish Free State.

I remember spreading out on the breakfast table before me on the morning of 7 December 1921 the newspaper giving the terms of the London settlement, the Treaty, and reading that politically our status was to be like that of Canada, Australia and South Africa, and that the British Army would be moving out. That was excellent, and I could see what was in Michael Collins's mind when he spoke of stepping stones and this being the first real step. There were features which were hard to swallow – an oath of allegiance for instance – so that the Treaty, while accepted by majorities in the Dáil cabinet, the Dáil itself and by the people at large, was resisted from the beginning by a sizeable minority. In our office, that was the way it went, too: the men, by and large, favoured the settlement, the two women opposed it, as did our minister, O'Connor.

Kevin O'Shiel, who was to become the Assistant Legal Adviser to a government which set out to implement the Treaty, provisionally wrote down what had influenced him. The Truce, he said, had intervened providentially at a critical moment in Ireland's fortunes. 'Our heroic little army had at that time practically reached the end of its resources and supplies of ammunition, and in the ordinary course would have had to surrender, or to permit itself to be slaughtered without any effective means of self-defence.'

A meeting had been called at our office of an Economic Affairs Committee, over which ordinarily Robert Barton would preside, and consisting of O'Connor, Etchingham, Ernest Blythe, the Director of Commerce, and Joe McDonagh who was directing the boycott of Belfast goods. It was called off, but O'Connor and MacDonagh got together in the Minister's room where I ordinarily sat and spent hours there. Both of them later declared against the Treaty, and O'Connor in time was to become President of the Republic, even in opposition to de Valera. He underwent a change, however, and accepted a judgeship when de Valera replaced Cosgrave as the president of the Executive Council of the Irish Free State.

I suppose I could not help being elated when I read in the paper the short announcement from Michael Collins that the Irish government had received the surrender of Dublin Castle! The Irish Tricolour had been raised over the building for the first time and the Union Jack lowered for the last time. There were pictures of Irish soldiers marching in and British soldiers marching out; and the public were told that the British Viceroy, Lord Fitzalan, who was also leaving, had been the centre and symbol of the British power that had held Ireland for 750 years. Then the evacuations began of British troops at the rate of three battalions a day. The Black and Tans and the Auxiliaries left. If everything else had been in order no Irish heart would have been unmoved; unfortunately, however, the dark shadow of disagreement on the Treaty was already gathering ominously, and I could see and sense it in my place of work.

I recall going down to Galway with Alec Maguire on the early mail train, enjoying a good breakfast and reading the newspaper while Alec read the stories of Anton Chekhov. The

Russians had become something of a literary craze. We did not discuss the political situation. Later that day Alec heard Land Settlement appeals in the city's courthouse, and I acted as his Registrar. I knew nothing at all about the cases, but that apparently did not matter. I had simply to look efficient and to make the most intelligent notes I could, which was difficult in the circumstances. We stayed that night in the Great Southern Hotel, sharing a large room with our beds miles apart. Most of the building was occupied by pro-Treaty troops. That, I think, was Alec's last appearance in a Land Settlement Court. A discovery that he had given a subscription to the anti-Treaty fund led to his being asked by Paddy Hogan, who had displaced O'Connor as minister, to explain himself. His reply put him finally in the anti-Treaty court. Years afterwards, when the anti-Treaty cause triumphed and de Valera came to power, Alec came into his own, becoming the Chief Justice of the Irish Free State and subsequently of the Republic.

Our new minister, Paddy Hogan, operated from an office in Government Buildings in Merrion Street. He came one day to our set-up in Westmoreland Street and took over formally from Martin Heavey to whom the leadership of the office had passed, Alec Maguire having been fired and Kevin O'Sheil being busy with the legal affairs of the new government. I had hitherto known Heavey only by name; meeting him in the flesh was not a pleasant experience. He was a self-opinionated big bullock of a man, and he destroyed almost in an instant the happy easygoing atmosphere of the place. He was in command and he wanted us to know it. He brought in an elderly typist to replace the two who had left to work with de Valera in his Suffolk Street office, taking their machines with them, and he reprimanded me for whistling as I went down stairs. It became evident later that he had more serious things to worry him, for soon enough he was to leave Ireland in a hurry, never to return.

Meanwhile things were steadily getting worse in the country as a whole. Guns were out. Groups were appearing everywhere, led by men whose names were mainly unknown nationally, to take over barracks and impose themselves on local communities. People read in their papers of seemingly endless meetings of IRA leaders which only increased the general confusion. Then a group, ignoring the decision of the Dail, occupied the Dublin Four Courts, making it inevitable that the government forces that were being assembled and trained would be compelled sooner or later to assail the building. When this happened we, from the upper back window of the office, could see the dome of the Four Courts and smoke arising occasionally as a shell was fired, and from a front window, after the Four Courts fell, we were distracted endlessly by movements up and down Westmoreland Street as the government attack switched to the hotel area in O'Connell Street now occupied by anti-Treaty forces. This was civil war, a war in which uncontrollable forces were being released to do unjustifiable deeds. Needless to say work was impossible, not that there was much to be done.

I had to bring a letter early one morning to our new minister in Government Buildings. The government was literally incarcerated in the office block they had taken over in Merrion Street which had been intended as an extension to the College of Science. The Ministers were living in, and there were soldiers all over the place. Hogan, when I met him, was in his shirt sleeves. He had just finished his breakfast and was looking in a drawer of his desk for a clean collar. I think I saw a revolver.

A decision was taken about this time – I don't know by whom – that we of the Land Settlement Commission should leave Westmoreland Street and go into Board of Works premises in Lower Baggot Street. This was our first contact with one of the many services that had been taken over from the British.

There were men with us at this stage that I was to know and admire greatly. One was Matt Flanagan who, having lost his job in the Irish Land Commission either because of 1916 or for refusing to take the oath of allegiance that was required of all civil servants later, went to work on the Liverpool docks. Another was Joe O'Byrne, the Land Settlement Commission's registrar, who had benefitted from the general release of prisoners consequent on the Treaty. He had been in Ballykinlar, but that was not his first experience of internment. A vigorous young man with particularly fine aquiline features, and an ex-law clerk, he had come back to take over a job which he had previously held briefly.

We turned in every morning, but there being by now nothing whatever to do, we just twiddled our thumbs and talked. The news from outside was grim indeed. Griffith had died of heart failure. Collins was shot in an ambush. We wondered what was to become of us. Was there anything we could do? It was Joe O'Byrne who came up with a proposal. He had been talking to the man who had become Chief of Staff in the Army, Sean MacMahon: they were old friends since Volunteer days. He had said that we might be useful to him at G.H.Q. and there we went. It was an utterly surprising development for me to find myself a commissioned officer employed on General Staff duties. I had no military experience whatever, of course, nor was I now given any training. Indeed I doubt if I could have done anything to defend myself if attacked; and I remember only too well my feelings as I first came out of Portobello Barracks in uniform having read that day that fellows like me would be shot at sight. Feelings were running desperately high, and a lassie I knew called me a traitor in the middle of Grafton Street. When Cáit's brother went to see his aunts in Navan, one of them told him straight out that she did not recognise him 'in that uniform'. The other aunt, however, countered by saying 'Come on in, Harry. Blood is thicker than water.'

In the army I did whatever jobs I was given to do, and as I was now a law student and had had some slight connection with the organisation of courts, I was given opportunities of looking at matters that had a legal aspect including compensation claims for damage to property that had started to pile in. I remember being selected as a member of a court that was sent to Athlone to try an officer who was charged with wilful negligence in an ambush which his platoon had suffered in the town of Boyle. We found the man guilty despite the protestations of John Hearne, the legal officer of the Western Command, who in later years was to become a constitutional adviser to de Valera and an outstanding diplomat. Despite his guilt the convicted officer was allowed to escape and to journey overseas. I suspect that the General Officer Commanding the Western Command, Sean MacEoin of Ballinalee fame, resented a G.H.Q. party courtmartialling one of his men.

John Hearne told us one evening that he had an urgent

case to settle in Strokestown and would we like to run out there with him. We said we would. It was a lovely sunny evening. There was no traffic on the roads, and rabbits everywhere, giving the impression of an area that had not been much touched, if at all, by the recent fighting. It was a most enjoyable trip. Hearne's business concerned a woman living in the town, but when we came to her house we were told she had gone to the Mission. We drove down to the church and John, the most urbane of men, made a modest enquiry. To our great surprise, out came the parish priest proclaiming in a loud voice that we would enter the church or take out a member of the congregation – I don't remember which – over his dead body. It was so ridiculous; yet it was quite clear there was no point in trying to reason with him. We would, I suppose, have gone away, and left him to boast of how he had disposed of those army fellows. However, as he went back to the church, a young priest came out of a house nearby and in a short polite conversation John Hearne explained that what he wanted would probably be to the woman's advantage. The woman was immediately produced and John's business with her was quickly and satisfactorily completed. I met John many times thereafter in many different capacities; the pleasantest perhaps was when as the Irish ambassador he entertained Cardinal D'Alton and myself to dinner in Ottawa during a Marian Congress.

Families were affected by the division in the country over the Treaty. My brother Séamus had worked at de Valera's headquarters in Suffolk Street and, when the fighting started, was with him in a hideout in the York Street area. Some of his papers I have seen indicate that before the National Army had broken the resistance in Dublin an attempt to capture a gun shelling the Four Courts was contemplated. Séamus went on the run, was arrested and sent to an internment camp in the Curragh. I had warned him to no avail. And he was saddened to learn from his captors, who beat him up a bit, that places he had taken messages to in England had been visited by the police.

All this time I was attending law lectures in University College and the King's Inns. Among the professors I met in the former place were two very kind but odd men, J. G. Swift MacNeill and Arthur Clery. MacNeill had been a member of

Parnell's party and had exploited his knowledge of parliamentary precedents to obstruct the proceedings of the House of Commons in the 1880s. He had quit politics on the rise of Sinn Féin. He was an erratic lecturer, seeming to depend for a subject on whatever newspaper cutting he fished out of the pocket of his overcoat. He was always encouraging us to ask questions; those put to him the year before 'by a smart fellow by the name of Binchy' had enabled him to write an article for the London *Times* or one of its subsidiaries for which he had been paid good money. His chair was in Constitutional Law and the Law of Evidence; but he appeared to me to act most erratically in setting an examination paper in Evidence without giving a solitary lecture on the subject. He never called the roll either, but would hand it down to the class occasionally with a 'Gentlemen, immortalise yourselves'. I am afraid some of the students availed of these opportunities to 'immortalise' their absent friends as well.

The other unusual figure, Arthur Clery, who had risen to prominence with the Irish revival and Sinn Féin, was well known for his opposition to the Treaty. We saw nothing of this in his Law of Property class, however. He was a gentlemanly fellow and completely devoted to his students. He had us all out to a meal at the end of the college year; and it was understood that if any of us went to practice at the Bar he would find us a small brief to start us off. He was a bachelor, and appeared to live frugally; certainly when I had tea with him in his flat there was little more on his table than a loaf of bread. Under a pseudonym he wrote for *The Leader* with which I became identified later, and as a student he was remembered for 'going quite mad' on the night the Chief Secretary, Augustine Birrell, came to the Literary and Historical Society to discuss university reform. Con Curran, my friend and Rathgar neighbour, said that he tore into Birrell, spitting on his promises, deriding his non-conformist conscience, and guying all his Liberal gods.

Once or twice I went to lectures in uniform; scarcely a wise thing to do, I now think. One morning as I walked towards Portobello Bridge I became uncomfortably aware that the barracks towards which I was facing was being sniped at from a number of directions. I decided to make for the canal entrance to the barracks and to put the bravest face possible on it. I returned the salute of the soldiers who opened the gate for me and walked towards my office which was over near the main entrance on the Rathmines Road. I was surprised that I saw no effort within the barracks itself to respond to the attack, other than what was being put up by one of our orderlies. He, a Belfast man with experience of the troubles in that city, was firing from the landing above our office at what may have been an imaginary target.

I paid an occasional visit to the Land Settlement Commission where the staff had been joined by Sean Collins, who became a fast friend of mine. He had been farming all his life in west Cork, had suffered considerably because he happened to be a brother of the Michael Collins whom the British wanted dead or alive. I loved to hear Sean talk. He had a modicum of native Irish which gave his forceful accented speech an unusual quality. He could hold you in thrall describing the beauty of nature as revealed, for example, in the rotation of crops. He let me see Michael's books, and I remember finding in one of them, O'Donovan Rossa's *Irish Rebels*, the moving Famine ballad of Jill and Andy which Sean knew off by heart. My colleague Joe O'Byrne was meanwhile persevering with his studies for the Bar. Unlike me, and despite his practical experience as a law clerk, he had to matriculate, with little to fall back on except the knowledge of Irish he had acquired in Ballykinlar. That meant that late at night, after he had seen the children to bed, he had to make up the other required examination subjects including Latin and Mathematics. How he did it I don't know. But he did; and when he had matriculated there was no stopping him. He won all the prizes that were to be won, not excepting the coveted Brooke Scholarship at the final Bar examination. He took silk in 1954, having in the meantime become the Registrar of Deeds and Titles. His was an astonishing career; and through it all he remained the humblest of men.

I had been seeing Cáit all this time with unbroken regularity, and from our meetings I naturally learned a great deal about her, and from her. The very first time we walked together she used a word I had never heard before. It was 'circumspect'. She was not saying anything about herself, as far as I recall. I just assumed that this was a casual word which showed how superior her vocabulary was to mine. That was undoubtedly true, but as I got to know her more intimately I could see that through that particular word she gave me a view of her inner self. It spoke of her attitude to life, of her aim to be circumspect herself. In the words of a song I first heard about that time 'she had a soul to keep'. I took her to hear a contralto who was much admired in the Central Branch for her singing of 'Softly awakes my heart' in *Samson and Delilah*. It was Cáit's first time ever at the opera, an art form she grew to love. She was musical of course, played the piano a bit and would sing for me a Percy French song with appropriate mimicry. Her favourite piece was *The Darling Girl from Clare*: 'I was sitting on the wall upon a Sunday/watching the girls go by/and thinking I'd be married to one one day/when Kate Flynn caught my eye.' Cáit, I suppose, was my Kate Flynn.

In the Dublin Gaelic League I knew, that Percy French song would not be amiss among young men and women who had probably more regard for Gilbert and Sullivan than for the sean-nós. I could enjoy G and S myself and not consider myself odd in any way for doing so. The oddities I became aware of in the League were of a different kind; men like P. T. McGinley (*Cú Uladh*) and Lord Ashbourne, two men who at different periods filled the presidential seat, were odd in the sense of being extreme. McGinley introduced an *Irish Only Day* which made no difficulties for him and his large Irish-speaking family, but for me it meant a day when I was mute, causing my mother to think I had lost my mind as well as my voice, and driving me out on to the unsympathetic street in search of fellow lunatics. Ashbourne, who wore his kilts short to the point of immodesty, would write me letters from France, each of which contained a conundrum or two. He, too, wanted Irish only; so that to mention, for instance, Winston Churchill or Hamar Greenwood he had to find an Irish equivalent for their names. In these cases the Irish form in translation would read Wind Stone of the Hill of the Church and Hammer of the Green Woods.

I once paid a visit to Cáit in Baltinglass, going down on the old branch railway line long since abandoned. I stayed a couple of days, and was charmingly greeted, housed and fed by her mother whom I was meeting for the first time. The old housekeeper Wardie I had heard so much about was dead, but there were stories about her that took me back to the Kiltegan area she hailed from, and of the local heroes of 1798, Michael Dwyer and Sam MacAlister. Indeed I got the strong impression that the whole of that countryside was rich in folklore, and I often pressed Cáit to get after it before it died. She was always reluctant to write anything, however, despite her obvious capability. I should, of course, have done something myself, even at second hand, for the life of the town as she described it was rich with personalities.

It was a garrison town of sorts, and occasionally an army band would play for a dance in the town hall. She sat once in the gallery there adoring her good-looking mother Jennie O'Reilly as she waltzed continuously through the night. Jennie attracted at least one suitor, the local stationmaster. He might have married her, widow though she was, only for the children, for Cáit *et al.* He may not have had much money, of course, or perhaps he was a bit tight with what he had. He took Jennie to lunch one day in Dublin and remarked that he did not like to see flowers on the table. 'You could always smell them in the bill.'

The call out of the militia was an important time in Baltinglass in British days; soldiers from a nearby camp would purchase enormous quantities of meat from a butcher who lived across the road from the O'Reillys and take it away in their own carts. Cáit spoke of the parish church, of the priests, some of whom went around on horseback, of the Presentation nuns and of a holy Augustinian brother who came down sometimes from Dublin to visit Wardie, his ageing aunt. She spoke of the life of the town, of what was thought of the new political leader W. T. Cosgrave – they called him 'old Cosker' – of the fact that all the good shops were in Protestant hands, and how girls she had played with ceased to recognise her when they came back from convent boarding schools. From Wardie she heard of the local belief that the lady who ran the hotel in the town went through the clients' pockets when they had 'drink taken'. She had a prime story of Mrs Hayden who looked after the Church so well that nothing connected with it could happen without her. A little child was being taken round the Stations of the Cross one day by her mother, and at the twelfth station it suddenly dawned on her that the good Jesus had been killed. 'Who killed him?' she said, amazed. 'The Jews', her mother told her. 'The Jews', said the youngster, 'and where was Mrs Hayden?'

I had often heard in Dublin of the jumble that was sometimes made of the Church's public prayers, of Blessed Michael the *dark*-angel, and the Holy *Imposters* Peter and Paul, but I really regret not recording, as Cáit told it, the Litany of Our Lady as it was overheard being said by an unlettered old man who had apparently picked it up as he knelt at the back of the parish church. Health of the Sick had become Hell to the Sick, Refuge of Sinners 'Rubbish of Cinders', and Ark of the Covenant was 'Ark of the Convent Gate'.

I heard of an experience Cáit's mother had had during the Black and Tan period. She got a call late one evening to a place some distance out in the country. A woman had come to her time, but to reach her a car was needed, and the people who hired cars ordinarily said they could not provide one. They were afraid to go out. Mrs O'Reilly spoke to the medical officer, hopeful perhaps that he would drive her to the case, but he had no intention of doing so; that became clear. 'Nurse O'Reilly', he said, 'you are under no obligation in these circumstances to go to that woman.' Nurse O'Reilly thought differently. She may have known the woman and considered it might be a difficult birth. She didn't give up anyway. She went down to the police station, and spoke to a Tan who was standing in the doorway. Without hesitation he said, 'I'll come with you.' He drove her out, waited till the child was delivered, and drove her home. Next morning the medical officer asked her had she any news about the case. 'Oh yes', Mrs O'Reilly replied, 'that came off all right. I was out there.' 'Oh, you were, were you?' he said, very surprised, 'and who took you?' She paused and then, very deliberately, said: 'A *friend* took me.'

Cáit liked to tell that latter-day variant of the Good Samaritan parable. It reminded her how important it was not to write off any body of people as being wholly bad. The Tans had had, as we say, a uniformly bad press; it was therefore necessary to be reminded that, even among them, there were good men.

I continued to write an occasional short story in Irish, and sometime in 1923 a friend – I wondered later if she was really a friend – suggested that I should put them together and publish them in book form. Having more vanity than sense I swallowed the idea in one gulp and made terms with a printer I knew. It never occurred to me, such was my innocence, to try and find a publisher. The book literally died at birth. There was no sales organisation to push it, and the result was that most of three thousand copies remained in the printer's hands while I struggled to pay off a bank overdraft. Then, out of the blue, something happened to lift up my heart. I read in the paper one morning that the printing works had been destroyed by fire. And assuming that they were covered by insurance, I saw that the *House of Dangers*, as I called my book, was going to pay its way after all. After a discreet interval, I rang up my friend the printer and tendered my sympathy. He was very grateful; it was just what he would have expected of me; but he hastened to tell me he had good news. My book had been saved from the flames. At considerable risk to himself one of his men had gone into the burning building, and among the parcels he pulled out were mine. With my tongue very much in my cheek I commended the man's gallantry.

My interest in the language itself, as distinct from being a literary medium, was stimulated at a course I attended in the School of Irish Learning which had accommodation in the building at the corner of Stephen's Green and York Street where the Gaelic Players rehearsed. In the course, which was conducted by the Norwegian scholar Alf Sommerfelt, and at which I met Osborn Bergin, Myles Dillon and Gerard Murphy – all of them vastly more learned than I – we studied the vowels and consonants of Munster Irish, using some splendid native speakers as guinea pigs. It was the first time I had seen the international phonetics system being employed.

I won the gold medal in the last year of a course I had been doing in the Leinster College of Irish and was then employed automatically to do a spot of teaching. One evening I went out to substitute for a colleague with a class of nuns in Glasnevin. Although it should have been a disturbing prospect for a young fellow, I was not really upset until I saw the class on a gallery before me; for there, sitting in the very first row, was a little lady I had not seen for years, the Sister de Ricci who had broken up the attempt to stage a school strike in 1913. She made no sign that she recognised me – maybe she didn't – but her very presence had a devastating effect on me. I turned my back to the class – a fundamentally wrong thing for any teacher to do – and half-heartedly gave my lecture to the blackboard. When the time was up I was led to an ante-room and given a nice tea from the community's silver service. I did not delay over it; I could not get out to the fresh air fast enough.

Some time in 1923 casually meeting Seamus Hughes, the secretary of the government's political party, outside Trinity College, he asked me if I could recommend somebody to him with Irish to be his office assistant. I recommended Cáit, and he took her on, increasing the salary of £2 a week she had from the Yorkshire Insurance Company to £3. Cáit had no political experience whatever, needless to say, but she soon found her bearings from working with Hughes. He was an idealist, a 1916 man and Irish-Irelander, and was deeply religious. Before the Treaty he had been employed by the Transport Union; after it he became the first Secretary of Cumann na nGaedheal. He was musical, and I had heard him singing at concerts before I spoke to him over tea in a restaurant annexed to Liberty Hall to which he had invited me. When Cáit was his assistant we often went together to musical evenings in his house in Glasnevin where Seamus would open up his repertoire to us, including songs that he had himself composed. I seriously doubt if politics was his metier, but he may not have been entirely responsible for the obvious lack of co-ordination between the party and the government. From 1924 and onwards was a bad period politically for the government; it was the time of the Boundary Commission debacle, the Army mutiny, and the resignation of ministers and T.D.s. With Hughes necessarily out of the office a lot, a considerable amount of work fell on Cáit especially during the by-elections, which Cumann na nGaedhael managed to win with the help of paid organisers sent down from Dublin. Cáit was with the government party too, when Hughes, put up to replace Hugh Kennedy who had become Chief Justice, was defeated in a by-election in South Dublin by Sean Lemass. In another by-election in the North city, J. J. Walsh, the Minister for Posts and Telegraphs, now the government's political supremo, sent word that Cáit was to go out canvassing after her day's work. That nowadays seems an extraordinary demand from an employer but, given the circumstances, Cáit would not have minded what was asked of her except that she had planned to go somewhere else with me that night. She phoned Walsh's secretary, Maurice Collins, and told him of her predicament. 'Forget about the canvassing,' he advised her, 'and keep the date with the boy friend. I understand perfectly. I was young myself once.' So, not by any means for the first time, affairs of the heart scored over the affairs of the nation.

Money was never flush in Cumann na nGaedhael and, mindful of this, Cáit suggested that they should cease sending out notices of meetings to members of the governing body who never attended. A particular case was that of Fred Allan, but Hughes insisted that he should continue to be invited to meetings whether he came or not. Allan was a link with their past; he had been a leading I.R.B. figure from the 1880s. The past was also represented on the committee by Jennie Wyse-Power who had worked with Parnell's sisters in the Ladies' Land League before marrying an I.R.B. man. She kept a close eye on the people with money but with no national background who came on the scene hoping to be adopted for political honours – membership of the Senate, perhaps. In 1924, the old Fenian John Devoy came to Ireland on his first visit for over fifty years. In the opinion of *The Times* (of London) he was the most dangerous enemy of Britain which Ireland had produced since Wolfe Tone. He stayed six weeks, received many courtesies, particularly from former supporters of the I.R.B., a body which had been recently dissolved. Cumann na nGaedheal sent him a telegram in Irish to be received as he came off the liner at Cobh. I wrote the telegram for Cáit, and many years later, when I was working on the Devoy papers in the National Library I found it. Devoy was obviously one of the breed of men who keeps everything, even their tram tickets.

Before I managed to pass the final Bar examination, leaving me wondering to this very day what the examiners thought of my attempted answers in Latin to the couple of questions in that language on the Roman Law paper, I found myself working in two of the former British departments. I was for a spell in the Irish Land Commission, and for a year or two on the Customs side of the Revenue Commissioners. It was there, in the building in Little Denmark Street where Radio Éireann first reposed and from which I did my first broadcast, that I encountered the writing tradition in Irish and English for which the Revenue service was renowned. It was there, too, that I met up with another Revenue tradition, that of lifting the elbow. Among my co-workers looking for dutiable commodities in the Parcel Post was one particularly able exponent of the art. He took to me for some reason and told me tearfully of the mess he had made of his life. While working in the London docks he had gone on a bad binge from which he recovered to find that he had acquired a wife and joined the British army. He got out of the army somehow, but he had made no progress when I knew him in the matter of ridding himself of the wife, and there may have been a child to add to the complications. He lodged near the cattle market and on Thursday, the market day, he would come in in swallow tails. He would have been drinking through most of the night before, and after a bath and a visit to the barber's would tog out in this formal way before facing another day. In the office he would soon begin to sag, however, and would fall asleep on the boring job of assessing the duty on the usually trifling things that were put before him. This was done by post office staff who consistently complained about the delays caused by my friend's drinking and sleeping habits. It was clear that a crisis was developing when, one Thursday morning, it was learned that a joint group of top Customs and Post Office people were on their way to Denmark Street. My colleagues accepted that the bounds of reason had been exceeded, but he was none the less a Revenue man and they were not going to allow the Post Office to score over them. So, they grabbed the sleeping figure, and stuck his head under a tap in the toilet until he had sobered up. When the inspection committee arrived, he was sitting up at his table as bright as a new penny and urging the Post Office officials before him to hurry up for God's sake. The last I saw of him was when he delivered to me a huge onyx clock that the Customs service gave me on leaving them. He and a colleague had carried the clock across the city and up the length of Leinster Road and were obviously exhausted when they reached the house where I was then living. A lovely bacon and cabbage and apple tart dinner was ready for them with the appropriate drinks. That revived them.

I was called to the Bar in Dublin Castle in 1924 by the Chief Justice, Hugh Kennedy, a rotund gentleman with a squeaky voice I had met socially a couple of times and of whose work on the constitution of the new state I was fairly conversant. Cáit and I celebrated the occasion by drinking a bottle of champagne, about which neither of us knew anything except that it was the thing you celebrated an occasion with. I took her home by taxi afterwards, another extravagance to which we were not accustomed, and she went to bed with a headache. That night she was as fresh as paint, however. I had bought a wig and gown in the famous Moss Bros house in London and toyed with the prospect of practising as a barrister, perhaps on the Western Circuit where I thought my knowledge of Irish would help, but I had to abandon the idea. I had no money, no solicitor friends, and to have survived without these for some years would have been impossible. The degree, however, helped to get me through the first Free State Junior Administrative examination in 1925 for which marks for army service were also awarded. I nearly missed the opening paper, however, and would in consequence have failed the exam. The circumstances were quite unusual. A colleague of mine in the Customs service was being tried for rape and I sat in the gallery in Green Street waiting to be called as a witness to character, if that should be necessary. My friend was an exemplary man and active in the Society of St Vincent de Paul; but broke a primary rule of the Society, however, in going alone to one of his cases. His co-visitor I think, had not turned up. The result was that he left himself open to a charge by a girl that he had assaulted her. He was acquitted, but that point had not been reached before I finally made up my mind that I had to leave and make across town to the Aula Maxima in Earlsfort Terrace. I was duly called to the Department of Finance to be looked at by two men in their late thirties, the round-faced Joseph Brennan, who was the head of both the Department and the Civil Service, and the bony-faced J. J. McElligott, his Assistant Secretary.

It was a brief interview that started badly, for I could not tell them which of the subjects for an essay I had chosen to write about, nor that I had done it in Irish. No question was asked about my knowledge of English. This was just as well, perhaps, because I had only made a scrappy preparation in the subject for the exam. I had found the set text, Pope's *Essay on Man*, quite beyond me. I have never looked at it subsequently, and was recently relieved to learn that Dr Johnson had spoken of the happy disguise Pope had made in it of 'such penury of knowledge and vulgarity of sentiment'; and that a critic of our own day saw no disrespect for poetry in hesitating to recognise as poetic the Essay's 'decorated platitudes'. My high mark in Irish must have been noticed by Brennan and McElligott and was probably the reason why they directed that I should go to the Department of Education, after a spell in the office of the Comptroller and Auditor General. The purpose of the diversion presumably was to ensure that I recognised the Finance idea of the need for authority in the spending of money. In the Audit Office I read some dreadful tomes, and actually audited a small vote on my own. It was the vote for the Dundrum Criminal Lunatic Asylum, and I remember that the only payment that at first sight seemed irregular was for a new dinner jacket for the Resident Superintendent, a Doctor Considine. I raised a query – that, I think, is what the regular auditors would say I did – and was told that one of the inmates had thrown a bucket of whitewash over Considine as he went out to dinner.

It was high time to take seriously the question of getting married, now that I had a good if poorly paid job with prospects. Cáit and I knew each other so well that it was most unlikely she would refuse. Nor did she when, sitting with me at the bandstand in Stephen's Green one night, I suggested we should go together to Geneva to a summer course in international law and politics I had seen advertised in College with special facilities for university students. Cáit, always so practical, said that would be very nice, but how would we do it? 'We'll get married,' I said, 'and go.' And go we did, in a rush. Sean Collins, who had promised to be godfather to our first child, backed a bill in the bank; Cáit resigned her job; and at 6.45 in the morning of 19 August 1925, we were married in Cáit's parish church in Iona Road so quietly that nobody seemed to know anything about the date except Cáit's boss, Seamus Hughes. When we left the church he was there, charming as ever, with a bouquet of flowers. We hurried from him to have a cup of tea with Cáit's family and were driven by taxi to the mail boat in Dun Laoghaire. On the other side of the Irish Sea, between boat and train and taxi, dinner and theatre and the rest of it, there was little time to remember that I had done something that was irrevocable, but next morning when I woke in that little room in the Russell Hotel in London and saw Cáit asleep beside me and wearing my ring I knew that this was *it*. We were now one, and as she used to say jokingly afterwards: 'I'm the one!' Another of her jokes was that she had got a husband for 7s. 6d., her annual Gaelic League subscription, and that would bring to her mind the story of a woman she knew who answered an advertisement in the matrimonial column of the *Irish Independent* and made a successful match on the head of it. It was, Cáit would say, good value for a twopenny stamp.

Our honeymoon was somewhat unusual. After a couple of romantic nights in Paris, we were installed in a pension in Geneva where, knowing nothing at all about it, we argued at table with students against the ban in Swiss law on Jesuits; we attended the formal lectures religiously, all of them given by international celebrities. We made friends, went to shows from which the unmarried students were excluded; we boated on the lake and saw something of the magnificent countryside. We went up to Leysin in the Alps one day to a sanatorium where our friend, the scholarly Gerard Murphy, was a patient. He was confined to his room, but through him we met Theo Dillon for the first time – he too, was a patient – and had tea with him in a mountainside café. It was possibly from him that we heard that the Irish TB sufferers, of whom there were a good number, were divided by their civil war politics. They only agreed to unite and fly the tricolour for St Patrick's Day. Myles, Theo's brother, was in Geneva at this time with Dan Binchy; and he came to visit Cáit in a clinic where, because of a slight mishap, she had to have treatment.

The International School to a degree was influenced by being held in Geneva, then the centre of the League of Nations. Ireland, as a self-governing state, had become a member of the League in 1923, her entry having been prepared by Michael MacWhite, a friend of Arthur Griffith and an ex-officer of the French Foreign Legion, who became the Free State representative in 1924. We went to see him in his office down by the lakeside and, at his suggestion, we also called on E. J. Phelan, who was the first Irishman to make an impact as an official of the International Labour Office. Cáit and I learned enough during those days in Geneva to swallow in part the optimistic thesis that, despite the absence of the United States, the League might succeed in preventing the big nations from again going to war. We joined the Irish League of Nations Society when we returned home, went in 1926 to Oxford to a League of Nations Summer School, and were members of an Irish delegation to an international assembly of League Societies in Aberystwyth. That was a splendid occasion which Cáit often recalled, especially the form of the hospitality she personally received. What, outside the formal sessions, I particularly remember is of an Irishman, obviously drunk, who at the unveiling of a statue in Tregarron, demanded at the top of his voice to know where the Irish delegation was. He did not succeed in finding us for, at the sound of his voice, we hid ourselves away in the deep charabanc seats. Sometime afterwards the Society asked me to speak to a meeting that had been organised in Lucan or Leixlip. There, to my horror, I was confronted by outright and noisy opposition to the League from a group led by a priest. De Valera had not yet declared himself about the League so that my critics were just taking the common line of assuming that any body the Free State government had joined was no good. De Valera in time was to become President of the Council of the League and occupied that position when it became necessary to defend the Covenant against Japan who had attacked the territory of China. The League was already in serious trouble by then: few members who professed faith in it really believed what they said, and the League, anyway, was without the means of enforcing its decisions.

In the headquarters of the Department of Education at No. 1 Hume St, I first saw the tall spindly figure of Joseph O'Neill, the Secretary of the Department, whom I had not seen since, as a secondary school inspector, he had examined me in the Brothers' school some years before. I had, however, read a series of articles of his in the *Irish Statesman*, which taken together with his friendship with Senator Alice Stopford Green, may have had something to do with his appointment. He suffered from the cold: so his desk was set behind a screen to keep out the draught, and I think he always had a fire. I saw very little of him while I was in Education but a lot of his private secretary who had a desk near mine where she read pedagogical publications endlessly and marked passages O'Neill might be interested in. O'Neill passed me on to his assistant secretary, Frank O'Duffy, and accomodation being scarce, I was given a seat in the general office which was near the entrance to the building. The general office was not the easiest place to work in: there was always someone coming or going. It was there I first met Peter Judge. He had earlier been a temporary clerk in the Intermediate Branch and used to drop in occasionally to see old friends. He was better known by his stage name, F. J. McCormick, and was, I should think, the most versatile player the Abbey Theatre has ever known. The theatre was at this time in deep depression, but Ernest Blythe and Sean O'Casey were coming to its rescue, the former with an annual subsidy, the latter to write plays that re-established the Abbey's international reputation.

I was aware, of course, that there was a Minister for Education, a political head, John Marcus O'Sullivan, who had not very long before replaced the victim of the Boundary Commission quandary, the historian Eoin MacNeill. I had little contact with O'Sullivan, and I was sorry not to have served under MacNeill. His private secretary, John McLellan, had an office in Hume Street and it was from him I heard of a dinner party of the Boundary Commission in Derry which MacNeill left early, taking MacLellan with him to visit the Grianan of Aileach. All of the really important people in the department, Minister, Secretary, Assistant Secretary and Intermediate Commissioners who had not yet been abolished occupied the spacious rooms on the first floor. Above them on the second floor were the General Inspectors, and it was in one of their rooms, George Nicholls', I was to spend most of the year or so I was in Education. Inspectors were fairly thick on the ground in fact and I have often wondered why a solid administrative cadre was not inserted below the level of secretary with the possibility of promotion to that post. Perhaps I was intended as the first of such a group. Until recently one got the impression of a fossilised top recruited from a highly unionised teaching class.

Reviving the Irish language was the principal burden that had fallen on Education. The difficulties were enormous, and P. S. O'Hegarty had commented on them in 1915, the year I joined the department. 'We are constantly told', he said to the Jesuit scholar, Lambert McKenna, 'that as Irish was threshed out of Irish children by the cane, so it can be threshed into them. But it was not the cane, nor any sort of direct compulsion, that lost Irish. It was the fact that English had more to offer. The Irish boy in the forties was offered official life, the churches, the professions, the British Empire and America as his scope. He was offered with them one of the greatest of literatures and the key to modern civilisation and development. Irish offered him none of these things. It has practically no modern literature save school text books, it has practically no translations, its vocabulary is centuries out of date, it is not habitually used anywhere in Ireland for official, church, business or professional purposes nor is it possible so to use it. It has no international value outside philology.'

To cope with the task of reviving Irish despite these difficulties was one for which the department and the teaching community in general were ill-prepared and ill-fitted; indeed Michael Hayes, who knew something about the subject, declared that 'once Irish was handed over to the Department of Education it was lost,' and Eoin MacNeill had earlier confessed that 'you might as well be putting wooden legs on hens as trying to restore Irish through the schools system.' Anyhow it is certain that by 1925 the edge had gone off some of the earlier enthusiasm. I had seen in the Central Branch of the Gaelic League and in the Leinster College of Irish the crowds of teachers, civil servants and others that flocked to learn the language in 1922, but the beginnings of a decline of interest had set in as a result of the civil war and through the discovery that Irish was a difficult language to learn. It was not high on the list of the ordinary person's priorities, and we did not know anything like enough about modern teaching methods. There was also a vast scarcity of reading matter, for books in Irish, other than elementary school texts, were regarded as economic monstrosities. It was to cope with that problem that I was brought into the company of George Nicholls and another inspector, Mícheál Breathnach. The outline of a scheme of publications involving the Department of Education and Stationery Office jointly had been given to us and we set about giving effect to it. In those early purist days a word like *scéim* for scheme was frowned upon, and it was Mícheál Breathnach, I think, who gave us the alternative *Gúm* from his North Galway vocabulary. This word was spat upon in the Gaelic League's paper, but it held its own and very soon, beginning with a trickle, there was quite a flood of books being produced under that imprint.

Pádraic Ó Conaire was probably the only professional writer of Irish in the country at that time, if you call him that, and we soon had a book of short stories from him. Little in the nature of original writing came in otherwise, and that fact compelled us to turn to translations on a large scale sooner than we might otherwise have done. I confess that I, as a young writer, found the terms for both original work and translations very attractive; so that, in those early days at An Gúm, I handed in, and had speedily published for me, two books of short stories and translations of Stephenson's *Kidnapped*, Wells's *War of the Worlds* and Jerome's *Three Men in a Boat*. This kept the wolf from the door as my family began to arrive, and brought me letters of thanks from Wells and Jerome for making their works known to readers of Irish.

We discovered early in the proceedings that An Gúm had to have a self-imposed censorship. After all, we were part of a government department subsidised from public funds, and our output was seeing the light of day through the Stationary Office. None of our troubles became public, however. Sean a' Chota's *An Fanai* was the first in which some changes had to be made to avoid criticism. Seán O'Sullivan, the painter who did the cover for my *Béal na hUaighe*, was asked to put more clothing on a female figure; and I felt obliged to comply with a suggestion that a nativity play of mine, which I considered religiously unexceptional, should adhere strictly to the infancy narrative of the New Testament. It was also quietly made known to me that an account of life under the Gilly which I had contemplated would not be acceptable. These were minor matters, however. The major matter, which all these minor matters pointed towards, was that a government department was not an appropriate place for the production of literature.

I met Nicholls and Breathnach almost every day, and we usually lunched together, over in Jury's in Dame Street. We were a happy trio, until an innocent joke broke up the party. Breathnach had a touch of blood pressure and was told by his doctor to give up eating the onion sandwiches his wife prepared for his supper. We commiserated with him, naturally, but the humour of the situation struck Nicholls and myself simultaneously a day or two later, as the two of us passed Knowles's, the fruiterers in Grafton Street. We went in, bought a Spanish onion, and had it put into an orange crate and sent to Mr Michael Walsh, Esquire. Christmas was around the corner and his house was full with his own and his brother's children when the Tramways Express delivered the crate into the hall. There was considerable excitement naturally about its contents, and no time was lost in prising it open and going through the sawdust until the single onion was revealed. To our surprise and horror Michael took the joke badly. He sent me a scorcher, breaking off relations with me. There were only two people who could have perpetrated such a mean and miserable trick, and I was one of them. He did not say that George was the other, or write to him for, after all, George was his boss. We did not speak for years and we had some clashes about radio comments on education when he was head of that service and I had responsibility for broadcasting. Indeed we were both retired when, running into one another one day in the National Library, we shook hands and behaved as if there had never been anything between us.

As you can gauge, George Nicholls was a more genial person altogether. He was musical; perhaps it was that that made the difference. He played the piano, and his house in Howth, where he often entertained Cáit and me, had Chaliapin singing Boris Godunov as a constant background to lively conversation. He had some responsibility for music in Education and once told me how he had had to disagree with an external adviser who believed incredibly that all music ended with Brahms. A greater love of George's was the Irish language. He was the complete revivalist, and allowed himself to be betrayed into making a speech in which he said that 'every hog, dog and devil' would have to learn it. His Minister, John Marcus O'Sullivan, could not, of course, stand over that statement when he was questioned about it in the Dáil. I was sorry about that, and now sometimes I think that that blunder had more to do with his failure to become the Departmental Secretary than the fact that he was a Protestant. George told me that he and de Valera competed for the same inspectorship. 'If de Valera had got it', he added, 'I'd probably be the Taoiseach today.'

I was by now inclined to dissociate myself from the Gaelic League, which was just as well perhaps, as the Department of Education and its officials had become cock-shots in the League's paper. I was tiring of the political atmosphere of the Executive Committee of which I had been elected a member and was giving more of my time to the production of plays in Irish by a Gaelic Drama League of which I was secretary, and to which Ernest Blythe had given a subsidy. This looked a promising venture with the return to Ireland of Gearóid Ó Lochlainn from Denmark where he had been acting professionally; but, after some years, the experiment failed due to a number of factors. The repertoire, even with translations, was slim; that there could only be one performance a month meant that the audience effectively saw only a dress rehearsal; and Ó Lochlainn made a cardinal mistake in being both producer and actor. The interest in Gaelic drama persisted for years after my time, however; indeed, so far as I was concerned, until Tom Derrig, a Minister for Education in the 1940s, asked me to chair a committee representative of both the survivors of the Gaelic Drama League and Abbey Theatre directorate with the aim of securing fairly regular productions of a professional standard. By then Blythe was the managing director of the Abbey and employing Irish speaking players. The earlier Gaelic Drama League had been competent, and gave some good performances, but they were amateurs – part-time actors – and that plus the other factors I have mentioned ensured a steady decline. I remember March 1926 when we did Liam O'Flaherty's one and only play, *Dorchadas*, where the dramatics were both on the stage and off it. We were told that some university students intended to prevent the play being done at all, as had been attempted before with Synge's *Playboy* and O'Casey's *Plough and the Stars.* I went to General Murphy, the Deputy Commissioner of the Garda whom I had got to know in the army, and he filled the house and wings with plain-clothes men on the night. There was no disturbance whatsoever, however, which I rather regretted, for there is nothing like a row to publicise a play.

Cáit took me one day to a sale of work in aid of the Save The Children Fund in Con Curran's house in Garville Avenue, a few doors away from where we had our flat. She had joined a sewing class that prepared articles for the sale, and had made the acquaintance in it of the wives of some celebrated men; Curran himself, of course, who had been with James Joyce in University College, Dublin, at the opening of the century; Bulmer Hobson, the great originator of revolutionary societies of whom I was in time to write extensively; P. S. O'Hegarty, who figures in this book; and George Moonan, best known perhaps as the associate of Mary Hayden in a history that for a time was widely read in the schools, but then perhaps bemoaning the demise of the Irish Party in whose interest he had been defeated in the 1918 election. The sale I remember because at it I bought a copy of Joyce's *Chamber Music* for a few pence. Joyce had not yet acquired the army of literary critics who nowadays devote their lives to his work, and what I knew of his published work was that his short stories and poems were readable, whereas his *Ulysses* and *Finnegans Wake*, for different reasons, were not.

Around the corner from our flat was Rathgar Avenue where, in number 70, I was aware George Russell, A.E., held a crowded court on Sunday evenings and hoped that somebody someday would bring me along as a guest. The hairy, bent, short-sighted A.E. I knew well to see. I saw him every other day moving in and out of his office in Plunkett House on Merrion Square which was within yards of Government Buildings where I earned my crust; and one day, I don't know how, he invited me to come and see him there. I climbed the stairs, entered an open door and found him sitting with a young woman on his knee stroking his beard. She rose and left when I appeared, and he, showing no sign of embarrassment or anger, beckoned me to sit down and talk, possibly about my interest in books. Anyhow he gave me one to take away to review. That was the only conversation I ever had with a man of enormous significance. In the British days everyone wanted to meet him, not so much because he was a poet, the editor of a periodical, an economist, a painter of landscapes into which he inserted something of the fairy world in which he believed, but rather because of his extraordinary conversationalist powers, his ability to say something of value on any subject at the drop of a hat. A French novelist said that he shook out ideas in dazzling improvisation, and each of his listeners carried away a spark to light his own fire.

I was not long enough in his company to observe anything of that quality, but he communicated his views on the Gaelic Theatre to me when I sent him an article on that subject for the *Irish Statesman*. He read into the article that I was proposing a form of drama that would be more acceptable to nationalists than the usual Abbey fare (I wasn't), but in rejecting the article he said some things that are worth preserving in extension of what he had written much earlier when criticising Arthur Griffith. He believed that a genius – a painter, poet or playwright – refuses to do what the sentimentalist exepcts of him. He follows a law of his own being which means that he can only express what is in him and not what is in the mind of other people. He was just as likely to kick his country as to bless it. 'People', he said in his letter to me, are as God made them, or as evolution has left them 'and not all the appeals in the world will produce genius or deflect it from the course which is natural to it. Arthur Griffith long ago was always appealing to the poets to write national ballads, but that kind of thing had died out last century. He wanted the ballads for political reason but the poets were interested in something else. I have the strongest objection to suggesting to artists or poets or dramatists the subjects they should write about or the character their efforts should take as I know all such advice is perfectly futile and everybody will act according to nature.'

Years before this, Norman Reddin, a solicitor who was sympathetic to what we were trying to do in the Gaelic Theatre and may have thought I was an up and coming young fellow, invited me to speak to a paper he was to read on J. M. Synge to one of Dublin's literary societies. I took note of the date, and turned up on the night but with nothing whatever prepared. I was late, too, through no fault of my own. Reddin was already on his feet when I entered the hall and, not to disturb him, I took a seat down at the back. I have no recollection now of what the lecture was like, and when he sat down W. B. Yeats – the great man himself – was called on to propose the vote of thanks. That shook me – I didn't know he was in the hall – and I don't remember his speech either; my mind was racing on to what I might say in such distinguished company, something perhaps along the line of an article I had read by Professor Tomás Ó Máille on the genesis of *The Playboy of the Western World*. As an habitué of the Abbey I was able to take all of Synge's plays in my stride. I loved particularly the treatment of the *Playboy* as an extravaganza and understood what an imaginative producer could do with it. Certainly when I stood up to speak nothing was further from my mind than to identify with the Sinn Féiners and Gaelic Leaguers who in earlier years had rioted against the play. Yet I fear that this was the impression I created. At any rate when I had finished, only one person applauded. I looked round and recognised her. She might well have been one of the rioters or an associate of theirs. It was that night I realised that if you are going to make a speech, you should bring a script with you, and stick to it.

That was not my only involvement with Synge. During the time I was doing those law lectures in University College I threw in my lot with the Irish language and Irish literary societies and got to know Douglas Hyde and Agnes O'Farrelly of the Irish faculty. Hyde asked me to take under my wing a young Japanese academic, Takaoki Katta, who had come to Ireland to do some work on the English of Synge's plays, especially *Riders to the Sea*. He, Cáit and I became great friends, and we corresponded for years, even after the 1939-45 war. I explained to him that one key to Synge's English was the Irish language and, accordingly, in typical Japanese fashion, he locked himself away from us for about a month with the large Christian Brothers' grammar and emerged with a fair idea of the structure of Irish. He had difficulties with pronunciation naturally: an *l* became an *r*, so that *Slán leat*, good-bye, for example became *Srán rat*. We went to Inishmore together for a weekend, and travelled about in a side-car. We visited the parish church, where he showed how little he knew about our Catholic ways by trying to stand his umbrella up in the holy water font. We came back on a hooker to Connemara and I left him in a house with his bags while I went looking for a car to take us to Galway. When I returned to the house I found him swapping songs in Japanese and Irish with the *bean an tí*.

In the summer of 1926 Cáit and I went to Carna in the Galway Gaeltacht where I was to teach at an offshoot of a summer school that was based in Galway city. Carna and its offshore islands were beautiful, the local community of nuns gave us a lovely house to live in, and we were fed like fighting cocks. I knew Carna already. A few years earlier, the hotelier and T.D. to be, Josie Mongan, had brought me down in an off-season period to do some quiet study – my final Bar examination was coming up – but when he got me down, nothing would satisfy him but to introduce me to what I was to learn was a folklorist's paradise. He had an old man living in a hut in his garden with whom I spent a lot of time, and every afternoon and evening I went visiting with Josie to meet every shanachie and singer of repute in the country-side. I never opened a law book. Teaching elementary Irish to some youngsters from Co. Wicklow was not too much of a strain and, as the weather was gorgeous, we were in the water a lot. I had teaching with me a splendid speaker of Irish from the area where Eamon and Sinéad de Valera had once taught a summer school. Cáit would later recall how she floated on an inflated tube from his motor car. It goes better in Irish, *ag snámh ar bholg an mháistir scoile as Tamhain.*

At the end of the school term we went to a feis at Barna near where Mícheál Ó Droighneáin, the head of our summer school, lived and ordinarily taught in a primary school. It was a glorious Sunday afternoon and, while on a platform children danced and sang, I sat on a wall and talked with Pádraic Ó Conaire. He had been teaching literary appreciation in Galway to adult classes in the school. He had done so without breaching an undertaking he had given to abstain from drinking for a month. That was a notable achievement for a man who was perpetually 'under the influence' and in a region where, it was said, pubs occasionally shut but never closed. I had not seen him for about a year. On the day before I got married I had run into him in Westmoreland Street. He was delighted to hear the news, and insisted we should celebrate. He brought me into the Pearl Bar and called for drinks which somehow or other he allowed me to pay for. He was always hard up and when I met him next, in the Radical Club in Dawson Street, where Liam O'Flaherty was holding forth, he and the poet Fred Higgins were on the stairs looking for the price of a drink. I was almost as hard up as they were: in fact, I had only the 10/- note I foolishly parted with. Fred, it will be remembered, wrote Pádraic's most moving panegyric. Had Pádraic been drinking that day at Barna it would have explained the proposition he made to me, which was that we should jointly write a book on the history of Irish language literature. He would do the first part and I would write the remainder which meant that in the contemporary period Pádraic would figure most prominently. The idea was all right, but to ally himself with me, an unproven writer, was preposterous. That was Pádraic. He was always romancing, inventing situations that would please those who happened to share his company.

Cáit and I, both members of the Gaelic Drama League, had been rehearsing in the Ó Droighneáin household in Furbo a one-act farce for performance that Sunday night at a summer school concert in the Galway Town Hall. The piece, a translation, was designed to end with the curtain dropping on me kissing Cáit as a demonstration to my elderly old-fashioned brother, Mícheál Ó Droighneáin, on how to make love. The kiss was to last just about long enough for Mícheál to say that he had seen enough, that he would take over himself from that point. Unfortunately at that point the curtain got stuck, and failed to come down. The kiss had therefore to be prolonged, and with Mícheál, a really funny actor, protesting furiously, there was uproar in the theatre. Our friend Liam Ó Briain was in the front row with Dean Hynes, the President of the University College. He was enjoying our antics immensely and, even more the embarrassment of the man beside him. 'It's all right, Monsignor,' he was heard to shout above the noise, 'they're married'.

THREE

IN JANUARY 1927 I had been changed from Education to the Department of Finance, why I don't know, though I can suggest reasons, all of them uncomplimentary to me. I was assigned to the Finance Division, one of the three divisions into which the department, then rather small, was divided. I worked to John Leydon, an ex-Maynooth man who had worked in the Ministry of Pensions in Britain, through an assistant principal, Larry Lynd, a brother of Robert Lynd, about whose connections with the national movement I knew a little and whose Y.Y. essays in the *New Statesman* I loved to read. Larry, a shy, kind Northern Protestant, smoked endlessly and, after hours, drank too much, I fear. He broke me in on Law Charges, a small vote and one where most decisions were taken on the basis of precedents which had to be unearthed and applied. It was a good training vote, and in later years I saw some very distinguished young men being trained on it much as I was. Lynd, who had come to Finance from the Office of the Clerk of the Crown and Hanaper in the Four Courts, was something of an authority on land purchase finance also and on bloodstock, an interest he had acquired from following horses at race meetings. He was also involved, while I was with him, in the beginnings of the Beet Sugar Industry: and there fell into his bailiwick a mysterious thing called Quit Rents on which no progress was possible, however, because it was still uncertain to whom the revenue from them belonged. This was an area, like others, where a case had to be carried against the British government. Brennan, the secretary of the Department, had won a high reputation in doing that sort of thing in relation to various funds whose destination had remained unclear after the Treaty.

Meanwhile, and for as long as I was with Lynd, scores of files on this subject accumulated, and an old-fashioned bespectacled fellow named Burnett from the Quit Rent Office on Ormond Quay, who rolled his own cigarettes, would come in to enquire if there was any news about the destiny of the rents he was raising on sheep being grazed on Maryboro' Heath and the Curragh of Kildare.

There was nothing in my Land Settlement work that was a help to Lynd with the Land Commission cases that came to the department. One morning, however, I was sent to the National Library to read up the law and practice of Treasure Trove. The Land Commission had asked for a direction as to how to deal with a claim that gold artefacts had been found on a holding in the West. My learned treatise was uncalled for, however, for it transpired that the whole thing was a hoax, that the man who had told the story to the Commission had been unable to get a response to earlier letters of his about his annuity or some such thing, and that he had made up the story just to stir the Commission up.

When the first Irish currency notes appeared I was sent to the Bank of Ireland to be associated with a very senior Bank Official in superintending the destruction of the old Bradleys. The notes were thrown from large sacks into a furnace and, at the end of the day, the two of us returned to see the ashes being raked through and the very few bits and pieces that had survived the flames being carefully destroyed. Then we sat down to append our signatures to a statement to the British Treasury or the Bank of England that we had that day witnessed the destruction of so many millions of their money. It was a strange performance, particularly when at that time I was getting about £5 a week, and I tell the story in the context of the temptations to which other civil servants of that time were subject.

Lynd came in one Monday morning to tell me that he had seen an alarming thing at Shelbourne Park on the previous Saturday night. He had seen a young fellow who worked in our accounts branch drinking overmuch, smoking cigars and placing five pound bets. He had scarcely told me that when local publicans came in looking for payment in respect of payable orders they had cashed and which they understood were for overtime. They had, in fact, been taken from a pile of orders for compensation which had been returned to the accountant for one reason or another. About the same time a similar defalcation occured in the secondary branch of the Department of Education. My suspicions had been roused when I saw the accountant, whom I knew, sitting up on a sidecar, obviously the worse for liquor, and eating fish and chips from a newspaper. He disappeared, like the chap in Finance, and was not seen again when an accountant from another branch was sent in to investigate.

The lease on the house on Leinster Road having expired, Cáit and I spent some time in a flat on Garville Avenue that my parents furnished out of their own resources. We went from there into a newly built terrace house in Seapoint. The rent was £24 a month which meant that one month in three we could pay no other bills. Hence debt began to accumulate willy-nilly and we were at times sorely pressed for money. I was glad to get anything extra I could from writing and from my work for the Comhar Dramaiochta, while Cáit earned whatever she could by typing plays. I was not alone in this plight among junior civil servants who had their own ways of coping. I heard a young engineer one day in the Dining Club of the Board of Works telling of a letter he had had from Switzer's, drawing attention to the state of his account. 'I tell you I knew how to deal with that one', he told us. 'I wrote to them and said that if I got any more of those impertinent letters, I would not include them in the next month's draw.'

I would not have had the courage to do anything like that, even if I had thought of it; but I was quite prepared to leave the civil service if I could have got a better paid job. I did apply for a secretaryship of a couple of County Councils, was placed by Local Appointments Commission, and on one occasion went down to interview a Council Chairman. He, very politely, told me to go home and forget it. My youthful appearance so militated against my chances that I often wished I had a few premature grey hairs. Tommy Murphy, who was the secretary of both the Civil Service and Local Appointments

Commissions, administered a small reprimand when I met him one day; he lived near me in Booterstown. I was trying too hard, he said. 'Take your time', he told me. 'In time all these things you are trying for will come your way.' It was easy for him to talk, I thought.

As was her wont, Cáit quickly struck up a happy relationship with our terrace neighbours in Seapoint. There were late night suppers with a childless English pair who lived two doors away; afternoon tea sometimes with another childless pair from the North who were our immediate neighbours on one side; while on the other side there was an engineer and his wife who had a baby about the same time as our first arrived. The two mothers met regularly every day at the wire fence as the prams were wheeled out. They seemed to be an utterly united family until one night in the middle hours we heard voices raised in argument and glass being broken. Next morning we heard what had happened. The husband had come home with drink taken, as the saying goes, and a row developed in the course of which he, a Protestant, but by no means a good one, proceeded to smash the holy pictures on the walls of their bedroom. That was a remote curtain raiser to deep tragedy. When Cáit last saw the wife, for whom and for her child she had formed a real affection, she was serving a term of imprisonment in Mountjoy.

From Seapoint Avenue where my two sons Eimear and Cóilín were born, we went to Marlboro Road. It was not a case of moving on rent day, but that this was to be the fourth move in three years did not go unnoticed. 'How long are you going to stay here?', Cáit was asked by one of my brothers. We only stayed in fact a few months. I have a painful memory of that Marlboro Road house, of audacious mice, bawling babies, a sick wife, another child on the way, a neighbour complaining about the bins, and no money. We felt we had to get out of that place – quick. And we did. To my intense relief, Cáit and her mother found a rambling old house, Rosevilla, on the seafront at Booterstown, and simultaneously an occupant for the house we were leaving. We had begun to have a maid. With the romantically exaggerated view some men have of their wives, I, according to Cáit, said to her, when I found her on her knees scrubbing the floor, 'do you think I married you to do that sort of thing?' and promptly ordered her to get help. I can't remember any of that, but it is true that from that on we had maids, the first an excellent girl who insisted on wearing a cap and apron. It looked wonderful, but it was a constant reminder to me that it was just a facade. Yet I couldn't ask the girl to dress more in keeping with the reality of the situation.

We loved Booterstown. Rosevilla gave lovely views across the bay to the Hill of Howth, and in the rere there was a long garden with glasshouses and vines in which I sporadically worked, though to little effect. We were on the main road out of Dublin, but Booterstown itself seemed to refuse to be absorbed into the city and seemed proud of its independent village character. We soon got to know many of our neighbours and they took us to themselves. We played cards with the stationmaster and his family. We were entertained to dinner by a former Irish Party M.P. in his house that subsequently passed to John McCormack. We discussed the political scene with a government official who was both an expert on elections and a church organist. Next-door we had the Montgomerys, the beautiful, brilliant, generous, but unpredictable Ethel, and her husband Jimmy who, among other things, was now the Film Censor. An intimate friend of his was Oliver Gogarty with whom at planned meetings he exchanged witty impromptus which may have been prepared with some care. A lady he could not stand he called 'The Snowy-Breasted Peril'. The difference between the Gate and Abbey theatres was like that between Sodom and Begorrah; and MacLiammoir's performance in a play about St Francis he described as the Francis of a Sissy.

I knew MacLiammoir, and corresponded with him when for a short time I edited the Gaelic League paper *Fainne an Lae*. He was living at that time in Menton and had started to write in Irish, in a Galway dialect, which was a strange thing for a Corkman to do. He had not yet formed that brilliant partnership with Hilton Edwards; and, though he would have laughed at how Jimmy Montgomery distinguished between their theatre and the old Abbey, he naturally saw the two places in very different terms. He and Hilton were bringing to the Irish theatre a repertoire of foreign masterpieces in the hope that they would guide young Irish writers to sides of Irish life that the Abbey had never explored, and to fresh forms of expression. Ireland had been transformed, he wrote somewhere, from a royal, restive, war-bedragled captive into a youthful, muddle-headed, ambitious debutante. There had been a decline in imagery, richness, colour and form, and the Gate would play its part in a re-stimulation.

Since my interview with Brennan and McElligott I had had no connexion with Finance, except only when H. P. Boland, the Assistant Secretary in charge of Establishments, invited the Junior Ads to join him in the Gresham for what was to be, we understood the first of a number of social meetings. But there was never a second. Boland was Irish, of course, and a Treasury man, whose most recent appointment had been in the House of Lords. When we met in the Gresham I got the impression that he wanted all of us to become civil servants on the English model. He spoke about how we should dress, and recommended that we should study the editorials in the London *Times* for literary style. Tommy Coyne, who later on was the Secretary of the Department of Justice, was caustic about this, and may have influenced his Minister, Kevin O'Higgins, to see to it that the Gresham experience was not repeated.

I saw very little of Boland at first, and our difference in status kept us apart. But following the reviews of my Parnell book, his attitude became noticeably warmer, and whenever I had occasion to visit him in his room he was always obviously glad to talk about the fallen leader. He greatly admired Parnell, wore the Ivy Leaf on his anniversaries, and was active in having a memorial erected to him. He was the surviving Finance link with the British Treasury, having replaced 'Corny' Gregg in charge of Establishments. In 1920 it had been thought to place Gregg in Belfast on the formation of a Northern Ireland government, but he was not wanted up there. When this was communicated by letter to the Treasury a sentence was added, saying simply 'I think you know the reason why he was not acceptable.' It was not necessary to be specific. He was a Catholic. Gregg came to Dublin in 1922, and having done his stint there, returned to London and rose to the very top of the Revenue service.

Boland was interested in music and played an important part in setting up a Civil Service musical society which had a short life. It appeared to die with a solitary choral performance under Jack Larchet in the Metropolitan Hall in Abbey Street. I remember the night well, and the exit at half-time to the pubs across the street of some of my senior colleagues. They had had enough of Hiawatha!

While Finance had a monastic appearance, with so many of the senior men occupying separate rooms, there was a certain camaraderie in the air at all times, what Ken Whitaker called an officers' mess atmosphere. However, there was one room, just across the way from where I worked, where something more than camaraderie prevailed. We called it the Tivoli, for the good reason that it was there that Frank Duff, Paddy O'Kelly and Jimmy Smith – all three hard workers – relaxed occasionally in the early mornings to play a practical joke or two. Frank was a past master at this game, having practised it across the street in the Land Commission in British days. When Paddy O'Kelly, a cousin of McElligott's, was promoted, Frank wrote a paper on how to apply the Theory of Relativity which was being discussed in scientific quarters at that time. I have given other examples in my book on Frank.

We young Administrative Officers were warmly welcomed into the department where, after Brennan, McElligott and Boland, the three most senior men were Arthur Codling, Walter Doolin and John Leydon. Leydon was to Frank Duff the W.L.M., the Wonderful Little Man, primarily because of his output which was quite prodigious. When I first saw him he was dealing with Civil War compensation. There were thousands of cases, of course, and many applicants chancing their arms. Their exaggerated claims had no success with Leydon; he must have saved the country millions but in the process he notably added to the government's natural unpopularity. He was a religious man, had been in Maynooth for a couple of years, shared Frank Duff's social ideas, and did what he could to lighten the burden on Frank's shoulders.

Codling and Doolin had also been British civil servants. Codling, a Yorkshireman, was an excellent man to dissect a problem and comment on it; and was a first-class trainer of men. Whitaker, reviewing Ronan Fanning's book on the

Department of Finance, remembers Codling as a gentle but meticulous person, a man of the utmost probity and of penetrating mind who gave loyal service of the highest quality to his adopted country. I would add that he was, or had been, a Gladstonian Liberal and brought to his work a certain religious zeal. He was a Methodist, and sometimes preached down town; at least I saw him at the top of a tram one night poring over notes for a sermon. He was involved in a charity called The Stranger's Friend; and he explained the meaning of the title when I pressed him about it. 'Don't you remember in your Saint Matthew', he said, 'I was a stranger and you took me in.' His first contact with the problems of Ireland was in the Local Government Board where he administered the legislation about Labourers' Cottages. He felt under an obligation to do what he could to make amends for earlier British misrule.

Doolin had long been a close friend of Brennan's and his colleague in the Chief Secretary's Office; and Brennan had stayed in the Doolin house on Fitzwilliam Square before he got married. I regret I saw too little of the man. He was always in good humour, and had a humourously cynical way of approaching the examination of a proposal. On the watch-out for a personal factor, he would say – while slowly stretching out his arms to full length and then drawing them back – 'Taking the broadest possible point of view, how does this affect me?' He made the farewell speech at the dinner we gave Brennan as he left us to become Chairman of the Currency Commission late in 1928. Brennan, he told us, could do anything; he could unscrew the inscrutable.

That was a dinner to remember. It was held in Mills Hall in Merrion Row which served good food but no drink, so that what we wanted to drink had to be brought in, which meant getting a licence. One of the organisers came round to us in our rooms to enquire what we thought we each would require in the way of refreshment for ourselves and our neighbours at table. The result was an over-supply. By two or three in the morning when the party broke up individuals among us were the worse for wear. The car in which I was being driven home was held up by a young Garda on the Merrion Road who wanted to know why we had no lights. 'There they are,' said the driver, switching them on. An argument ensued and next day we got a couple of summonses. For such an apparently solid body of men we managed, apart from the drink, to entertain ourselves more than adequately. A brother of the comedian Jimmy O'Dea played on the piano anything anyone ventured to sing, whether they had brought music with them or not. George Fagan, who came from a musical family, and who had won a Military Cross in the War and been gassed, was full of fun that night. He was in everything, and sang with me the always popular 'Moon' duet from *The Lily of Killarney*. Jimmy McElligott, Brennan's successor, gave us, not too tunefully, the sea-shanty, *Blow the Man Down*, while John Mooney initiated us, in Dublinese, into the five quid in the boot which he alleged sustained the amateur soccer player.

As I have written in another book, most of us that night had no idea why Brennan was leaving us. The Chairmanship of the Currency Commission was a step up for him, we supposed, though it would turn him away from the centre of things and deprive him of the sort of authority he had wielded as head of the 'boss' department. It was a long time after before we realised that he and his Minister, Ernest Blythe, had grown so seriously away from each other that he had to go. Thus it was fortuitous that a job was coming along into which it suited everybody that he should be placed. It is not always easy for higher civil servants to live with politicians.

The first politician I was to meet officially, but briefly, in the Department of Education, was Dick Mulcahy. I was secretary to a little committee of which he was chairman, and whose remit had to do with the extension of teaching through Irish in University College, Galway. My duties were made minimal by Mulcahy who did any writing that had to be done, and impressed me by his speed in doing so (I sort of remember, too, that he drafted in shorthand). He was at that time, I think, making a re-entry into politics after the Army Mutiny crisis of a year or two earlier. In Finance, I made the acquaintance of Michael R. Heffernan, Blythe's Parliamentary Secretary, who between 1927 and 1932 was in political charge of the Post Office. He was a farmer's representative, and put their view for retrenchment in government spending by Cumann na nGaedheal which since 1923 had been carrying the unenviable stigma of having, in Blythe's first year as Finance Minister, cut old age pensions by a shilling a week. To mollify the farmers an economy committee was set up in May 1927 with Heffernan as chairman and with civil servants as the ordinary members, among them Diarmuid O'Hegarty, the secretary of the government, and McElligott and O'Friel who were departmental secretaries. Johnnie Hanna and I from Finance were the secretaries. It soon became painfully evident that it was going to be hard to find any fat to cut into. Indeed in the run-up to the forthcoming election the government found taxation necessary for the balancing of the budget which was considered to be vital rather than a reduction in public service expenditure. The Economy Committee exercise may have been intended as an education for Heffernan: it was for me, certainly. I remember Sir Joseph Glynn, who was Chairman of the National Health Insurance Commission, explaining why appeals cost so much more in Ireland than in England. There were three appeals possible for persons feeling themselves aggrieved. An English complainant would be satisfied with the result of the first appeal. The Irishman explored all three. We were a litigious people.

Economically, this was by no means a good period; and we were facing into the Great Depression which broke over the world towards the end of 1929. It began in the United States and its effects spread dramatically. Ireland did not escape its effects on trade and employment and the government's political decline became more evident. Fianna Fáil, now in the Dáil, shared with the British an interest in Protectionism, for which Cosgrave's government showed little enthusiasm. Their only concession was to strengthen a Tariff Commission which had hitherto effectively operated as a barrier to the obtaining of a tariff, but little had been achieved by 1932. In the area of political independence, however, the government had been making steady progress on the road to the greater freedom Griffith and Collins had spoken about, by removing in negotiation the objectionable features of the Anglo-Irish Treaty. Patrick McGilligan had become Minister for External Affairs after the assassination of Kevin O'Higgins. He had wanted to leave politics and go to the Bar, but O'Higgins had dissuaded him from doing so. The next five years would be pivotal politically and economically, and he encouraged

McGilligan to stay on and fight. 'You are one of a few that know how,' he said. McGilligan stayed, and made an enormous impact upon the evolution of the Commonwealth, wholly changing the role of the British government within the system and determining that as far as Irish affairs were concerned, the British monarch functioned entirely in accordance with the will of the Irish government. That was a development which de Valera would build on when he assumed power and found the star of Neville Chamberlain rising in Britain.

Cáit and I were living in Garville Avenue that Sunday in July 1927 when we heard that O'Higgins had been murdered. The morning before – we still worked on Saturdays – he was in the lift with me in Government Buildings; his office in the Department of Justice was above mine. I did not know him to speak to, but like most people I was horrified by his cruel death. Not that I was surprised that he had been physically attacked. He was regarded as the strong hard man of the government and was hated by his enemies. Cáit told me of a meeting at 5 Parnell Square where she had worked, and of a mob of screaming women outside waiting for him to emerge. 'Good night, ladies,' he said, doffing his hat. His death produced something like a political miracle. It brought de Valera, who condemned the assassination as murder and inexcusable from every viewpoint, into the Dáil, thereby carrying a form of normality into our politics. I say a form of normality, because the abnormal has always to be allowed for; and an example of that occurred within weeks of O'Higgins's death. On a vote of no confidence in the Dáil Fianna Fáil, in combination with Labour and Captain Redmond's National League, were to have brought about a change of government by a single vote. I was travelling back that night by boat from Brittany where I had been attending a Celtic Congress, and managed to get invited to the radio room to hear the BBC news. The abnormal, the unexpected, had indeed happened. One of the National League deputies, an Alderman Jinks, had been missing from the chamber on the division, there was a tie and the government was saved by the speaker's casting vote. When I got to Dublin I heard variants of the story of the missing Jinks: of how an Independent, Major Bryan Cooper, with help from Bertie Smylie, the editor of the *Irish Times*, had been drinking with him in Buswell's Hotel, which is just over the way from Leinster House, and left him to sleep off the effects. He was, therefore, literally unable to be present when the division bells rang. It would be almost five years later before de Valera would get as good a chance again.

It is extraordinary how a political murder fixes in one's mind for ever where one had heard the awful news. Who does not remember where they were when they heard of John F. Kennedy's death? My mother could recall in detail where, and with whom, she was playing when the news broke of the Phoenix Park murders in 1882. I, likewise, can recall that Cáit and I had gone down to the garden to inspect an aerial that my brother Paddy had put up for us, when the news reached us there that Kevin O'Higgins had been shot dead in Booterstown on his way to Mass. Later we heard the details, how lying on the roadside with a bullet in his head and six in his body, but without losing consciousness, he had dictated a will, and directed that the ambulance, when it came, was not to take him to hospital, but to his house and wife and children. He knew he was dying, and forgave his murderers. 'God help the poor devils,' he whispered.

Nobody yet appears to know who they were, and all sorts of suggestions have been made as to what faction they belonged to. Were they official IRA; relations or associates of the many men who had been executed since 1922; or ex-Irish Army officers, affected by the mutinous troubles of 1924; or had some British or Northern Irish individuals, worrying about what he was doing to break up the unity of the Empire, done it? He was, after all, O'Higgins of the comma, the comma which changed the King's title from George V, by the grace of God, of the United Kingdom of Great Britain and Ireland etc. to 'of the United Kingdom of Great Britain, Ireland, etc.' In pursuance of the idea of a dual monarchy, he was said to be thinking of having the King crowned as King of Ireland in the Phoenix Park by the Primates of the Catholic Church and Church of Ireland, with a flag and anthem more acceptable to the North, and perhaps a parliament in Belfast for local business.

As to who murdered O'Higgins, Ernest Blythe, who was well placed to hear things, had a name or two but they were not those whose names have been recently revealed. I thought once I was going to hear something really convincing when my neighbour Sean MacEoin told me of a visit he had had in the early days of the inter-party government of 1948 from O'Higgins's brother Tom. Both MacEoin and Tom O'Higgins were members of that government: MacEoin was the Minister for Justice and Tom O'Higgins the Minister for Defence. In MacEoin's office in Government Buildings Tom O'Higgins, without introduction, asked MacEoin two questions. Was he a friend of Kevin's – MacEoin said he was – 'then, if I put the evidence of who murdered Kevin into your hands, will you prosecute?' MacEoin said he would. Six weeks passed, leaving MacEoin in fear and trepidation that the evidence would incriminate a ministerial colleague, but no sufficient evidence, if any, was produced.

Kevin's daughter Una told me of an extraordinary incident that occurred as she walked up the centre aisle of Westminster Cathedral one Sunday morning in the sixties. As she passed a rather unkempt figure who was muttering to himself she heard him say something like 'And then there was that awful shooting of Kevin O'Higgins: I never meant to get involved in that.' She enquired afterwards about the man, and found that he was Irish, had been educated in a top Catholic school, and that he had suffered some form of mental collapse. Una asked the priests in the Cathedral to tell the man to cease worrying and be at peace, that O'Higgins before he died had forgiven those involved in any way in his killing, and that that was also the position of his family.

Since I started to write these memoirs it has been my good fortune to read the letters O'Higgins wrote to Birdie Cole, the girl he married. They confirm an opinion I formed long ago that O'Higgins was one person from Ireland's past that I would have liked to meet. He had a refined, gentle side to him to balance the sterness which enabled him to confront the difficulties of government, and he was an able judge of individuals. During the negotiations arising out of the Treaty he was in London a good deal and described some of the British representatives he met: 'I only straighten up when

Dublin Castle, represented by Hamar [Greenwood] and Sir John Anderson, is facing us across the green table. Hamar *is*, and looks, the complete charlatan, full up of loud-mouthed insinuations – crossing his hands over his stomach and turning his eyes to heaven at any suggestion that he has any motive other than effervescing affection and good will towards ourselves personally and the new order generally. The other fellow [Anderson] is a more dangerous type – the well-trained civil servant sneak – plausible, vigilant, malevolent, and false as Hell. . . . We met the Prime Minister [Lloyd George] on Sunday afternoon; we were about an hour with him – he's certainly a remarkable devil – he flirted with his eye-glass and faced us now with the beaming ingenuous face of a boy and now like a very very old fox. Michael Collins stands the test well with any of them and certainly does not suffer by comparison – you will say that not unnaturally I am partisan, but I am telling you what I see reflected in their own behaviour while they are dealing with him.' Kevin O'Higgins, as I see him in his letters to his young wife, was so refreshingly open-minded and frank that he might, had he lived, have cut a path through all our ingrained anglophobia, jingoism and bigotry to a united Ireland.

I was soon to see something of the contemporary Irish political scene. It was conventional at that time in Finance, and may still be for all I know, that the Junior Ad. on his way to becoming the Minister's Private Secretary became first the Estimates Officer, and then the Parliamentary Clerk. In the first of these roles he edited and saw to the publication of the estimates volume for the supply services. I travelled that road, and in the Parliamentary Clerk's job I had to keep an eye on bills as they progressed through the Oireachtas, and see to the drafting of such financial resolutions as they required. Most of the bills needed a money resolution because of the expenditure involved in implementing them. The Finance Bills were in a category of their own. In any event I had to learn something about the attitude of the Ceann Comhairle to these and related matters, which meant that I was frequently in consultation with Sean Malone, the official on whom Michael Hayes, the Ceann Comhairle of that day, and everybody else appeared to rely. Nearly every day there would be parliamentary questions affecting Finance and on those, and on the briefing of the Minister for Finance, I had to maintain an especially close watch. Inevitably I saw something of the daily proceedings of both Dáil and Senate. And when, in 1931, I became Private Secretary to the Minister, Ernest Blythe, I saw a great deal more, and was frequently for long stretches in the officials' gallery in the Dáil to be in close proximity to Blythe who had to spend so much of his time there. Important things were happening behind the Ceann Comhairle's chair, other than that concerned directly with the conduct of parliamentary business. I saw at close quarters the work of the translation staff and frequently turned to them for guidance in the matter of terminology. For years their work was rather looked down upon but they obtained full recognition, I think, when de Valera, who was slow to change, became dissatisfied with the quality of the work of miscellaneous scholars he had commissioned, and handed over to the translation staff the task of producing an Irish language version of his Constitution; later he asked them to produce a standardised grammar. Among the translation staff were many native or near-native speakers of Irish from all parts of the Gaeltacht, but I single out two geniuses amomg them who were Dubliners and whose native language was English. These were Tom Page whom Canon Peter O'Leary said was the finest speaker of Irish he had ever heard; and Liam Ó Rinn, a lonely introspective figure, who learned Russian so as to get to the inner core of Russian literature. He could knock off a translation of an Act of the Oireachtas as easily as he could write a piece for *An Branar*.

Ernest Blythe had been Minister for Finance since 1923, but, following the assassination of O'Higgins he became the No. 2 Minister in the government and Vice-President of the Executive Council. His political career had otherwise been quite unique. A northern Protestant with a unionist background, he had, through the influence on him of the Irish language, become an advanced nationalist, had gone to the Kerry Gaeltacht to improve his knowledge of the spoken language, and there increased the membership of the Irish Republican Brotherhood and the Irish Volunteers, before being deported by the government for his activities. He was in England when the Rising of 1916 occurred, and was kept in custody until the general release of prisoners when he resumed his Volunteer work, was re-arrested and served a term in Dundalk Gaol. He was elected M.P. or T.D. for Monaghan in the 1918 election, became a Dáil Éireann Director of Trade and Commerce, and voted for the Treaty. In the Free State era he guided the provisional government towards a policy of non-violence in relation to the North and as Minister for Finance he gave vent to his abiding love of the Irish language by sanctioning all sorts of projects, including An Gúm and the establishment of Irish-using preparatory colleges. He rejected advice from within the department to act more moderately in dealing with projects affecting Irish; to avoid delay to such projects he made an order that any papers affecting Irish that had not been disposed of within a month were to be brought to his desk for decision. When a well-intentioned official suggested that to help civil servants to improve their knowledge of the language they might be given some monetary assistance to spend their holidays in the Gaeltacht, Blythe wrote on the file that any concentration of officials in those areas should be dispersed, if needs be by machine-gun fire. His fear, of course, was that the shrinking Gaeltacht would be swamped by English speakers. This attitude no doubt made him unpopular with the officers of the Supply Division who handled the Education Votes, and especially Walter Doolin.

One thing I learned from my association with Blythe was that elections are won by organisation. You may have good leaders and good policies, but if you have not an organisation on the ground your prospects of gaining and retaining office are very slight. That was at least in part why there was a change of government in 1932. Fianna Fáil had an excellent organisation whereas Cumann na nGaedheal had virtually none. Blythe certainly had not: when an election was announced he contrived to have something *ad hoc* created but while he got in in 1932 on the strength of being a Minister, as soon as he lost that position he lost his seat and never thereafter seemed likely to be able to regain it. I don't think he realised the importance of having a party organisation, nor did his colleague Desmond FitzGerald. I remember Desmond telling me what a bore it was to go out to Sunday morning chapel meetings in Carlow-Kilkenny which was his constituency, and, standing up in a ditch, to try and hold the attention of the handful of people who came to listen to him.

The Cumann na nGaedheal period in office was therefore coming to an end when I became the Minister for Finance's Private Secretary in 1931. The name Cumann na nGaedheal or Confederation of the Gaels, as the police papers in the State Paper Office for an earlier period have it, had been revived in 1922 to organise popular support behind Griffith, Collins and their successors, but in organisational terms they achieved nothing approaching de Valera's Fianna Fáil. At the beginning Cumann na nGaedheal ministers may have been too busy running the country to find time for organising a party, and some of them would seem at times almost to have hoped that they could do without one. Their fear of a popular organisation like the United Irish League and the Ancient Order of Hibernians of earlier days was that it could only increase the number of people pulling strings to get government jobs. Even the defeat of Seamus Hughes, their General Secretary, in 1924 did not jolt them seriously, I think. That, I believe, only happened when de Valera got the better of the extreme republicans in the anti-Treaty ranks and started to move towards the Dáil.

A man I got to see a lot in Finance was H. P. Boland the head of the Establishment Branch. He kept a constant flow of files to Blythe, and saw him quite often about them. He had played over the years the unpleasant role of economising on staff costs, and was naturally criticised by friends and foes alike of the government. By the time one of the inevitable economic recessions arrived, everything seemed to have been cut to the bone, so that the government 'obligingly falling on their own swords', as Leland Lyons said, cut teachers' salaries and old age pensions, with little regard for the consequences. That no doubt was a government decision, but Blythe was ever afterwards referred to as the villain of the piece. Boland, at the time, was likewise violently disliked among civil servants, some of whom must have carried their tales of woe outside their offices for, in my parish, a violently political curate told me that when 'we come into power, we will crucify H. P. Boland!' Yet, when the 1932 election came on, Fianna Fáil publicly criticised the high salaries that were being paid, and, in government, went through the charade of passing an Economy Act. I can't remember much about that, except that guineas became pounds and that Boland was the principal official that saw to its implementation. He was a formidable man, and paid little attention to what narrow-minded people were saying about him. I have a copy of a letter, probably typed by Cáit in 1924, which was sent to Cosgrave in that year by the Coiste Gnó of Cumann na nGaedheal, saying that the control of the personnel of the Irish Civil Service should be exercised by a man in whom the country could have confidence, or at least be above suspicion of English or Masonic influence. Otherwise, a further impetus would be given to the disintegration with which the party was threatened.

The Private Secretary in Finance was more than what the title implies. He had to be an intermediary between the Minister and the Department; to represent each to each other, to keep them well informed as to what each was thinking on matters that immediately concerned their joint work. This was done to a large degree through the Private Secretary's everyday contact with the Secretary of the Department. In my time the Secretary, McElligott, and I talked over things nearly every day. This was a change for me indeed; to be not at the top but to be in the regular company of the top man, the head of the Civil Service. I also met the men in the next line: the Assistant Secretaries and Principal Officers. Doolin did not come down to Blythe too often, if at all. I think the passages at arms that had occurred in Brennan's time, and the attempts to restrain Blythe's ardour in the matter of the Irish language, kept them apart, which meant that I had to act as an intermediary more frequently than I would otherwise have had to do.

I have said earlier that many of the schemes for the advancement of Irish were produced during Blythe's time as Minister for Finance. There was no Minister for Irish nor yet a Minister for the Gaeltacht; but in a sense Blythe discharged both roles. He had a Gaeltacht map on the wall facing his desk and often on late evenings I stood there with him talking about the problems of the language. He knew the Kerry Gaeltacht himself, having worked there as a labourer and as an organiser for the I.R.B. and the Volunteers; he was in regular touch with Josie Mongan about the position in Connemara, and no doubt had contacts as well with other places where Irish was hanging on. He believed that a multiplicity of small schemes was needed to sustain the revival, and argued that in their totality the cost would not be significant. He was, therefore, always on the look-out for new ideas, and thought up a few himself. When Mongan, for instance, told him that, as the Shannon Scheme had not yet reached Connemara, students from that part of the world working towards a university degree were at a disadvantage, he told him to have a form of illumination called Coleman's Quick Light that had come on the market installed, and the bill sent to him. He had a hand, I am sure, in the promotion of the writing of biographies which turned me on to Parnell; and he examined with care the returns of sales of An Gúm publications, asking questions to which I had to find the answers. With Mulcahy he supported the Irish Christian Brothers in the building of Colaiste Mhuire as an all-Irish secondary school in Dublin city; and I have a letter he wrote to me from Brittany, where he was taking a holiday in 1931, on that subject. Incidentally he was not interested in folk tales which had hitherto formed a great part of the literary diet, and directed An Gúm away from them. Blythe had always been a man of the theatre. He took a close interest in the events that led to the establishment of the Taibhdhearc in Galway, in the bringing of Edwards and MacLiammoir into that theatre, and in the training of Frank Dermody, an army man, as a producer. He went down to Galway for many of the Taibhdhearc productions, and took me with him to see a performance of *Arms and the Man*. He was what you might call a moderniser. He directed the Civil Service to follow the translation staff's system of orthography which involved modifications of the spelling given in Dinneen's dictionary; and that the Roman script and simplified spelling should prevail in an English-Irish dictionary which was being prepared. This direction was reversed on the change of government in 1932, however, at, it was said, the instance of the Gaelic League.

The Shaw play was the only Taibhdhearc production I ever saw; I did not even see an adaptation of a French farce of my own they put on. What I would have been delighted to see was the original Irish-language production of Diarmuid and Grainne, of which I later heard many stories. (I saw, of course, and greatly admired the English version in the Peacock.) In both productions MacLiammoir himself played Diarmuid; in Galway Maire Scully was Grainne. During the rehearsal of the love passages, into which Hilton the producer was urging the couple to put more and more passion, he noticed a man in the stalls he called Buffalo Bill – it was as near as he could get to pronouncing his Irish name – becoming quite agitated. 'I believe that fellow is in love with Grainne, and jealous', he whispered to Michael. He was right. Buffalo Bill, otherwise the university lecturer and erstwhile cooper Liam Ó Buachalla, had begun to fear that his intention to marry Grainne might be frustrated. It was not, but Maire Scully's stage career may have been.

I can't remember if Blythe ever talked about politics, certainly never by way of criticising his critics; and I must disappoint readers who might expect that, through my association with him, I have anything to reveal about what was in the minds of Cumann na nGaedheal as they approached the vital 1932 election. Men like Sean MacEoin and Batt O'Connor would call to see the Minister, but I only conversed with them when the Minister was not available, and then only about matters affecting their constituents.

I saw Desmond FitzGerald, the Minister for Defence, who deputised for Blythe at holiday time. Again we did not talk politics but of his consuming interest, the *Summa* of St Thomas Aquinas. He was later to lecture in the United States on that subject and to write the *Preface to Statecraft*, based on Thomistic principles. Though acting Minister he would not talk to me from the chair in the Minister's room. He preferred to sit on the corner of my desk outside, smoking a cigarette, and talking at length in that distinctive accent of his; he was born and brought up in London, and had lived in France. He became a good friend of mine in the years we shared membership of the Mercier Society. He was strongly political, as Blythe was, and would no doubt fight his corner with vigour; but he welcomed people who would talk to him about something other than politics, and he retained old relationships despite everything. When MacEntee replaced Blythe, I found him and FitzGerald one day amicably Dessing and Seaning each other in the minister's room while in the House you could cut the bitter political atmosphere with a knife.

I often wondered if those close friends, Blythe and FitzGerald, who had both made mixed marriages, ever talked about religion, even accidentally. I feel sure that Desmond would have liked to, but might have considered it indelicate to do so. In the Mercier Society he was considered by the Protestants as excessively controversial, but I can well realise he would be inclined to avoid discussion altogether where there was any risk of close friendships being affected. I imagine that is why Annie Blythe hoped that I might be able to lead her husband towards the Catholic Church, and said so to me when we happened to meet on Stephen's Green one day. But, of course, she did not understand how more difficult it would be for a young civil servant to speak to his Minister about such a topic than it was for her. Perhaps there was an opportunity for raising the matter when I saw him one afternoon in his room with a copy of the Maynooth Catechism on the desk before him. I did not do so, I just remarked humorously about his taste of reading matter, and he explained that young Earnán had started to ask questions about religion and, rather than that Annie and he should confuse the boy with different answers, he had gone into Browne and Nolan's on the way back from lunch so that from the Catechism he might understand what the Catholics taught on these difficult subjects.

I went over to Leinster House the afternoon Blythe's government was overthrown, and saw him chatting with his colleagues in the ante-room. They were in good spirits, apparently, though defeat was staring them in the face. I have a feeling that they thought it would not be long before they were back in office again. To obtain office, as they did that day, Fianna Fáil had found support elsewhere in the House; but how long would they retain it? That was the question.

That night I stayed with Maurice Moynihan in his room waiting to see whether we were needed by the new government for any purpose. They were having their first meeting in the Council room and sat late; obviously the discussion was tense at times judging by the tone of the voices that reached us from the floor below. I left near 11 o'clock to catch a late tram or bus home, but Maurice stayed behind. His brother, John, was succeeding Diarmuid Ó hÉigeartaigh as Secretary to the government and would in time be replaced by Maurice himself. The new government were fortunate in having such excellent men.

The Civil Service had already learned who their new ministers were to be. We, in Finance, were to get Sean MacEntee. We knew later, from MacEntee himself, if we had not surmised it, that none of the new ministers had been consulted about their portfolios beforehand, that Mr de Valera chose his men because of his understanding of their interests. But there were few, if any, experts among them for any portfolios. And so far as Finance was concerned, I doubt if much was known about MacEntee's real views other than what had been picked up from his political speeches, and the senior men no doubt feared he might have leanings towards some of the unorthodox views that were surfacing at that time.

I was naturally concerned to know what my personal position was going to be. I was told by H. P. Boland, who was one of the first senior men to see the new Minister, to carry on for the time being as private secretary: and I did in fact remain with MacEntee until after his first budget, which was a few months away. Like the good Establishment officer he was, Boland had circularised all the heads of departments, as to what the proper dispositions as regards the private office of a Minister should be on the arrival of a Minister of a new government. The view, which he got Blythe to authorise, was that the private office should be completely cleared of the existing staff, including the private secretary, before the new man came in, and that he should find nothing which would in any way imply even a suggestion to him that he should accept the services employed by his predecessor. The outgoing government obviously intended to facilitate in every way the transfer of power to Fianna Fáil; nevertheless some of the incoming men believed that their entry would be resisted; and MacEntee told me that his colleague Frank

Aiken gave him a gun so that the resistance he anticipated could be overcome; he laughingly added that Aiken had forgotten to give him any ammunition. De Valera feared that the Civil Service would refuse to co-operate, and went over the list of past students of Blackrock and Rockwell Colleges occupying key posts on whom he thought he could rely.

The change-over was effected without fuss or ostentation. The seating in the Minister's room was changed slightly, and a few of MacEntee's personal books on financial topics appeared in the bookcase. After a few days his small political staff arrived to share my room with me. This was a new thing in Finance. Hitherto, the staff of the private office had consisted of the private secretary and a typist, and in my experience little of a party political character passed between the private secretary and the Minister. Now the Minister had a man and a woman with whom he could speak quite openly on political matters.

I must say that from the outset I found MacEntee a nice person to work for. I had not met him before; but he would probably have known me from seeing me supporting Blythe on the official benches of the Dáil at Question Time, or during Finance debates. He was among the more tempestuous members of the Dáil, however. When he was on his feet, there was trouble about; I have seen him described as practising a form of clinical surgery that would make most knife-men of the 1980s look like butchers. He belonged to the old school of orators, he and, pre-eminently, James Dillon. People flocked to hear them. If you shared their politics you loved them; if you didn't, you hated them; if you had no party affiliations they were an excellent free turn. I heard both MacEntee and Dillon on the hustings and can vouch for what I say. There was another side to MacEntee. In debate with Blythe, for instance, he could be as nice as pie, so nice in fact that when a young friend of mine from Cois Fharraige saw it, he concluded that the rows he read about in the papers were put on to fool the people. Blythe liked and respected MacEntee and tried to be helpful to him in the Dáil. His verbal bitterness in public, Blythe found, was in complete contrast with his courtesy in private. His occasional harsh utterances did not reflect his real feelings.

The budget was to be his first big test, and I remember

how surprised he was when I told him that it had been Blythe's practice to write the budget speech himself. Not out of the top of his head, of course, but following discussions with the Revenue Commissioners in person and with the officers of the department. In my biography of Joseph Brennan – *No Man's Man* – I tell how this practice began. MacEntee, like Blythe, had no difficulty in expressing himself on paper, but he was desperately prolix: and it became evident around lunch time on budget day that he would not be able to meet the time fixed for the delivery of the speech. There was a mild stampede. The time was changed and, while the office did some substantial pruning, the Minister went off to the Grafton Street Picture House. A feature of the speech was the use of gold ounces as a recurring statistic: that prompted Paddy McGilligan to say that, like Midas of old, everything the Minister touched turned to gold. McGilligan, an even more acerbic Ulsterman, used one of MacEntee's published poems to poke fun at him; and I can remember how devastating he was when, referring to the Minister's oratorical movements, he said that the best part of the Minister's speech was the footwork.

MacEntee was woefully long-winded. He was always anxious to cover every point in his opponents' arguments. I counselled him to take a leaf out of Blythe's book. Blythe would listen to a debate that might run on for weeks but, when his turn came to reply, he would make a relatively short speech, just picking out a few salient points and dealing with them effectively. MacEntee saw the wisdom of this, but the next time he spoke he was as bad as ever. The habit had become ingrained. We, in the official benches, would, of course keep every Minister we had supplied with material for reply – perhaps we overdid it – but it was for the Minister himself to decide what use he would make of what we gave him.

MacEntee had an insatiable thirst for information, an extraordinary inquisitiveness about things. He wanted to see the files; he wanted memoranda on this, that, or the other. In no time the presses in his room was chock-full of files and, being busy otherwise with meetings and interviews, he could barely find time in the early afternoon to run round to the Shelbourne Hotel for a sandwich and a glass of sherry, his favourite drink. The result was that he cracked up quite early on. I remember the shock of being told, when I came to the office one morning, that he had been taken ill and had three doctors with him. I rushed out to Ballyboden where he lived, to find that he had gone into a nursing home. His health thereafter was quite good, but in those days before public address systems I often wondered how he stuck those long platform appearances.

MacEntee, whatever he thought of the nostrums that were around before he took office, was a pillar of orthodoxy by the end of his period as Minister for Finance. He learned a lot in the department, from McElligott primarily no doubt, but also from Joseph Brennan whom he and the Fianna Fáil government appointed to a succession of important chairmanships and ultimately to the Governorship of the Central Bank. If you look at my biography of Brennan you will see MacEntee defending Brennan in the Dáil against a combined attack from the Opposition and his ministerial colleague Sean Lemass. This was a remarkable episode. I don't think he altogether liked Lemass, and may have been jealous of him. He was disappointed when he was not chosen on the delegation that went in 1932 to the Imperial Conference in Ottawa, where, as I have also shown in my Brennan book, silk hats and formal dress created a problem for one member. That would have been no problem whatever for MacEntee. He liked to dress, and was probably out of line with his colleagues in government when they decided not 'to dress' for the Eucharistic Congress.

After the 1932 budget I resumed a normal sort of existence in the Finance Division. I was there in June 1932 when two British ministers, J. H. Thomas and Viscount Hailsham, came to discuss with de Valera the first steps he had taken to dismantle the Treaty agreement. At the end of the first day's discussion they were said to have told enquirers that de Valera in an historical survey of Anglo-Irish relations had got as far as the Battle of Kinsale. I saw my Minister a few times in his office to take his directions regarding a Folklore Commission the government proposed to set up, and in my house where he dropped in to have a cup of tea and to discuss Post Office and Trustee Savings Bank figures that arose in my bailiwick. The decision about a Folklore Commission pleased me very much, and I was delighted to be the Minister's representative on it for a number of years. I had an amateur's interest in the subject myself, since realising as I opened my notebook in a Gaeltacht cottage that it was to record bits of an old world that might not be there to record a little later. The passage of years, with luck, might not mean so much to an archaeologist, but the folklorist had a different problem. If he did not get the material down on paper when he first encountered it, it might well have vanished when next he came looking for it. Hamilton Delargy had been pushing his ideas on de Valera. I imagine there had been no difficulty in reaching agreement as to the need for action to put the recording of material on a permanent footing, and to enlarge and expedite it, but there may have been some hesitation to leave this entirely in Delargy's hands. At any rate many different points of view, academic and non-academic, were represented on the Commission, and I could sense a certain tension at the first meetings. Delargy was short-tempered, and usually raised his voice unpleasantly till he got his way.

There was now more time for the family, and for writing. I had that book on Parnell to finish, while the apostolic interest that Frank Duff had awakened in me was demanding more attention. That October I got the first promotion every Junior Administrative Officer keenly awaits, particularly if he was as hard pressed for money as I had been. I was now an Assistant Principal, the man I was assisting being Owen Redmond, who had come up from the ranks and was notoriously meticulous. He changed the format of letters so often that his assistants found it quite impossible to give him one that he would not tamper with without affecting its substance. He had been given the task of preparing a Revaluation Bill – the existing measure had held the field since the nineteenth century – and MacEntee was keen on fundamental changes. With Redmond I spent many months, day after day, toiling over various drafts, and I imagine that at the same time MacEntee was tiring out his Cabinet colleagues as he argued in favour of proposals that were likely to be politically unpopular. At any rate when Dr Jim Ryan was Minister for Finance in 1959, and sending John Mooney as Commissioner to the Valuation Office, he told him that he did not want to hear another word about Revaluation!

The five years between 1932 and 1937 were full of political

excitement. De Valera's first administration depended for its existence on the support of Labour and a number of independents. Early in 1933 de Valera went to the country again, won the biggest vote any party had received in the history of the State, and shed his dependence on Labour. His policy of retaining the land annuities hitherto paid to Britain led to an economic war with Britain, while on another front the release of Republican prisoners and the breaking up of Cumann na nGaedheal meetings created a troublesome Army Comrades Association which in a short time developed into a National Guard which, under the leadership of General Eoin O'Duffy, a former Commissioner of the Garda Siochána, was distinguished by their wearing of blue shirts. That was a most unfortunate development and normally sensible men like Ernest Blythe made themselves rather ridiculous by appearing in this quasi-Fascist garb. The Blueshirts petered out however, in the Spanish Civil War which began in the summer of 1936. O'Duffy, affected personally by the need to support Franco in his stand against international communism, led an Irish brigade to Spain and led them back about a year later. They had not covered themselves with glory. De Valera meanwhile produced a new Constitution and, in the run-up to the Second World War, did a deal with the British which ended the economic war and gave the Irish Free State control of the ports that had remained in British hands since the Treaty. The deal was initiated in 1935 by Malcolm MacDonald, the Secretary of State for Dominion Affairs, in a series of secret conversations in London, at League of Nations meetings, and elsewhere, and was supported by Neville Chamberlain, the Chancellor of Baldwin's coalition government, and who later, when Prime Minister, became de Valera's 'very dear' friend.

By the time we moved into that house on the seafront, Rosevilla, we had three children – Eimear and Cóilín who were born in Seapoint and Eithne on Marlboro' Road. We stayed in Rosevilla for four years, and there the family was completed. Nóirín and Blánaid were added to my company of daughters. There was a sixth child – the son we called Eoin – but he arrived prematurely in 1935 and the gynaecologist brought a death certificate for him on each of the ten days he lived. I was happy in Rosevilla; the view over a bird sanctuary towards the sea was always enticing. Many friends made the journey out from town to see us, among them Cearbhall Ó Dálaigh – a future President of Ireland – and Fionan MacColuim who startled me once by telling me that he believed in the existence of fairies. It was an old-fashioned gas-lit house with a long passage running from the front door to the garden.

I had got immersed in the St Vincent de Paul Society while I was there and made many friends among the people I was directed to visit. I made progress on my *Parnell* there, smoking so many cigarettes as I did, that once at least I was forced out into the night air for breath. From the upper windows, we saw the Papal Nuncio pass on the way to the Eucharistic Congress; and on fine mornings I loved walking down to the Blind Asylum to the early morning Mass. It was on my return from that walk one morning that I found Eithne, who was then perhaps a couple of years old, standing up in her nightdress in her cot, terrified. She had brought a box of matches into the cot, and lighting one of them, had let it drop on to the bedclothes, setting them on fire.

From Rosevilla we moved in 1936 just around the corner to No. 3 Vernon Terrace, a fine double-fronted house with a large garden on Booterstown Avenue. It was the end house of a terrace of four that had been built for Jessie Leitch when she was a baby. The architect, I gathered, was he who planned the Mater Hospital. In the next house to ours was a judge's widow, next to her lived Miss Leitch herself, and beside her a doctor, a general practitioner. On the first Sunday afternoon we were installed in No. 3 Cáit suggested I should go up to No. 7 and pay my respects to the landlady. I did. Miss Leitch herself, a tiny wizened little thing, opened the door, brought me into a scantily furnished front room, with religious texts hanging on the faded wallpaper, and introduced me to Miss Mellone, a tall very plain woman who shared the house with her. She was a good deal younger than Miss Leitch, yet not young by any means, and totally blind. Cáit and I had seen them together for the first time years before on a crowded train to the South; they looked so remarkable as they moved towards the dining carriage, the little old woman leading the gaunt blind woman along by the hand. That blindness had changed their roles, but had not separated them. Miss Mellone had been a most active person, and 'a real fighting suffragette'. Augustine Birrell, when Chief Secretary of Ireland, who thus described her, warned his Civil Service Under Secretary to be careful when she was around. 'She'd chuck an inkpot at you as soon as she'd look at you.' When her sight went, the roles of the two women were reversed. Miss Leitch was now *her* companion. And, indeed, that afternoon when I rang her doorbell, Miss Leitch had been reading to her out of Trevelyan's *History of England* and would later, I gathered, read something in German to her. They were keeping in touch. The house was full of books – some of which later became my property, among them major English poets, and bound collections of anti-Roman Catholic sermons from the nineteenth century.

Miss Leitch talked to me about the neighbourhood and the house I had taken from her. She told me that an earlier tenant, Dr Richard Robert Madden, the historian of the United Irishmen, had died in the house in 1886. She spoke as if she had known him and his wife Harriet rather well, and it was she no doubt who told me about the condition of Madden's house – my house now – with books flowing out of the rooms on to the stairs and being added to every time Madden came out from Dublin by the train to Booterstown railway station which was just below the house. From Miss Leitch too, I heard of the long nights Dr Madden and Harriet spent working together, being sometimes only interrupted when the maid came in in the morning. She described how the old couple were dressed as, arm in arm, they made their way to Mass in the Parish Church up the Avenue. That was a church Cáit and I and our growing family were to know and love.

In 1936 in a house quite near us a young man named Edward Ball killed his mother with an axe. He put her in the back of her Baby Austin, drove to Shankill and tried to drive the car into the sea. Finding that impossible he took the corpse out of the car, dragged it over the ground and pushed it into the water, from which it was never recovered. Ball had committed the crime either because his mother had accused him of homosexual behaviour or had refused to give him the money to go on a tour of Egypt with the Gate Theatre with which he had some association. He was found guilty of murder, but instead of being executed he was committed to the Dundrum Lunatic Asylum, where he spent many years. He was likely to have met there an acquaintance of mine from my days with the nuns and the army who, with some drink taken, as we say, and in a fit of temper had killed a man in a family row. This normally quiet and pleasant fellow was also detained in Dundrum but for a relatively short time. At any rate I was surprised to run into him one early evening on the top of a tram at Nelson Pillar. I avoided the 'long time no see' formula, needless to say. He was then a temporary clerk in a tax office.

The Ball murder greatly excited Booterstown. My sons still talk about it. They, that year, had gone to the Brothers' school in Dun Laoghaire, as a result of Dr McQuaid, the President of Blackrock, suggesting that they had not enough English to enter the junior school. They were to get a tutor, and then return. Clearly, English was a vital subject for Blackrock, though Myles na gCopaleen would say that in his time there only two people could write it, the President and himself. From Dun Laoghaire Eimear and Cóilín went to Colaiste Mhuire on Parnell Square. Being both more or less native speakers of Irish I naturally considered that that was the place for them. I took them away, however, when a stiff-necked brother insisted that Eimear should turn out to play football when he wanted to go to a music lesson. Incidentally I should say that the lot of being Irish speakers was becoming difficult in an English speaking environment. Eimear and Cóilín were often greeted with shouts of 'Tá sé mahogany gas-pipe'; and Blánaid, a child of seven, was pushed one day up against a wall by youngsters from a nearby housing estate who shouted something similar at her. For self-preservation, she gave up speaking Irish.

From that Sunday afternoon with the Misses Leitch and Mellone I began collecting copies of the many books Dr Madden wrote as well as bits of information about himself. I searched under the stairs for a manuscript Madden was said to have mislaid, and looked in the out-offices for the death masks of United Irishmen he had collected and which an over-zealous servant had whitewashed. In one of his United Irishmen volumes I read Madden's account of the vaults of St Michan's in Church Street and his identification of one of the mummies there as a Miss Crookshank. This gave me the inspiration for the book of that name which was published in 1951. It was, more than anything I had hitherto done, a work of serious research. Miss Crookshank was said to be a nun, so I searched for her in the convents that were located in that part of Dublin, one by one, and I described the search and what I found or did not find till I reached an unexpected denouement. I won't say what that was lest I should spoil the tale for future readers. What I will say is that I neither devised nor expected the ending which led people to regard the book as a sort of modern thriller. For that reason alone, perhaps, Miss Crookshank was the most successful book, in terms of readership, that I ever wrote in Irish.

I got a good deal of pleasure and education from the search for the nun, as indeed did Eimear and Cóilín. They were now day pupils in Blackrock College and involved in a society, the B.V.P., (Bonum, Verum, Pulchrum) which encouraged its members during their summer holidays to prepare a lecture on some subject that interested them for the coming year. Eimear began some musicological studies. Cóilín looked for records of what had been written about the vaults of St Michan's in the past. All three of us discussed at length all the possibilities of tracing the background of Miss Crookshank whom we frequently went to look at in her poor shriven state. Research among the convents or in the records of communities that had once had convents in that area yielded a considerable measure of interest. I got to know a good deal about the Benedictines who were in Dublin in the short reign of James II and wrote something about them, and about the Dominicans, the Poor Clares, the Carmelites and the Presentation Sisters, and was often surprised by what I saw and learned. In the Presentation Convent in George's Hill, for instance, I saw the finger of a saintly Father Tasborough and in the Carmelite House in Ranelagh the pictures of contemporaries of Miss Crookshank that later illustrated my book as well as the signature of the poet Tom Moore on glass: he had been a pupil there in his youth.

FOUR

WHILE still his secretary I was bold enough to ask Ernest Blythe to read the first draft of my *Parnell.* I don't think he liked it: at any rate he just handed it back to me without comment, which was comment enough perhaps. I took it away and began to work more seriously on it. Since my promotion I was now working normal hours in the department, and that enabled me to devote a lot of time to the book. I worked hard and late on it. Circumstance, of course, prevented me from engaging in what is generally called research, but I made up for that, as far as possible, by correspondence and by reading everything that had heretofore been written about the subject.

I wrote to St John Ervine to enquire if publication of his recent biography of Parnell had brought him any new information of value. His reply began with an apology for the abrupt opening of his letter; there was no 'Dear' anything. 'I cannot do otherwise,' he said, 'because I cannot decipher your surname, although I have tried several times to do so, and, presently when I come to address the envelope, I shall have to drop a blot where your name should appear. I suppose you have signed yourself in Gaelic of which I am entirely ignorant. The daring part of me urges me to write "O'Brien," but the timid part says "Throw up your hands and confess you can't make head or tail of his signature." And the timid part of me won.' He naturally hoped my work would be a success, but 'why not translate it,' he asked 'into the language that the Irish people can read?' He had no information, new or important, to impart apart from something he had heard from T. P. O'Connor, but which I was not to divulge. Parnell had enthralled him, and left him unable to stop talking about him. But immediately the book was done, his interest left him. 'I am not, I hope, superstitious, but I began to feel I was possessed by Parnell, that he was driving me to write the book – I have never written any book with so much ease and eagerness as I wrote his – and that when I had finished it and he had no more use for me, he tossed me aside. I am now working on a life of General Booth, another amazing figure, but he does not possess me. I am not driven by him: I have to drive myself.'

I met Joan Haslip in Dublin when she was working on a life of Parnell and after its publication I wrote to compliment her on her achievement. I had questions to ask, of course, and she graciously replied. I had thought that the critics had not been very kind to her, but she told me that what seemed to me faint praise was for her absolutely overwhelming.

Henry Harrison, with whom I also corresponded following the appearance of his *Parnell Vindicated*, had been Parnell's private secretary and had stood behind him and Kitty O'Shea at the time of the split. He had promised then that 'the truth would be given to the world.' He had been eager to solve the 'enigma' of Parnell; the startling contrast between the man who had bridled a revolution between the shafts of constitutionalism and the man whose mad love for Kitty was made grotesque by the rumour that he had slid down a fire escape to avoid the husband. And then, the statuesque silence of Parnell in the Divorce Court. In Harrison's book no new facts were produced; what was given was Harrison's interpretation of facts already known. His broad thesis was that the quality of the love the man and woman had for each other and their transparent honesty overbore every other consideration, Parnell believed he was morally justified in overriding the law, ecclesiastical and civil. But he was no deceiver and he would engage in no traffickings over the complaisance of Captain O'Shea. It had been suggested that Kitty was a Juliet unworthy of her devoted Romeo, which appears to have been Frank O'Connor's judgment, as we shall see.

In a letter to me, Captain Harrison set out what I take it was the Parnellite position, assumptions, allegations and all, at the time of the split. 'My view of Parnell,' he wrote, 'was that he was the only real and practical Nationalist in the party. . . . He had the stateman's view when the rest had only the politician's view.' He knew in 1886 that if he compromised with Gladstone in order to secure a parliament and control of the Irish customs houses, everything else, if the nation held together true to its aim, would necessarily flow. But of this the public did not know. Davitt was being cited (together with Archbishop Croke) as an authority *against* a separate Irish parliament while Tim Healy could be seen, in documentary evidence, to have been intriguing with the English and ridiculing the idea of Ireland having a separate economic and financial policy. Parnell had made no move to retain his leadership after the Divorce Court until Ireland had pronounced (at the Leinster Hall meeting and elsewhere) in favour of his continuing in that office. Gladstone wrote his letter and the English started to stampede the Nationalist members against the *newly* re-elected Irish leader. That raised a major issue of Irish independence. Nobody ignored the fact that the divorce and the stories that went with it were a bitter blow – peculiarly bitter to Irish Catholics – but that was not the cause of the revolt against Parnell. The avowed, *openly avowed*, cause was the necessity for preserving the Liberal alliance by placating Gladstone. On the day that this view, the anti-Parnell view, prevailed parliamentarianism, Harrison said, died the death. It could only have been revived by Parnell himself, if he had lived to triumph once more. How could a Nationalism that sacrificed its leader to an English demand for the sake of the Liberal alliance, imperil that alliance by demanding immediate Home Rule in 1906, or in 1914 or in 1916? Harrison's view was that Sinn Féin was mistaken – not in its aims or spirit – but in its tactics. If it had taken over the Irish representation at Westminster in 1918 it could have got what it wanted – at least, as much as it had now – *and* it could have prevented partition. It threw away a very useful weapon in a very difficult fight – and a mutilated Ireland was paying the penalty. He had always held that Sinn Féin originated in reactions provoked by the Parnell controversy and in disgust at the development of anti-Parnellite parliamentarianism when it had lost his guidance, control and virile nationalism.

My neighbour Jimmy Montgomery, anxious that I should get a genuine taste of the atmosphere of the split over the

Mrs O'Shea affair, had brought me to Con Curran's house in Garville Avenue where I talked with, among others, Willie Dawson, the son of the Lord Mayor of Dublin in the Parnell period and the writer Pádraic Colum. In my own family I had heard surprisingly little about the subject; it was not one to be discussed before children. My mother, I imagine, was a Parnellite but she never said a word to me about a matter on which feelings ran so high at the time that someone told me at the gathering in Con Curran's house that, if guns had been available, the Civil War over the Treaty would by comparison have been a minor affair. Men had ceased going to Mass to show how they felt about the attitude of churchmen and lights ordinarily before the Sacred Heart were now burning before pictures of Parnell.

Tim Healy, of course, was regarded as the villain of the piece. When in the turbulent leadership debate in Committee Room 15 of the House of Commons, John Redmond had claimed that Gladstone had become 'the master of the party', it was bitterly remembered that it was Healy who had asked who was 'the mistress of the party'. The playwright Lennox Robinson once described to me, as we stretched out pleasantly in the sun one Sunday afternoon in Blackrock College, a couple of incidents affecting Healy of which he was personally aware. When Governor-General of the Free State, Tim came to the Abbey to see a performance of Lady Gregory's *Le Bourgeois Gentilhomme*. After the play was over Lennox, then the theatre's Managing Director, bowed him out to the Viceregal car. It was known that he was in the theatre and a small crowd had gathered in the street to see him leave. Across Marlboro' Street stood an old woman from the slums in a shawl, and when Healy appeared she shouted 'Who betrayed Parnell?' Lennox said he would never forget Healy, who was old and stooped, becoming more and more stooped still, and getting into the car as quickly as possible.

The second incident occured at a small dinner Lennox gave Healy in the Shelbourne Hotel. There were eight or ten people present, certainly not more. Everything went off pleasantly: they had a private room and, after the meal, the party returned to another room where they had coffee and suitable drinks. At about 10.30 Healy got up and said his adieux and went round the room courteously shaking hands with everyone until he came to Sarah Purser, the assertive little doyenne of Dublin's artistic life, as Lennox called her. He passed her, she passed him, and then Lennox realised that she would have died rather than touch Healy's hand and that Healy knew it. There was no embarrassment on either part; there was only Lennox's embarrassment afterwards, as host, in thinking that he might have placed them side by side at dinner. I asked him did not Miss Purser know she was to meet Healy and did not Healy know he was to meet her, but Lennox could not remember the circumstances. 'Perhaps I was so ignorant', he said, 'that I did not know that a Governor General should be told in advance the names of the guests.'

My *Parnell*, when it appeared in 1937, was well received; even a poet was moved to write some verses in praise of it. By then Blythe was no longer a minister, but he reviewed it warmly in the *Irish Independent*. I had written a solid book that would dissipate the confusion and misunderstanding about Parnell and his position in Irish history, he said. Frank O'Connor sent me an enthusiastic letter. My *Parnell* was as good as any biography in English which was saying a lot because Parnell attracts writers and competition was keen. He liked the way I defined my characters; doing it with Captain O'Shea, for instance, so that one isn't really surprised at his final twist. He suggested I might do a biography of Kitty O'Shea for he did not think I had said the last word about the fair lady. There was something diabolical about her, and I, with my storyteller's knack of conveying character, could do a real portrait of her. What was she like? Brainless? Intelligent? Difficult? Authoritative? Did she give a damn about Parnell? Frank added that it was a great relief to read an Irish book that was first and foremost a book. Curtis once recommended a servant as 'a Roman Catholic but with the virtues of a Protestant'. It was well to be able to praise an Irish book as though it were in English and without making reservations to cover the non-existent standard of writing in Irish. Clarity and conciseness were my virtues.

Frank O'Connor was right in thinking that the last word had not been written about Kitty O'Shea. Quite recently I read a correspondence that passed in the mid-1950s between a Father John Maunsell and Shane Leslie and from it I gathered quite a lot about Kitty's children. She had seven children in all: three by Captain O'Shea (Carmen, Norah and Gerard) and four by Parnell (Sophia Claude, Clare Gabrielle, Katharine, and a fourth who was stillborn after Parnell's death). Sophia Claude lived only a couple of months, Katharine or Katie married and died in an asylum; she had one child that was also stillborn. This left Father Maunsell to concentrate his interest largely on Clare Gabrielle, a beautiful girl who became the first wife of Dr Bertram Maunsell, Father John's father by a second wife. Clare Gabrielle was born in 1883 and died in 1909. She had one child, a son they called Assheton Clare, and he, Parnell's only surviving grandchild, a British army officer, died of enteric fever in India in 1934 and was buried there.

The Parnell relics, such as they were, passed to Father Maunsell on his father's death in 1941 and he was glad to be able to make them over to Shane Leslie. The most important of them were the rings Parnell and Kitty exchanged when they married following the O'Shea divorce. Father Maunsell thought he would have to describe these as unholy relics, yet he was loath to condemn what Parnell and Kitty had done. 'Our Lord on occasions used harsh words', he wrote, 'but they were never used towards those who had fallen into the more shameful faults and sins which are due so much to man's inevitable frailty and weakness'. The O'Shea children were not so charitable. One of them, Gerard, writing in 1923 to Dr Maunsell, claimed that he had been the means of causing Parnell to hide and slink about under cover of darkness and under many aliases like the cowardly wretch he was. Finding him unexpectedly in their house one day he had smashed a bottle of wine over the blackguard's head: his sole regret was that he had not shot him.

Among writers Daniel Corkery reacted to my book, as Frank O'Connor had done. *Parnell* was a book of good texture, he said, every sentence signed by the one hand. He invited me to lecture in Cork, and entertained me in his house at Ovens. Sean O'Faoláin, who was at that time putting the finishing touches to his biography of Daniel O'Connell, said, in a very long review in the *Irish Press*, that I had wisely allowed the moral issue to make its own impression, the arguments and conclusions to run out of the interest of the recorded event, uncushioned by those comments and analysis and conclusions that too often turned a biography into an argument *a thèse*. He, like O'Connor, had almost forgotten the book was written in Irish.

The Leader, D. P. Moran's old paper, announced on a poster that Michael Tierney, the future head of University College, Dublin, had reviewed the book for them. Tierney was critically enthusiastic. I had broken new ground, he wrote, not alone by writing the first Irish biography of Parnell, but also by writing the first Irish work of this kind on any serious scale since the revival movement began. It was, indeed, an odd experience to read a life of Parnell in Irish. I had written naturally as an admirer of Parnell, he went on. My account of conditions in Ireland after the Famine was touched by the passion that no Irishman could help feeling, and in dealing with the final tragedy, while recognising the soundness of Archbishop Walsh's view that Parnell should have resigned, I was perhaps a little too severe in my judgment on both his English and Irish opponents. Tierney's own judgment on the outcome of the split was that it was fortunate that Parnell had not been victorious, otherwise he would have won with the Fenians against the Church, and could thereby have inflicted a wound that generations might not have healed. As things turned out, his death was, after all, probably the lesser misfortune.

These reviews were read no doubt by people who could not read the book. But that did no harm. The next time I was in the Secretary's room in Finance I noticed that McElligott had a copy of the book standing out prominently in the book case behind him. That pleased me. Otherwise I derived little satisfaction from the publication. It did not sell well. After many years there were still copies available of the second printing, and a good number of those that had been sold went as prizes at feiseanna, which meant, I fear, that they were unlikely to have been read at all.

Being aware of my interest, Jimmy Montgomery rang me up in Finance one day and invited me to see a film on Parnell he was about to censor. I naturally dropped everything and, going from the rere of Government Buildings through Leinster House, was soon in the little studio in Molesworth St. It was already full, with some people sitting on the floor. There were a few survivors of the old party there as well as men who had written about Parnell or acted in plays about him. The lights were lowered and we saw a poor film with Clark Gable in the leading role but without a beard, as if he feared his fans would not accept him otherwise. When it was over and the lights went up we turned to Jimmy on the dais behind us. He was stroking his chin. 'Ladies and Gentlemen' he said, 'I don't know what you thought of that. I thought it was a *barefaced travesty*.'

Among the people I interviewed in connection with *Parnell* was Dr Mark Ryan. He, who had spent most of his life as a medical doctor in London, was now living in retirement in Dublin and I was brought to him by a mutual acquaintance, Fionán Mac Coluim. Dr Ryan had been an I.R.B. man since his schooldays; there was a circle in St Jarlath's in Tuam and some of the members at least had rifles. In London he was deeply involved in most Irish activities but managed somehow to avoid being arrested, though Scotland Yard kept a close watch on him and on anybody who had associations with him. I got to know about this in a curious way. In the days before the Second World War the British Post Office wanted to do some confidential business affecting radio wavelengths with their opposite numbers in Dublin. The Irish Engineer in Chief, T. J. Monaghan, was a splendid and utterly reliable person but the British were slow to approach him because his father, another London doctor, had worked with Ryan. To ensure that T. J. was 'all right', they spoke to the assistant Engineer in Chief, John Willie O'Neill, a T.C.D. man, who told me in later years that they had done so. There was clearly nothing wrong with the British Intelligence system: they had the files since Fenian days and had studied their implications in the 1939-45 generation.

If there had been a second edition of my *Parnell* instead of a second printing, I would have liked to elaborate on some aspects of the story; for instance on the circumstances in which Captain O'Shea, having delayed divorce proceedings for several years, finally acted. He had held his hand for a mixture of reasons, but his restraining motive was a fear that public scandal might shock Mrs O'Shea's rich old aunt and cause her to change her will. This aunt, Mrs Benjamin Wood, was supposed to be worth £200,000, which she might leave entirely to her favourite niece. O'Shea was determined to have his share, though as trustee for his children, as he said. Other relations of Mrs Wood were ready to contest the will. If he threw in his lot with them it could make all the difference to the result.

The old lady held up everything by living to the age of ninety-eight. Her will, as expected, made Mrs O'Shea sole heiress and executrix, putting her in the position, if she felt like it, to square the Captain, though the price might be high. But Mrs O'Shea and Parnell decided against doing this, fearing that by making O'Shea financially independent they would put themselves more than ever in his power. So, on his part, O'Shea, having no further reason for restraint, and every conceivable personal reason for action, joined with Aunt Ben's disappointed relations to dispute the will, while simultaneously he sued for divorce. This came as a horrible surprise to many people, particularly in Ireland, and was the direct cause of Parnell's political downfall; but the Irish leader's entanglement with Mrs O'Shea was fairly widely known all the same. I quote some examples in the book. The Home Office knew about it as early as February 1881 and, in May of the following year, Sir William Harcourt, the Home Secretary, told the whole Cabinet that the 'treaty' with Parnell, then a prisoner in Kilmainham Gaol, would not be popular when the public discovered that it had been negotiated by Captain O'Shea, the husband of Parnell's mistress. O'Shea at that time did not know what the Home Office knew.

My interest in Parnell did not, of course, end with the publication of my biography. For years afterwards I kept running into him here, there and everywhere, and in a book of mine in Irish published in 1963 – it appeared in English later as *The Prime Informer* – I told of the collaboration of William Henry Joyce, a district inspector of the Royal Irish Constabulary, in the complicity of the British government with *The Times* of London to substantiate the charges made by the paper against Parnell and his party in a series entitled 'Parnellism and Crime'. I had had possession for many years of an unpublished typescript of Joyce's which my friend Dr T. W. Moody believed cast a flood of new light on the subject. Joyce's revelations were fired with a hatred of a government that he believed had treated him badly, and they impressed Roger Casement and Eoin MacNeill the historian when they saw them. Some of Joyce's writing was done *sub rosa* in the Irish Republican Office in New York and, knowing two men who had worked in that office, I was able to fill in some interesting details about Joyce who was naturally inclined to lie low. Another friend of mine, Kevin O'Shiel, told me how he was sent by Arthur Griffith to interview Joyce in Dublin. He found him at his residence off the Palmerston Road, a dingy little house that reeked strongly of boiled cabbage. Joyce was a small, sharp-featured, stooped and shabbily-dressed old man with a moustache, who smelled of drink and had a shake in his hands. On the strength of O'Shiel's report, Griffith agreed to talk to Joyce in a neutral setting although he had a dislike of policemen and distrusted turncoats and was convinced that he had a story of importance to tell and arranged that he should go to New York to write it. De Valera when he was in the States, also learned of 'the Joyce affair', and thought, in November 1921, that if there was anything really in it 'this would be a valuable time to bring out the Joyce manuscript'.

Evidence continues to accumulate that there was 'something really in it', something sufficient to create alarm in government circles. My attention was drawn quite recently to a letter in the Balfour papers at Whittingham in North Berwick which Sir West Ridgeway, the Under Secretary, wrote on 12 April 1896 to Gerald Balfour, who was then the Chief Secretary of Ireland without Cabinet rank and whose brother Arthur was the First Lord of the Treasury. Ridgeway spoke of 'a very disagreeable complication' and suggested that before any action was taken the two brothers might confer. Joyce, still serving as a Resident Magistrate, had lost favour with the powers that be and was now believed to be going into league with the Nationalists who would be happy to revive the old issue of the government's collusion with *The Times* to down Parnell. Ridgeway believed, on the strength of a letter from Joyce, that he should be immediately suspended. A court of enquiry should be established; but he warned Gerald Balfour to be very careful who to put on it, so few Irishmen could be trusted. 'In Ireland two classes are certain to be your enemies (1) those whom you have admonished; (2) those whom you have benefited'.

Robert Emmet, 'the darlin' of Erin' as the ballad singer

called him, was another figure to occupy a lot of my free time. He, at the age of 23, had been executed in 1803 for leading a rebellion, had made a famous speech from the dock, and interest in him was almost continuously stimulated by the search for his headless body. Dr Madden had joined in the search and, in the *Lives of the United Irishmen*, had written at length about him and his equally distinguished brother, Thomas Addis Emmet. Somehow I got involved in the recurring discussions about Emmet and, at the instance of an office colleague, gave a public lecture which was heard by the publisher of *Miss Crookshank*. He came up to me after the lecture and suggested I should turn it into a book in Irish. This I did in 1954 and the book was deemed good enough to be given a Douglas Hyde award. Somebody reviewing the book said that I had brought two advantages to the writing of it, my native acquaintance with Emmet's Dublin and an understanding of the period. Whatever about that, it was inevitable that I should do a version of the book in English, a language in which I had previously written little, apart from articles and book reviews.

Brian O'Nolan, who found the Irish original a pleasant book, had said (under one of his pseudonyms, Myles na gCopaleen) in his Cruiskeen Lawn column that he was sorry that the book was written in Irish, if only to assess it against the not inconsiderable corpus of existing works about Emmet and his time in English and French. Emmet had no interest whatsoever in the Irish language, O'Nolan said, though he lacked the undisguised hostility of O'Connell, and he had the sense to refrain from ludicrous utterances about it such as those made by Thomas Davis, who knew not a syllable of the tongue – I am not sure if he was right there – and who could, therefore, speak freely about it. Many politicians of the present day, Myles continued, quoted the Davis idiocies with solemnity. The worst Myles could remember, without raiding his vast library, concerned a passage in Davis's famous essay, where he rounds on critics who said he was advocating an Irish-speaking Dublin – law courts, mart and street saturated with Erse, the peasant ascendant, the Bayrla barred. 'That', Davis said, 'is a thing that cannot happen for a century hence.' It was over a hundred years since he said it.

O'Nolan then added a typical passage. 'O'Broin clearly likes Emmet. But it is improper for the true historian to like – or dislike – his subject. It would be a nice state of affairs if the success of an operation depended on the degree of skill brought to its performance, or depended on the extent to which the surgeon liked the patient. The study of individuals who have a place in history should be far more anthropological than was customary. If their personalities were to be judged from their own letters and other writings – many written for the eye of the historian – what use was history, except as a pretext for the trashing of school children? Had the science of scholarly intuition progressed not at all in the last century or so? A proper approach to the anthropology of history would reveal that the most active public figures of a century ago and earlier were fellows, like Pitt the Prime Minister of England and Robert Emmet, who attained great things very early in life in the arts and sciences. It was not until they were over 40 that a lot of fellows of to-day even thought of looking for a job.'

I enlarged the text considerably drawing particularly on my friend Dr F. S. Bourke's remarkable collection of papers, and I called this 1958 version of the story *The Unfortunate Mr Robert Emmet* to emphasise Emmet's own conviction that he had been the victim of misfortune or sheer bad luck. One arms depot exploded; in another the pike-shafts would not fit the heads. A rumour turned back a large force of Kildare men coming to join the rising; and Emmet had no sooner given the word to march than the whole affair got out of hand and turned into a street brawl. These may not have been chance events, however.

I availed of the biography which Billy Wicklow published to deal with the theory that the government had instigated the revolt, and with James Connolly's view of it as part of the world-wide upsurge of the working class; and I was able to say something about Archbishop Troy and the Catholic community who were the first to be blamed for 'the disturbances'.

In an office shuffle in 1928 Frank Duff had become my boss, replacing Larry Lynd, and we worked together for a year or

Called to the Bar, 1924.

In the National Army, 1922.

With Ernest Blythe on Budget Day, 1932.

In attendance on Robin Flower (*front row, left*), Osborn Bergin (*middle row, second from left*), Ernest Rhys (*back row, left*), and other scholars at a Celtic Congress in University College Dublin, 1924.

Our first baby, Eimear.

Above: Emergency Year 1940. Cáit and I, together with our sons Eimear and Cóilín, in Connemara with the Commissioner for Co. Galway, C. I. O'Flynn. *Below left*: Cáit and Frank Duff outside the GPO. *Below right*: Cáit among the pigeons in Trafalgar Square.

Secretary of the Department of Posts and Telegraphs.

With my Minister, James Everett, and J. F. Dempsey, the general manager of Aer Lingus, at the inaugural flight of mails from Dublin airport.

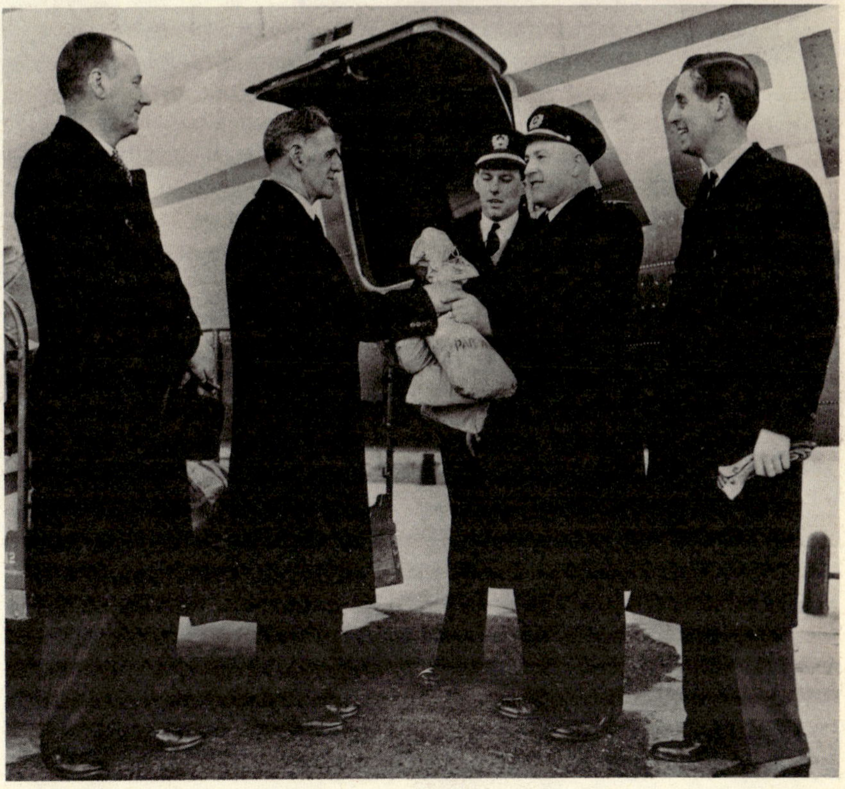

Choosing a meal with Cáit at a broadcasting function.

Giving my daughter, Eithne, away.

Golden Jubilee, 1975.

Cáit with Eithne and her daughter, Marion.

Coming up to my eightieth year.

two. It was a privilege, of course, to share Frank's company in this way and to be given an opportunity of seeing something of the double life that he was living. For this was the period when his Legion of Mary was beginning to expand internationally, while in Dublin his hostels for down and out men and women and prostitutes and a variety of Legionary activities were making an impact. Frank would have desired to separate his commitment to the Legion from his office job, but that was impossible. If he could not be seen after hours, he would have to be seen in Government Buildings, and I am afraid that too many people encroached upon his office work and in such a way that he could not dismiss them abruptly as other people would have done. Frank was not made that way. However, he recognised that the interruptions could not go on, and he applied for permission to retire on pension, relying on the fact that his official position had worsened since the Treaty. It was 1933 before he was able to do so, benefitting from an Article in the Treaty which provided for such situations. Somebody said that he would have been asphyxiated had he had to remain in the Service. Whatever truth there was in that remark, it is certain that by leaving he was set free for his monumental activities in the order of Grace. In the order of nature, Frank had what the Germans called *fingerspitzgefühl* (tip of the finger feeling), a sense of opportunity allied with clearness of mind and a decisive purpose.

Though he was now outside the Department I was actually seeing more of him than before. Before he left I had told him I was thinking of 'doing something useful', feeling perhaps that he would find a corner for me in some Legionary field. He did not do so, in fact, but recommended that I should join the St Vincent de Paul Society where his own social career had begun. Nevertheless, what was being done in one particular hostel, the Morning Star, continued to appeal to me. Living in, as clients of the hostel did, for long periods the Legion had to provide entertainment for them, indoor and outdoor games, a debating society, and an amateur theatrical class, as well, of course, as bed and partial board. I spoke once at least to the debating society, and gave some help to a group that were preparing a play for a local feis. There was talent in the group, which contained some fellows who had been in jail, and I believe that when the time came they gave a rather good performance. However, for financial reasons probably, the feis abandoned the competition in dramatic art, leaving the Morning Star players high and dry, without an objective to work towards. To prevent the class from breaking up, the Legion, rather typically, started its own feis which went on for the best part of a fortnight, the adjudicating of plays being done by Andrew E. Malone, the critic of the *Irish Times*, and myself. It was an incident during the adjudication that made up my mind to become an active legionary. From where my colleague and I were seated in the middle of the improvised theatre in the Morning Star building I became aware of a scene being enacted at the door that led from the women's hostel next door, the Regina Coeli. A lassie insisted upon being admitted while a play was in progress, and struck in the face the sister on duty who tried to prevent her. This left me wondering afterwards why a girl who could have been amusing herself elsewhere should for an ideal put herself in a position to be treated in that way. In the Regina, insults to legionaries were not unknown, and I had heard of sisters taking punishment while striving to separate women in angry brawls. Here was another example; and it impressed me.

I became an active legionary and president of a praesidium which, with Father Senan Moynihan, the Capuchin, as its spiritual director, began with a number of artists, writers and actors for the most part as its ordinary members. Father Senan did not stay long. Group piety did not appeal to him, I think, and he had ideas as to how artists could help him with the *Capuchin Annual* and *Bonaventura* of which he was the excellent editor. Anyhow, most of my artist friends followed him, without the praesidium altogether losing its intended character. Two men who stayed with me until their deaths were Peter Nolan, whose playing in Lennox Robinson's *Whiteheaded Boy* in the Abbey I had always admired, and Gerard O'Byrne, a stained glass worker who adorned the oratory in the Morning Star and illustrated Joseph Plunkett's poem: *I saw his blood upon the Rose*, which Frank, not very wisely, I feel, introduced into the Legion Handbook.

In 1937 the praesidium took on the publication of a Legion quarterly, for which Frank found a name, *Maria*

Legionis, and which I edited for ten years. It brought me even more closely into contact with him than before. We met in his house or at *ad hoc* meetings of the praesidium to review progress, and the editing was largely a tailoring job, fitting and illustrating the copy Frank supplied from his own limitless larder. The praesidium was excellent. In it and in another group of which I had personal experience later, I saw the Legion of Mary working on all classes of people, moulding them into a family, disciplining them, instructing them in their faith, and causing them to occupy themselves with problems that as individuals they might never know or would be unable to confront. Of course, a lot depended on the personalities concerned, and particularly on the officers, but it was quite amazing to observe what persons with limited talents and education could be made to do. I have seen officers literally sweating to give expression to the thoughts they had put together for the allocution which the spiritual director was expected to give, but with spiritual directors hard to come by, they had to do themselves. One of these officers, a labouring man, would have his pint in the local on the way home and recruit among the men he met there to join him on an enclosed weekend retreat. On Sunday mornings he would lead us first to the mortuary in a public hospital to pray for the dead, and then send us to visit the sick in the hospital wards. I learned a lot from those Sunday mornings. I learned what St Paul meant when he told the Thessalonians to go on encouraging one another and building up one another's faith. My faith always needed building up. I was just about able to say the Legion prayers when once I found myself in the mortuary alone, but I was not brave enough to draw back the shrouds, as my colleagues would have done, to see who had died since the previous Sunday. That would only confirm what I was afraid of, that in some cases death had come with pain to waste and make ugly, and with terror perhaps of what lay beyond the next desperately drawn breath.

In the Legion I got to know many remarkable people. One of them was Edel Quinn, and it fell to my happy lot in time to appear before the tribunal which examined the cause for her beatification and canonisation. I gave them a typescript I had already shown to her biographer, Cardinal Suenens of

Maines. This told, largely in their own words, what six lady friends of Edel's had told me, and which I had carefully written down. The tribunal had already taken evidence from a number of these women, but death had forestalled two of them, increasing thereby the importance of the typescript. What I had to say about Edel of my own knowledge was not valuable; it certainly did not add anything at all new to what her friends and co-workers had said; but I gave the tribunal a picture of a slim, good-looking, nicely dressed, attractive girl who spoke rapidly and whom I had met at Legion meetings or travelling home by train, I to Booterstown, she to Monkstown further on the line. She had written to me from tbe boat on the way to Africa a characteristically happy slangy letter, and I had published in *Maria Legionis* extracts from a diary of hers. I surmised that, as we journeyed homewards after a Concilium meeting, we could have talked about Tim Barry, an auxillary legionary I had recruited in the course of my Vincent de Paul work. He was a holy soul, and I may have asked Edel to look after him as he travelled as a T.B. patient to Lourdes on a Legion pilgrimage. Tim spoke to me, on his return, of how kind she had been to him. He preceded her to heaven, from where no doubt he prayerfully followed her extraordinary African apostolate.

In the early autumn of 1937 a number of Irish agricultural workers died in a bothy fire in Kirkintilloch in Scotland, and, under public pressure, the government set up an interdepartmental committee to look into the circumstances in which seasonal migration occurred and to make recommendations to mitigate it. The chairman was Lemass's parliamentary secretary, Sean Moylan, who had been a senior I.R.A. officer in the war of independence and later. I was nominated to represent the Department of Finance on the committee; two of my colleagues came from Industry and Commerce, and Agriculture and the Land Commission each nominated an official. The Land Commission man had served in the Congested Districts Board till its dissolution in 1924 and seemed to be attached to the idea that the Board should be revived. We travelled, all seven of us, through those congested and largely Irish-speaking areas and inspected what had been happening in Co. Meath as the result of the transfer there of Gaeltacht families; and we had no difficulty in agreeing that an extension of that policy be recommended. We disagreed, however, as to whether a separate department should be set up to supervise and control the various schemes that were operating in favour of these areas, and I, with the representative of Agriculture and one of the nominees of Industry and Commerce, constituted the minority. After almost fifty years my memory is not clear as to what the government did on the Committee's recommendations. Worry over the war situation developing in Europe may have constrained them from doing anything very positive. One thing I do remember from our tour of the West was my conversations with Moylan on bookish subjects. He was a great reader and the possessor, moreover, of a fine sense of humour.

I represented Finance also about this time in a group that was given the macabre job of arranging the details of the funeral of President Hyde, whose death was expected hourly. A lead coffin was bought, but, happily, remained unused by the time Hyde left the presidency. It turned in useful, however, when Cardinal Glennon, a guest of President O'Kelly's, died in the Aras.

FIVE

WHAT WAS to be the Second World War could be seen coming a long way off. The issues were better defined than on the previous occasion, but the line-up was likely to be more or less the same. The British and the French and whatever others they could muster would stand up to the Germans who were led this time, not by an Imperial Kaiser but by a National Socialist, Hitler, who was intent on recovering what had been lost at Versailles. There were uncertain elements in the picture. What would Russia and Italy do? And where did we, the tiny Irish state, stand?

I had been to Teelin in Donegal in 1938 to learn something about the local Irish dialect, and found myself sharing a room in a cottage with a German, a Professor Ludwig Mulhausen. He, too, I understood, was a student of Irish language dialects, and had worked his way up to Teelin from the Kerry coastal Gaeltacht. He was studying other things besides. He photographed untiringly, and local people observed that, when returning to Dublin, on his way back to Germany, he never ventured through the British-controlled area in the North. He would take the longer journey round by Sligo. When he woke the first morning we were together he took out his Nazi song book and sang a verse or two: I responded by kneeling down and provocatively blessing myself. He then put on his dressing gown, walked with me to the pier head nearby and dived into the bleak sea. Not to be outdone I did the same; and nearly died of the cold. I gave this morning exercise up; the Nazi, a man of tougher breed, did not. We ate our meals together in the kitchen. I, conscious of the demands of Irish hospitality, began by passing things to him, but I gave that up too, because he never passed anything to me, so that meals would end with an accumulation of dishes at his side of the table, and little or nothing at mine. When the war came he spoke to Ireland from Germany in Irish by radio to remind us who were our friends and who were our enemies. The latter he reminded us had sent us the Black and Tans.

In 1938, during the period when Chamberlain was negotiating the Munich agreement which he believed assured us of peace, I had a long series of conversations about the international situation in the Cistercian monastery of Mount Mellary with an Englishman, W. H. Flear, who was 'making his soul' there, as I was. He was a most charming fellow, a convert to Catholicism. His father had been a Quaker, his mother a Baptist, and his current job was as secretary to a London electricity company. We agreed on many things. He had been all through the 1914-18 war, and served as an infantry officer in Ireland during the Black and Tan period. He had hated what he had seen and heard, he told me, and used the opportunities that came his way to soften the bitterness. He still wished to make amends. I believed him, for he was manifestly an unusually sensitive chap. One of his jobs during his service in Ireland was to patrol on a Crossley tender the railway line between Cork and Cobh to prevent attacks on troop trains. One day he saw a boy with a basket on his head leaning against a railway crossing gate. He jumped from the tender and ran forward, revolver in hand, and drove the boy back into the centre of the road and kept him covered until the train passed. The Manchesters who were on the train wondered as they watched what this was all about. When the train had gone, Flear turned to the boy. 'Come on now,' he cried, 'let's see what you've got in the basket.' It was full of raspberries; and Flear had to endure some leg-pulling when he returned to barracks.

He also spoke to me of going in mufti with another Catholic officer to the church in Blackpool 'to hear a rebel sermon'. Instead they heard the most beautiful sermon Flear ever heard on love for one's neighbour. They both left rather ashamed of themselves. 'We should go to Mass,' Flear commented, 'with better dispositions.'

He was desperately upset by the prospect of another war. Like his Prime Minister, Neville Chamberlain, and most of his countrymen, he did not want war, and was not averse to helping Germany to eliminate the worst features of the Treaty of Versailles. At the same time he was fearful of what would happen to Austria, Czechoslovakia and Poland if Hitler had his way. Since becoming Chancellor of Germany, five years before, he had lifted the morale of the people and given a new impetus to German industry while displaying an ugly ruthlessness in his treatment of Jews. Another great war appeared inevitable and Flear feared that his country was drifting into it. What would Ireland's policy be?

I thought that, while we would do anything we could to prevent a war which was not likely to be much, we would not participate if one did occur. I had a slight reservation as to whether that in fact would be Ireland's position. The head of our government, de Valera, had become a close friend of the British Prime Minister, Chamberlain. Together they had ended the economic war, Chamberlain conceding more than any other British statesman would possibly have done in the expectation that we would face a war with Germany together or, if that was impossible, that Irish neutrality would be qualified in Britain's favour. And concessions in that direction were made, though not as regards the availability of the Southern naval bases.

As war drew nearer and nearer, it naturally occupied more and more of one's thoughts. Ireland was to have a pavilion at the World's Fair in New York and I went over to London one night with a colleague from Industry and Commerce to settle some business urgently with the firms that were constructing the building for us. It was a balmy night at sea and I spent most of it chatting with an Englishman about the unavoidable subject. It seemed to be ridiculous to be concerned with World Fairs and Irish pavilions with a form of warfare that could be terrible in its ferocity just round the corner. On the Sunday morning, 3 September 1939, before Chamberlain announced that Britain was at war with Germany, I was in Blackrock College on one of those days for non-Catholics that through the Legion of Mary I had got involved in. At home nearby in Booterstown the family with Cáit's sister Eileen gathered round the radio set to hear what Chamberlain had to say. At his words announcing that Britain was now at war Eileen broke down. Cáit went to her aid, realising in a flash what this meant, and she gestured to the children to leave the room. Eileen in the previous war had lost a fiancé. That the war might impact seriously on Ireland was realised on the very first night when the British liner *Athenia*, carrying about 1,400 passengers, was torpedoed by a German submarine north-west of Donegal with a loss of 112 lives and some of the survivors were brought ashore in Galway.

I was promoted to be a Principal Officer that September and served as such through the years of the war or what we in Ireland called the Emergency. When the war threatened, the departments likely to be affected most, including our own, had looked into the crystal ball and tried to envisage what a prolonged conflict had in store for the country. We had none of the special skills the modern Department of Finance appears able to command; we, therefore, could only do the best we could with whatever common sense God had given us. Whether our prognostications were of any real value I doubt. We tended to be pessimistic, and some of the things we wrote about inevitably occured, the shortages of basic commodities, for example. That required no particular foresight. They created problems for the Department of Supplies from the moment of its inception, which Sean Lemass and my old superior John Leydon tackled with more success than may have been anticipated.

I don't think anybody in 1939 could have foreseen how the war was to develop in its early stages; the phoney period when nothing seemed to be happening, with France apparently secure behind its Maginot line, the evacuation of children from English built-up areas to the countryside in expectation of air raids; and the distribution of masks, even in Ireland, for fear of gas which was never employed. But by June 1940 a calamitous situation had developed for the Western allies with France signing the most humiliating armistice in her history, and the remnants of the British Expeditionary Force being saved as if by a miracle at Dunkirk. That was a period when Britain might also have given up but Churchill, now Prime Minister in place of Chamberlain, declared that they would go it alone to the bitter end.

Quite quickly my family learned how near the war really was. A widow lived in a mews at the end of our garden whose boys were in the British navy. One of them was lost on the

H.M.S. *Courageous* in mid September 1939 and the other, a submariner, was nearly drowned off Narvik the following year. Our boys followed the news with particular interest after that, and were allowed to stay up to hear the B.B.C. 9 o'clock bulletin, as well as 'Lord Haw-Haw' and my Teelin acquaintance Mulhausen. In time the shortages of certain commodities began to tell. Tea was scarce so we started to drink shell cocoa in its place. Butter, too, but as it was unthinkable that 'fear a'tighe' should have to do without it the girls from the West who were working for us returned to something they had not practised for years and somehow managed to churn a little for me. Coal was scarce too, all the time, but some of Cáit's male protegés went up into the Dublin hills and cut turf for her. Drying it was a problem and I remember the competition to get hold of the bellows, wielding which gave more heat than the sods of turf in the fireplace. Gas restriction was severe because of the coal shortage, and to prevent the law being broken a glimmer-man went about, and rumours that he was about caused panic sometimes in our kitchen.

I remember well the day France fell. That her condition was critical we all realised, and not having a radio set, a number of us in Finance hurried from our rooms into Merrion Street and piled into a car to hear the 1 o'clock news. Charlie Almond, an Englishman and a realist, was with us. When he heard the news he just said 'that's the effin end,' and ran off. Nobody thought otherwise, except Arthur Codling who refused to lose hope. He pinned some of it on an inevitable American entry, and showed me from the maps he kept in his drawer how things would then change. Nevertheless an overwhelming German victory looked a money-on proposition until a Russian recovery began at Stalingrad. Meanwhile, we were under pressure from the British to abandon our neutrality policy. There was a moment when it was possible that the British might be constrained to invade us before the Germans did, or that we might have both of them in on top of us in order to get at each other. That was the situation in July 1940 when, with seven other Civil Servants, I became peripherally involved.

Whatever form the invasion of Ireland might take it was obvious that an Irish government would have serious difficulty maintaining a central administration; and out of this realisation came a decision to set up a stand-by administration in eight regions, each of which was to be directed by a commissioner. I was to be one of these. The whole scheme was improvised in a hurry by the Department of Supplies with some advertence to the British model, and an outline of it was given to me and my colleagues. We would be expected to preserve order, to maintain essential services, and to control supplies. The Taoiseach, Mr de Valera, spoke to us briefly in the Cabinet room before we left for our regions. He was grim, but said no more than we already knew. He certainly gave us no indication whatever of the direction from which we might expect trouble. We knew already that if an invasion occured we would have the father and mother of a job on our hands. As we paused for a minute outside the Cabinet room, some one raised a laugh by saying that in all the uncertainty one thing was certain; we the Regional Commissioners were going to be shot. He was thinking principally of a German invasion, no doubt, because of the apparent unstopability of the German armies. The gauleiters, he said, would shoot us if we refused to collaborate, and the common people of Ireland would do the same if we did collaborate and became Quislings. Yet we felt there would have to be some measure of collaboration in the interests of the people we were being appointed to serve.

Our lack of knowledge as to the likely first-comers reminded me of a situation I was witnessing every night near our house in Booterstown. Two of my neighbours, elderly men and members of the Local Security Force, a police auxiliary, went out night after night to patrol a strip of the coastline. They were excellent fellows, intelligent and sturdy, and would give a good account of themselves in a crisis. But the crisis they expected differed from one to the other. One was a man in the republican tradition who, as between Germans and English, would prefer the Germans but would follow a government lead strictly. The other could only foresee a German invasion and this he would fearlessly oppose. If, by some unbelievable chance, the British came he would not oppose them, believing with Churchill that this would be for

Ireland's ultimate good. Our neutrality policy was rarely discussed. All the political parties were at one on that issue, and were represented in a National Defence Conference. Because of our propinquity to Britain, our trade connection and so many other ties, it was necessary to explain to the Germans that our neutrality to an extent would have to be qualified, but that I only know since reading the post-war literature. How really neutral we would prove to be in all circumstances was another matter.

In the process of time the Americans joined the Allies and there was talk, stimulated by the known utterly unfriendly attitude of their ambassador in Dublin, that they might seize Ireland as a base for their campaign. That raised again a question as to the nature of our neutrality. I remember walking along the seafront at Galway's Salthill and being rather surprised when Liam Ó Briain, a University professor with a national record and a member of the defence forces, doubted whether we should oppose the Americans. 'How could we?' he said. 'They are in a sense ourselves.'

I should make it clear that, from my own reading or otherwise, I knew nothing about the German 'Operation Green' which envisaged a possible German landing on an eighty-five mile front between Wexford and Dungarvan, either as a diversion from a major assault on Britain and to draw off British troops in Northern Ireland, or as part of a plan to occupy the two islands ultimately. Nor had I heard of the publicity the Germans were giving to 'Operation Green' with the object of stretching the British defence preparations. Neither did I know anything about the British code-named 'W' Plan which covered an invasion from the North to repel a German force coming in expectedly towards Cork, and an occupation by Royal Marine units of a bridgehead the moment the Germans landed. Some of this British plan was apparently communicated to the Irish army with the idea that, when the crunch came, British and Irish soldiers would together oppose the invading Germans. We could surmise that some preparatory talks on these lines would be going on, but nobody, no doubt rightly, thought it would help the national position if the Regional Commissioners were informed. It was reasonable to believe that in the talks with the British, once their pressure on us to declare war on Germany had failed, the Irish government would undertake to operate a neutrality policy that took seriously into account Britain's vital strategic interests. It would, for example, allow Irish Free State citizens without restriction to join the British armed forces as volunteers; it would permit British soldiers, sailors and airmen to take leave in the Free State area provided they wore civilian clothes; it would convey to the authorities in London any intelligence it could about German naval activities off our coasts, which explains, no doubt, the haste I had seen in installing a telephone to Belmullet. This was certainly not justified on commercial grounds; but a watch-out post had been set up on the coast nearby. The control of information about weather conditions was so rigorous that when de Valera's parliamentary secretary, Paddy Little, while skating on the lake in the Phoenix Park, fell and broke his arm no word of it was allowed to be published. MacDonald said that de Valera could scarcely have promised more benevolent co-operation short of declaring war against the enemy. He thought that there was quite a lot of sense in the Irish position, but when he reported the results of his talks, Churchill was deeply disappointed, and continued to the end of the war to be bitterly critical of de Valera. One wonders how much his subordinates allowed him to know. The British demands on Ireland continued to the very end; it was February 1945 when their request was approved to establish a radar station on our territory for use against the latest form of German submarine activity.

As part of their invasion feasability studies, the Germans had available to them an impressive volume of photographs, and a map of the Irish-speaking areas from West Cork and Kerry to Donegal. When I read about this in Robert Fisk's *In Time of War* I wondered had the photographs at any rate been taken by Mulhausen, the Nazi I had met in Teelin, and who was regarded by some of the local people as a spy.

My region was Galway and Mayo – I asked for it myself because of my old attachment to the West – and I got down to Galway by train the night of my appointment with my family. This was a strange turn-up. I had arranged with The O'Mahony, who was a T.D., that in the event of anything serious happening I would have one of the houses of his estate in Grange Con, Co. Wicklow for my family, whereas here I was making across the country to the West. I was met by a Garda Chief Superintendent at the city railway station, and going up Eyre Square, where a large muster of the local Defence Force was being drilled, I could sense a feeling of expectation that something quite dramatic was on the way. The government had put out a statement stressing 'the colossal tasks' the Regional Commissioners might have to face, and calling for maximum help for them. Our orders would have to be loyally obeyed, and disobedience would be disloyalty to the nation. We would be the last bulwark against anarchy, and on our ability to discharge our duties the health and lives of the people would depend. The public were warned that arrangements, no matter how carefully planned, could break down if any stampede occured. The real danger of panic and large scale evacuation following a landing was borne in on me when a young man I knew came to see me a day or two after the German blitz on Coventry. He was frightened out of his wits – I never saw anything like it – and was looking for a job at home. He had certainly no intention of returning to England. From the middle of July 1940 the Germans had attacked from the air a variety of British targets and this developed into what became known as the Battle of Britain. My friend had watched these developments, rather dispassionately I fear, believing perhaps that he was safe where he was in Coventry. And then the Germans arrived overhead one night and kept dropping their appalling loads until morning, wreaking enormous destruction and terrorising the population. I had only to look at my visitor to see what could happen, perhaps in my region. The next year we had the North Strand bombing. Dublin was apparently not too safe either. What if Galway were on the list?

The danger of panic was very much in our minds when I met the County Secretaries of Galway and Mayo, Clem O'Flynn and Michael Egan, who had been appointed to work with me as County Commissioners. They were good men who knew their counties like the backs of their hands and did everything I asked them to do. Indeed when I met Egan he was suffering from a poisoned hand which he had got helping to put obstacles in fields round Castlebar to prevent aircraft from landing. He was almost too eager, and yet when I saw his office staff I was disappointed, it was so small. Clearly in a real emergency we would have to supplement that and the staff in Galway considerably. I warned such civil servants as were in Galway and Castlebar to be available if called upon.

I was very fortunate in the Chief Superintendents and Superintendents of the Garda Siochana. They gave me their complete support, and had already built up a useful security force. There also existed various civil defence groups and a multitude of parish councils. All of these, and some key men we thought it well specially to alert, constituted the framework of an organisation which we hoped – and *hoped* was the word – would function tolerably well in a crisis. I made it my business to see each bishop personally to bespeak their close interest in what we were doing, and one of them actually introduced me to a meeting of all his priests.

In Galway the bishop was the formidable Michael Browne – 'Cross Michael' – and my old friend Liam Ó Briain suggested that, if the balloon went up, the bishop was quite capable of asserting that he, not I, was the Regional Commissioner. He was a strange man. I had gone to the Shelbourne Hotel with Frank Duff to meet him when he was first appointed. Though I wondered about his hoity-toity accent and the venue he had chosen for our conversation, he was charming that night and insisted that whenever headquarters officers of the Legion were in Galway they must always come and see him. Frank was delighted, and when some time afterwards, I, with another legionary, were leaving for a meeting in Galway, he reminded us of what the bishop had said. We duly called. The bishop opened the door himself, brought us in, and got rid of us as quickly as he could. It was a freezing experience. By contrast, not very much later, when I was the Regional Commissioner he received the Taoiseach royally, and I shared in the honours. He behaved towards me then as if the earlier episode had not happened.

It was impossible, of course, to foresee what form the crisis would take within the region; what worried me most was the likelihood that supplies of essential foodstuffs *to* the region, and distribution *within* it, would be disrupted if an invasion took place. The crisis might be long or short, who could tell? And we were particularly concerned about the areas of concentrated population, about the city of Galway and the larger towns. These obviously required special attention. We had to think of such things as a voucher system, and what to do when the money in circulation ran out. Finance had given me some money with which I opened an account in the Bank of Ireland on Galway's Eyre Square, but I was asked to refund it, as soon as the invasion cloud lifted and close the account. I never saw anything like the speed with which that transaction was completed. McElligott, I feel, did not relish at all the idea of Exchequer monies lying out in the regions.

The rural areas, we anticipated, would be less demanding than Galway and the larger towns; and yet it was from a rural area, when the immediate danger of invasion seemed to have passed, that we got the first hint of trouble. My Mayo Commissioner, Michael Egan, one day hurried me over to an Irish-speaking area in the extreme west of the county on the Atlantic where a serious problem was said to have arisen because of a shortage of flour. The relieving officer was with us, and Cáit, who was in Castlebar at the time, also came along. It was a long journey, but as we came towards a little village in the heart of the distressed area we could see people moving down from the hills in our direction, some of them with sacks, expecting perhaps that we would be able to fill them. In the village itself there was quite a crowd; and as Egan and I listened in one place to a representative group of men, Cáit was harangued in Irish by a group of women in another. She got the impression from them that they feared a recurrence of the Great Famine of the 1840s which was still a lively memory, and they appealed to her to use her influence with the great man from Dublin to see that the threat that hung over them was speedily lifted. As far as I can remember the flour shortage had arisen because the travelling shops, a feature of that time, had suddenly stopped going into that remote district to conserve their petrol. That was bad enough, but what caused near-panic was that messages to Dublin, even those sent by telegram, had not been answered. Anyhow we cleared up the problem, and no further trouble of that sort arose in that or any other quarter.

The Emergency passed without our arrangements, such as they were, being put to the test. I was aware of belligerents making emergency landings from the air – one plane full of

American brass hats making for North Africa lost its way and came down on the Department of Agriculture's farm at Athenry – and of planes being flown from the States to Britain just making it to the Irish coast. I also heard stories, whether true or not, of cocks of hay, blown into the air by high winds, being mistaken for German parachutists. And we had one scare. It occurred, I remember well, on a Sunday night. I was in our house on Booterstown Avenue listening to a favourite B.B.C. programme of mine after the 9 o'clock news when the phone rang. It was Michael Egan, calling from Castlebar, and his voice betrayed alarm. Something like an invasion, he understood, was under way. A fleet of ships had entered Killala Bay and a landing was expected shortly. The ships were British, he told me, and everybody in the West was moving to confront them. When I had time to think about it I was surprised at the idea of a British invasion through a harbour as remote as Killala though the French had come that way in 1798. What I did immediately was to ask Cáit to pack a bag while I sought confirmation of Egan's message from the Army. Their story, the real story, was much less dramatic. There were British ships off Killala alright, but their intentions were entirely pacific. They were part of a convoy that had taken a plastering from the Germans in the North Atlantic, and had run in under the cover of the Mayo coast to reform before continuing their journey. That was all there was to it.

There was more excitement to be found in Dublin. German aircraft came fairly frequently, and my children got to know the sound of their engines, and, while maintaining the black-out, would try to spot the planes from the upstairs bedroom windows. On 31 May 1941, the night of the North Strand bombing, we all heard the firing from anti-aircraft batteries and wondered was it that which caused the bombs to be dropped that did so much damage. In the previous month we had heard the Dun Laoghaire fire brigade ringing the bell as they passed the corner of the avenue. Nicholas O'Brien wanted us to know that he was on his way to Belfast to put out the fires the German bombs had left behind them there. Between the attacks on Belfast and Dublin there had been seven such incidents apart from that on the North Strand; all of these occurred on or fairly near to the east coast which looked suspiciously as if radio beams were being tinkered with. I got up to Belfast twice during that time and stayed with friends in a lovely house on Derryvolgie Avenue. I remember a taxi drive from the railway station in a blackout, a scary experience, with the driver occasionally using a small torch to find the kerbstone, and a halt at a place where through a muffled doorway we could hear Lord Haw-Haw from Germany telling his doleful tale to the Irish.

There was no need for me to stay in the Region once the immediate danger of invasion appeared to have passed. I returned to Government Buildings, therefore, and in the Department of Finance worked successively in the Supply and Establishment Divisions, evaluating the financial merits of whatever was thrown up by the congeries of departments that were assigned to me, and claims for compensation arising from the German bombings. But, till the war ended, I kept in touch by correspondence with my county commissioners and occasionally paid them a visit. It was pleasant to find an empty railway carriage on the way to the West to catch up on my reading; and, one afternoon, with nothing better to do, I sketched out from a folktale a ballet that I called *An Boiscín Ceoil*. It was never danced, but my friend Arthur Duff wrote the music for it and played it over the radio. I don't know if the score has survived.

It was in this period that I began to realise the value of a good radio set at home. Eimear and I listened to the sounds coming out of occupied Europe, and scoured the bands for orchestral music. We discovered some unexpected sources of enjoyment nearby. I remember a B.B.C. programme of words and music on Sundays that gave unalloyed pleasure. One night I heard James Stephens reading extracts from *Finnegans Wake* and somehow the rhythm in his voice told me more than I had otherwise found in Joyce. Another night a reading of Gerard Manley Hopkins's *Starlit Night* so moved me that I called on the boys in the office next morning to listen while I read it to them. Hopkins is of course notoriously difficult and I failed completely to reproduce what I had heard on the radio. It is only now, many years later, that I can approach to doing justice to 'Look at the stars! look, look up at the skies/O look at all the fire-folk sitting in the air. . . .'

At one stage I had felt rather done up and a local doctor, rather baffled, took me into the hospital where he had an appointment and introduced me to the experts. One said I had too little of something, another that I had too much of it; and so it was until Frank Duff told me to come down with him to Navan to his brother-in-law Dr Vincent Monahan who had a reputation as a diagnostician. I must have looked pretty bad the day I met Frank and his mother at the bus stop on Aston's Quay, for he immediately took off his scarf and put it round my neck. The emergency restrictions put thought of travelling otherwise than by bus out of our minds. We had a pleasant journey nevertheless, an excellent lunch, a good talk; and then Vincent took me to his study and gave me the most thorough examination I so far had ever had. He diagnosed that my thyroid gland was malfunctioning, and put it right within a few days.

A couple of years later Cáit became ill and I took her to see a leading Dublin specialist in his rooms in Merrion Square. He took me aside, after briefly examining her, and astonished and frightened me by saying that at the most she had only a month or two to live. He spoke of a raging blood pressure and sent her into a nursing home. This was the first time we were separated, and the experience told on the children, too. One of them wrote to her a sublimely innocent letter: 'I am,' she said, 'awfully lonely without you', and added that she was getting a new toothbrush because she was going to clean her teeth for Lent. That, no doubt, would help Mammy to get better. I kept to myself the shattering piece of information I had received from the specialist, until I told Frank Duff about it. He laughed at a judgment that had been made after a minimum of testing and, as before, he insisted that we should see his brother-in-law in Navan. He, having examined Cáit as thoroughly as he had examined me, declared that there was nothing wrong with her that could not be put right in time, and he set about doing this with a very co-operative patient. The result was that Cáit lived, not a month or two, but about forty years, and saw Frank Duff, Vincent Monahan and his wife Geraldine, Frank's sister, into their graves. Frank thought that what he called 'a funny nervous factor' operated in Cáit's case, and there was something in this. She certainly could shoot her temperature up as soon as a visit to a doctor was contemplated.

Geraldine usually presided over the hospitable table whenever we went down to the Monahan's beautiful house, Moatlands, and took a lively share of our discussions about national and international affairs. She was an eye specialist, and consultant to a couple of counties, and Frank consulted her when I was waiting for a minor operation that had suddenly become necessary on one of my eyes. She advised me to wait overnight and, of course, I was only to pleased to do so. During the night the infection and pain left me, for which a drop of Lourdes water Cáit produced may have been the cause.

What Lourdes meant in the world of suffering I discussed one day with a man whose name was revered in the Post Office as an authority on postal history and stamps. Dr Stafford Johnson, an ear and throat specialist, was less known as a member of the Medical Bureau at Lourdes whose function it is to establish whether claims to have been cured there are genuine or not. Though since the apparitions 130 years ago there have been thousands of such claims, less than 70 have satisfied the Bureau's rigorous standards. As Stafford Johnson said to me, 'Our Lady has no need of miracles', and, of course, the normal pilgrim to Lourdes is not primarily concerned with bodily cures. Indeed, when I was there quite recently with a large organised party, I never heard the word mentioned, though there were some sad cases among us who would greatly have benefited from a miraculous intervention. The spiritual miracles in a sense are more apparent, in the behaviour and speech of the ordinary pilgrim.

Stafford Johnson's postal expertise was always available to me when I went to the G.P.O. One day he rang me up to suggest I might be interested in purchasing portraits of a father and son, Sir John and Sir Edward Lees, who were Postmasters-General in Dublin from about 1794 till the Act of the Union and filled the jobs notoriously for their personal advantage. We went down together to where the portraits of these men and their wives were to be seen; all four to be sold in one lot. The elderly owner, a direct descendant of the postmasters-general, was leaving to marry into a modern house in the North where the portraits would be out of place. His large glebe house was out in the middle of the Bog of Allen and, while I was enjoying a glass of sherry, Stafford

Johnson negotiated a price for the pictures, without revealing that he was buying for me and the State. We brought our purchases back to Dublin the next day, had them cleaned, and were offered a large sum of money for one of them. It was a Gilbert Stuart for which, we understood, there was a distinguished customer in the White House whose offer, however, we were neither in a position nor willing to accept. It was still hanging behind my desk when I went into retirement.

In the early days of the war the Legion of Mary, under Frank Duff's presiding genius, founded two societies in Dublin in which I became involved. The second, in order of starting, had a very short life, so I can dispose of it quickly. It was a society in which it was intended that Jews and Catholics would come together to discuss their mutual religious and social positions. It started on the model of all Frank's societies with a talk on a chosen subject, and a discussion which would be interrupted for a cup of tea. Frank believed strongly in the break for tea. It gave people a chance to make friends and encouraged them to air their views conversationally if they were reluctant to participate in the formal debate. I gave the first lecture to this Pillar of Fire Society, as Frank christened it, speaking of the heritage Christians shared with the Jewish people – we were all Semites – and going on to air some of the problems that arose from living side by side with one another in Dublin city. I was able to introduce the subject of the abuses of money-lending; and my acquaintance with senior members of the Jewish community enabled me the better to handle a Moneylenders Bill that was before us in Finance. We rated that meeting, in which Cáit and other Legion sisters shared the serving of the tea with charming Jewish ladies, as moderately successful. A month later a distinguished Dublin Jew spoke, but then, we were told to close down; to this day I don't know why. I had the painful duty of telling my Jewish Civil Service friend, Larry Elyan, that certain difficulties had arisen on our side of the Pillar of Fire which had not been surmounted; in the meantime we were unable to hold meetings. I promised to let him know as soon as I had something to communicate, but the Society never reopened, and neither the Jews nor ourselves ever learned the facts.

The same effectively happened to the Mercier Society, though after a longer trial, during which what the Canon Law said on the subject of meetings of this sort was considered by the Archbishop and the Vatican authorities. This Catholic-Protestant Society was named after Cardinal Mercier of Malines who, years before, had discussed the possibility of reunion with Lord Halifax and other High Church Anglicans. That stirred Frank to admiration, of course, but he was perhaps drawn to Mercier even more because Mercier had inspired Rome to approve a Mass and Office for Mary, the Mediatrix of all Graces. Frank saw Our Lady in that light, by which he by no means meant that Mary displaced Jesus as the one mediator with the Father but rather that when we come to Jesus seeking his favours we receive them through the hands of Mary who is both Christ's mother and ours. Frank was hopeful, I feel sure, that the Vatican Council, to which he was invited, would reach a position on the subject of mediation in similar terms. However, the Council went off on a different tack, situating Our Lady as the Mother of the Church. The mediation question was apparently deferred.

The Mercier Society was directed by a joint committee of Catholics and Protestants of which I was a member. One member, during the couple of years he was the press attaché to Sir John Maffey, the British Representative in Dublin, was John Betjeman who died in recent years as the knighted poet laureate. I got to know him rather well. With his wife, Penelope, he came with me to Blackrock College one Sunday to a course in the Catholic faith for 'interested enquirers'; but he and I talked mainly, I believe, about the *Quest for Corvo,* A. J. A. Symonds' brilliant biography of Frederick Rolfe, which I had loaned him. Symonds believed biography to be the most important of all forms of writing after poetry, and that it was destined to supersede the novel as a form of personal instruction. We discussed that theory and Betjeman was also aware of my Irish language interest, and, believe it or not, he sent me two letters in that language on official British notepaper. Was he helped by Martín Ó Cadhain? Learning Irish and pursuing Irish antiquarian studies were part of his technique for winning over influential Irish people to the British side; that, and the practice of having Irish writers into the office for drinks. At a small farewell dinner which I attended with Mícheál MacLiammoir and Hilton Edwards we learned something of John's eccentricities, particularly in the matter of dress and his dependence on Penelope. Stories were told of how he dealt with enquiries for information during the tense days of the Battle of Britain; an *Irish Times* man said that when he phoned one day Betjeman explained that Maffey was not available; he was in fact out playing cricket in the Phoenix Park and had just been bowled for six. Maffey was painted as a man who knew little or nothing about the Irish literary scene, leaving that to his attaché. One day, the story went, coming into Betjeman's room he saw on his desk a book by an Irish author from the nineteenth century and long deceased. A brief Question and Answer session then followed, like this: *Maffey* (pointing to the author's name on the book): 'Irish?' *Betjeman*: 'Yes'. *Maffey*: 'Important?' *Betjeman*: 'Yes'. *Maffey*: 'What about having him in?'

Among the Catholics on the committee of direction of the Mercier – and remember this was during the Second World War – were the present Taoiseach's father, Desmond FitzGerald, and Joe Walshe, the serving Secretary of the Department of Foreign Affairs. Both these men and the chairman of the formal meetings of the Society, Jimmy Cummins, shared Frank Duff's apostolic concern and in one way or another were important figures in the conduct of business. FitzGerald was a keen debater of theological issues while Walshe, who had a Jesuit background, read a paper as I did. In later life Walshe was a rather cynical representative of Ireland at the Vatican. Among the visitors from England who spoke to the Society was the Dominican biblical scholar, Father Hugh Pope. He was an extremely able speaker and enlivened a lunch we gave him with an account of a recent visit he had paid to the Royal Air Force centre with his cousin, Sir Hugh Dowding of Battle of Britain fame.

When in 1944 we were told to suspend the meetings of the Mercier we notified the members in a letter which did not tell by whom we were being suspended and for how long, nor did we say anything about when we might resume. Years passed, and with no sign of a revival, a harsh note crept into the communications we received from some of our non-Catholic friends. A letter from a Quaker written in 1947 spoke not of suspension but of a suppression, which he deemed to be not only a calamity but a crime.

During those years – the forties – I acquired in the Jesuit Father Charles Mulcahy a spiritual friend to whom I had every reason to be grateful. He 'hung out' in Room 15A of the Retreat House in Milltown Park. 15A was a large, high-ceilinged, rather cheerless room, that had little in it beyond a table, a raft of books, a typewriter, an armchair for visitors, a plain chair, an iron bedstead and a prie-dieu. He was sixty-nine when I first saw him entering the chapel downstairs to give the opening lecture of a weekend retreat, but he did not look it. He was 'an old fraud', he told me, for his features were those of a man in his middle years, and his light brown hair was strong and plentiful. His walk gave him away, however; though quick and purposeful he shuffled noticeably. His speech was rather like this, too; quick and abbreviated.

In that first lecture of his he laid the basis for much of what he taught me in the next ten years or so, namely the supreme importance of understanding where all of us stand before God, our essential creaturehood and its obligations; the absurdity of an independent creature. That came straight out of the spiritual exercises of St Ignatius on which he had himself been reared. In 15A where I went at his invitation 'to talk myself out', he insisted that, in the matter of assent to the truths of religion, I should understand the difference between what was merely notional and what was real, and he set me reading Newman on that subject. My problem was not uncommon, I am sure. I wanted to do better. I was always starting to do better, but found it hard to maintain the momentum. I had had one long, painful period of scruples, and never completely got over the habit of looking back. (I know that this book would be better if I described the basis for this scruple but I am not going to do so.) So Father Charlie had to seek to replace my fears with a real love of God. I was too serious altogether, he told me, and suggested I might read Lewis Carroll's *Through the Looking Glass*. That I was too serious – rather gloomy in fact – I had been told years before by a Belgian Benedictine. His cure for me, like

Fr Mulcahy's, was to look for joy, and to ask Christ for it; to be joyful in God's creation; in my wife and children, my neighbours and my work; and to take joy and consolation in God's use of me to do good works. This was excellent advice which was repeated to me by a Carmelite confessor, but I have always been defective in responding to it.

Father Mulcahy and I became close friends, and to turn me away from being self-centred he showed me the outline of the talks he was giving to nuns and brothers and asked me to pray for students for the priesthood who were in his care. His interest extended to my work, my literary interests, my aging parents, my wife and family. Our chats had sometimes to end abruptly when he would explain ever so courteously that he had another 'tough' waiting for him outside. He wrote me many a letter and, going through them recently, I rediscovered some fine things.

He had for example, a deep affection for Our Lady – the Great Mother he called her – and kept flowers growing in profusion around a petite figure of Her in the garden. And he moved me once with the tale of an old continental Jesuit who taught in a house near Canterbury and who went practically every afternoon to say Compline in the Cathedral so that Our Lady might know that she was not forgotten by her own people in that place which had once been Catholic. I had heard earlier a rather similar story from Frank Conway, a colleague of mine in the Department of Finance, about a neighbour of his in Howth who had just died. One Ascension Thursday she went to the 11 o'clock Mass and returned at a quarter past two. Her niece, who kept house for her, remarked that the lunch had been spoiled waiting for her. 'I know, my dear,' the old lady replied, 'but you see the chapel emptied after the Mass and no one came in until a few minutes ago.'

When my father died in 1949 Fr Charlie's concern was most touching. He was anxious about my mother, 'the dear old granny' as he called her, fearing she might be unsettled; and, feeble though he was himself now, he went with his Rector one day to see her in her little flat. He remembered her in two Masses, putting her especially 'in God's care and guard'.

The first sign that Father Mulcahy's own mortal end was not far off appeared in his letters. They were suddenly shorter, disjointed, with words misspelt or omitted altogether. He tried to behave normally, insisting that his 'toughs' should take the armchair and, when that courtesy was refused, sitting bolt upright himself on the edge of it. He could read no more, or read only without fully comprehending. It was pathetic and yet somehow significant that, when the end came, all that this lover of books had was his rosary beads and a crucifix. When I last saw him he was lying awake but silent, his whole body covered in a white powder whose purpose was to mollify the burning sensation of his poor flesh.

In the forties, Frank Duff and I had dinner one night with Sean O'Faolain and Peadar O'Donnell, in the former's house in Killiney. Those two distinguished writers were complaining of the rigours of the official censorship which they contended, not without reason, was blessed openly by the Church in its national manifestation. Elsewhere a *modus vivendi* had been worked out between creative writers and the Church, but not in Ireland. Here the situation was abnormal, leaving writers utterly frustrated and driven into a kind of underground life like troglodytes or, as it were, forced to live in cellars like conspirators under the Czars. O'Faolain had led the attack on the censorship system in *The Bell* which he edited, and he believed that the Legion of Mary, as represented by Frank Duff, were to a large degree responsible for the atmosphere in which the repression of writers become possible. I remember him telling me, but not from his personal experience, of Legionaries asking people on their doorsteps how long it was since their last confession. I denied that any such thing was happening, though one would have to admit the possibility of an odd, unauthorised case. I suppose it was I who, on Frank's prompting, brought about the Killiney meeting. That such excellent men as Sean, Peadar, and Frank could not fail to like each other I knew. Peadar, talking of Frank, once said to me, 'I love that man. He came to see me when I was ill. He was always bright and cheerful; none of the long-haired penitent about him. The priests would have nothing to do with the Morning Star and wrote offensive letters. None of them would take on the chaplaincy. Tell them, said Frank, we have Father Tom Counihan a Jesuit.'

I remember that dinner very well. Frank soon made O'Faolain and O'Donnell realise how well he understood their worries; but he made them realise, too, that by comparison, their worries were as nothing to what he had been going through with the ecclesiastical authorities. Why should the Legion of Mary be criticised by the writers? Wouldn't it be better for all of them to get together to talk over their problems and see where that would lead them.

As editor of *Maria Legionis* I was well aware of one aspect of the interference from ecclesiastical sources that Frank Duff was complaining about. That March, the acting censor, Dr Kelly, had phoned me to say that, knowing that the Archbishop, John Charles McQuaid, did not like Frank's serial about the cleaning up of the area of prostitution in Dublin city, he had referred to him in proof the instalment intended for publication in the current issue and had got back a note which he read out to me. It said: 'I wish the series to be discontinued as being unsuited for general reading.' I expressed my astonishment, but was told that the decision was final: there would be no point in looking to have it reconsidered. He personally quite agreed with the Archbishop, Dr Kelly added. That was that. Frank was wild when I told him; but he was not surprised. As far back as 1937 he had described the whole recital to me as covering very delicate ground, and he was fearful of the censorship. He counselled me not to mention this to anyone; it might only put the objection into their minds. Word had reached him that some priests were saying that the story was giving Dublin a bad name. He had by now, however, almost finished the serial and he appealed to Dr McQuaid to let him finish it. This personal request was rejected. Appropriately enough, the title of the instalment was 'Enter the Police'.

Frank read into the Archbishop's direction more than mere concern for the name of the archdiocese and city of Dublin. It meant that truthful history was not to be written. The story of the area he called Bentley Place he saw as a testimony to the power of grace, how it had stepped into ordinary life to conquer a great evil, and to achieve a wholesale conversion of souls. He was profoundly sad, for Dr

McQuaid, whose appointment to Dublin he had welcomed enthusiastically, was also about to close down the Mercier and the Pillar of Fire societies.

The talk in Killiney with Sean O'Faolain and Peadar O'Donnell led to still another Society that we called Common Ground. The title came from O'Faolain; the format was that of Frank Duff's other societies. Papers would be read and discussed with a break for a cup of tea; but, at O'Faolain's suggestion, a Question and Answer session was to be fitted in, the questions to be sent in in advance to Father John Heuston who, without the word being used, was to be a sort of spiritual guide. Father Heuston, the brother of one of the men executed in 1916, was a Dominican theologian and had made something of a name for himself at the Mercier.

I am trying to recall who attended the early meetings of Common Ground. From the writing community Sean O'Faolain certainly, with Roibeard Ó Faracháin, Mervyn Wall, D. J. Giltenan, Michael Farrell, Frank Gallagher, Peter O'Curry, Paddy Kavanagh, and M. J. MacManus; while others who came in from time to time to represent other points of view included Joe Walshe, Desmond FitzGerald, Michael Tierney and Gerard Murphy. Frank O'Connor never came, though at an early stage he had discussed the possibility with Sean O'Faolain and had suggested that Bishop Browne of Galway, whom he suspected was an intelligent man might be invited. O'Faolain, who had been to see Dr McQuaid, told O'Connor that he had found the Archbishop sympathetic to writers, which prompted O'Connor to say that perhaps 'His Grace might honour us, at least once, by dining with us.' The Society did not live long enough, however, to try out these ideas. By a date in August 1943, two papers had been read by Sean O'Faolain, and one by Frank Duff. Roibeard Ó Faracháin, Joe Walshe, and Peter O'Curry contributed one each, as did Frank Sheed when he happened to be in Ireland. We had hoped that he would talk to us about the experience of Catholic writers in Britain but that had not apparently been explained to him, with the result that he spoke entirely about the Blessed Trinity which was a subject then very close to his mind but did not stimulate the kind of discussion the aggrieved Irish writers wanted.

Sean accepted an invitation to see something of the Legion's work for the down-and-outs which O'Donnell, I imagine, already knew something about; he considered the Legion was a very liberal-minded organisation. Coming back from the hostel Sean and I encountered the worst fog in our experience, we linked arms, made our way down to the Liffey wall and, with considerable difficulty, got as far as Butt Bridge. It looked as if we would have to spend the night in a hotel, and had done some phoning from the *Irish Press* office to alert our wives when the fog suddenly lifted. But another fog of sorts appeared to descend on Sean's attitude to hostels. In a letter to Frank, he called the Regina Coeli a slum, a description that Frank accepted as meaning that it was a very poor and overcrowded place. Frank in his reply cried shame, however, on those who beslimed the place without making the slightest effort to help it. Sean he thought had been misled by someone into believing that hostels, and the Legion itself, were maintained by capitalists. If so, said Frank, they were making a very poor job of it. The Legion had no money and paid no workers, and he invited Sean to come up and look at the accounts. He could not believe that Sean was dishing out the old tripe about 'dulling the revolutionary edge of poverty'. If a girl comes to the hostel in trouble – most of them almost demented – should we refuse her, he asked, because of some doctrinaire stuff or other? Likewise, was the down-and-out man or the prostitute not in the interests of world revolution, or a future reform of the situation? Frank was a doughty fighter; but he ended that letter by saying that he would be glad to have Sean's friendship, and would remain anxious to make *his* path easier.

In an odd way the demise of Common Ground came about when Frank ceased to attend meetings. He had, as Father Michael O'Carroll has noted, a certain sensitivity that made him vulnerable to personal hurt, and a vivid imagination that could sometimes fill him with anxiety about the future. Something in a paper of Mervyn Wall's upset him; and when Frank Duff came no more, Sean O'Faolain lost interest. He told me he did not feel like wasting his sweetness on the desert air. He did not wish to be regarded as responsible for Common Ground in any way. At the same time he had not spoken to anyone about it, and he would not influence anyone against it. He admired our sticking power and wished us well. I got him to promise that he would come occasionally to a meeting on that basis. The sticking power he had commended was not one of my attributes. With Frank gone I pulled out, leaving the society to carry on, as it did, for a while, under Gerard Murphy.

SIX

ONE PLACE I had never any connexion with, save in relation to its savings bank, was the Department of Posts and Telegraphs. I was not prepared, therefore, in any way when one morning the Secretary of Finance, Jimmy McElligott, called me down and, without any preliminaries, asked me would I like to go to the Post Office; there was a vacancy there for an assistant secretary and I could have the job if I wanted it. This came like a bolt from the blue. I was not aware that there was any question of looking outside the Post Office itself for an assistant secretary, which, I later gathered, was being caused by the retirement of P. S. O'Hegarty, who had been the Secretary since the formation of the State, and the elevation in his place of the serving assistant secretary, R. J. Cremins – we called him Joe. Because of the suddenness of the suggestion, McElligott would not have been surprised if I had asked for time to think it over. So I imagine he was more surprised when I said right away I would be glad to go, and thanked him and the Minister for making the offer to me. I said this, although what I then knew about the Post Office would have fitted on the back of a postage stamp. I had never taken any particular interest in the Post Office and I remember well that when I was being interviewed as a prospective Junior Administrative Officer, to a question – it may have been from P. S. O'Hegarty – as to how the telephone worked I could only reply that I didn't know. I often told that story later at social gatherings, and was reminded that the telephone, under me, still didn't work. That I was able to say 'yes' immediately to the proposal that I should go to the Post Office was due to a belief that 'there's a divinity that shapes our ends, rough-hew them how we will.' My mother used to say, when tempting us with something sweet, 'close your eyes and open your mouth and see what God will send you' and it was in some such spirit that I took on a job about which, as I say, I knew little or nothing in advance. What I did know was that those who were involved in the appointment considered that I had some relevant qualifications, but please don't ask me to spell these out. I know that P. S. O'Hegarty wrote some nice things about me to his Minister as I think H. P. Boland, the Establishment Officer in Finance, did.

Arthur Codling had retired some time earlier, his colleagues forgathering in the Cabinet Room to make a presentation. He had been asked what he would like, and opted for books about Ireland. He intended to spend the rest of his days in Ireland increasing his knowledge of Irish history and growing roses. He sent me a message of congratulation when I went to the Post Office and promised to come and see me when I became Secretary of that department. That was a promise he kept, but the decision to declare a republic in 1948 was more than he could take. Dejected, he went to live in the North.

Before I left Finance McElligott brought me in to see the Minister, Sean T. O'Kelly. It was a short, pleasant occasion. Mr O'Kelly I had known on and off for years, but not intimately. Then, and later when I met him as the President of Ireland, he showed his normal genial side. He liked company, particularly the company of women, and he could drink a glass or two or more of whiskey. Quite abnormal was the occasional absurd flare, as when he talked of whipping John Bull or was involved in a tussle with the admirable E. P. McCarron which resulted in McCarron leaving the public service. I can't say what sort of Minister for Finance he was. I imagine that he must be judged in that capacity in association with McElligott with whom he had an easy relationship.

P. S. O'Hegarty I never met, and I now deeply regret it. We had similar interests, the language and things national generally, and he knew my literary work as indeed I knew his. We nodded to each other in recognition when our paths crossed but never had a conversation; and the day I came to the G.P.O. he moved out. I was at the farewell dinner in the Dolphin Hotel that his colleagues gave him, but somehow had no conversation with him. Memorable on that occasion was Charlie Kelly's drawing of a new penny farthing stamp for the menu card. It showed P. S., with his old bike, standing on a letter box which carried, not the V.R. or G.R. that was then common, or the S.E. that had not yet arrived, but simply P.S. He had an umbrella under his arm and a bundle of books. At the base of the letterbox a dog was furiously barking and, on the top of the G.P.O., a couple of female figures were dancing as if showing how happy they – the girl telephonists perhaps – were to see him go. It was a magnificent piece of work.

When some years ago I was working on a book about the Irish Republican Brotherhood, the I.R.B., I recognised what I had lost by not knowing O'Hegarty. He was steeped in the separatist tradition and, as a member of the Supreme Council of the I.R.B., knew more than most people about the policies and practices of what euphemistically was called the Organisation. When he was employed in the Secretary's Office in London he swore Michael Collins into it, and also Pádraic Ó Conaire and the two Ulstermen, Robert Lynd and Bulmer Hobson, to whom many years later he dedicated his *History of Ireland under the Union*. When the Treaty came he was for it from the first day. He believed that nothing more could be won by fighting. He instinctively disliked the style and personality of de Valera who was, he wrote 'ambiguous, argumentative, theoretical and tendentiously didactical' (Cian Ó hÉigeartaigh in the *Irish Times*, 4 January 1980). He edited *The Separitist* in 1922 for the I.R.B. and I remember particularly his tribute to Arthur Griffith when he died that August. 'Ireland to-day,' it began, 'lies in the shadow of the greatest and most unexpected calamity that has befallen her since the death of Davis. By the death of Arthur Griffith we have lost not only the most constructive and political intelligence in Ireland, but the man upon whom for the last twenty and odd years has lain the whole burden of the travail of this nation, and upon whom by rights it should have lain for at least another ten. Arthur Griffith was not alone the greatest Irishman of his time, but he was the greatest Irishman since Davis and Mitchell and perhaps the most gifted all-round nationalist since Tone.'

P. S. was deported in 1914, lost his job as Postmaster of

Welshpool in the aftermath of the 1916 Rising and, having run the Irish Bookshop in Dawson Street for a number of years, became the first Secretary of the Department of Posts and Telegraphs in 1922. He brought his capacity to write to the job, and the minutes of his that survived on the departmental files gave me enormous pleasure to read. In 1925 he was invited by the Chairman of a Commission on Education to give his views on the subject. He did so at length and, in a covering note, explained that what he had written was, of course, all coloured by his own temperament and experience. 'Of education as a science', he said, 'I know nothing.' He continued:

> I left school at fifteen and have never been inside an educational establishment since. But I do not think there is any obligation on the State to educate any or all of its children. I believe education nowadays is too easily got and that there is too much of it. I disbelieve in educating the lame, halt, blind and mentally unfit. I disbelieve in compulsory school attendance. I think education should be more difficult, something to fight for. Security kills initiative. And I disbelieve profoundly that all this pampering finds any more talent than would naturally find itself. The boy of talent will find his way to his own level, whether you stuff him with education or compel him to fight for it. I believe in the old Intermediate system and in money prizes. I believe in teaching out of books, by set lessons, and in letting a boy's mind develop its own way. I disbelieve utterly in the modern devices for making a boy think and understand, before his mind is ready, which in most cases it isn't until sixteen or seventeen. And it is not necessary that he should think before then. I know that at fifteen I had been through the four grades (as there were then) of the Intermediate, with Exhibitions in all four. But it wasn't until my last year, in the Senior grade, that I ever began to have an intelligent understanding of my subjects. That came of itself (our master was a wise man who set the lessons, left us alone to puzzle them out, and lashed us with wise sarcasm if we failed to puzzle them out). It never would have come through explanations and dis-

sertations and trap questions. So I'm afraid I'm quite helpless.

P.S. was a staunch believer in the need to revive Irish, though I don't think he spoke it very well, and his son Seán, whom he greatly influenced and whose premature death is still deplored, did more perhaps to stimulate quality writing in Irish than any man apart from Ernest Blythe. But P. S. was a figure of controversy, a man who often trailed his coat as if looking for trouble. He had a ready answer when Bill Norton, the Secretary of the Post Office Workers' Union, came complaining of Dill Smith's treatment of the girls under her in the Accountant's Branch. Dill, P.S.'s sister-in-law, was the Dill of Sairséal and Dill, the publishing firm. 'What are they complaining about?' P. S. demanded. 'They've only got to work with her, I've got to live with her,' which was the case. In his *Who's Who* entry, he described his recreations as journalism, controversy and telling the truth. His books show this. To his *History of Ireland under the Union* he appended an epilogue, carrying, as he says, the story down to the acceptance in 1927 by de Valera of the Anglo-Irish Treaty of 1921. De Valera would deny that he had done any such thing, and he might also deny what O'Hegarty accepted as true, that the same Treaty which he said Griffith had secured with a couple of pamphlets was the beginning of the end of the British Empire. Another, and earlier book, *The Victory of Sinn Féin*, written in the immediate aftermath of the Civil War, must have given greater offence still on a wider front. I was not, therefore, very surprised to hear in the Post Office, when I got there, that there had been no personal contact between O'Hegarty and his Minister, Gerry Boland, for years. Boland, who had lost a brother in the Civil War, could not tolerate P. S., and I'm sure that that was P. S.'s mutual sentiment. There they were next door to each other on that first floor of the G.P.O. with communication between them conducted through intermediaries. Joe Cremins would have done much of the talking with the Minister that P. S. should have done in normal circumstances. Some people would wonder why P. S. hadn't been sacked or moved to some other office. I'm sure this was discussed among politicians, but if it was the decision was to avoid making a bad situation worse.

I didn't go to the Post Office under false pretences. The publicity hand-out said among other things that I was a writer. I mention the point because I was to hear a question being asked as to how the head of a department could also be a writer. That I thought was a silly question, and still do. Why shouldn't I write instead of playing golf or bridge or do in my spare time any of the hundred and one things people turn to after their work? There were precedents. In the Post Office there were among the secretaries Arthur Hamilton Norway and P. S. O'Hegarty, and long before them a Londoner, Anthony Trollope, began his profitable career as a novelist in Ireland while he was a postal surveyor in Banagher.

In my twenty years in the Post Office I served no fewer than ten Ministers and one Parliamentary Secretary. They were a mixed bag and came from two of our political parties, Fianna Fáil and Labour; you have to go back to the first government to find Cumann na nGaedheal or Farmer Ministers and Parliamentary Secretaries of Posts and Telegraphs. Among the politicians I worked under in the G.P.O. were men like Paddy Little and Michael Hilliard who had entered government through the national movement; Little was a lawyer and Hilliard an auctioneer. There was a national teacher, Sean Ormonde; a couple of trade union officials, James Everett and Michael Keyes, and an engineer, Kevin Boland. The backgrounds of the others are harder to label. They were, for the most part, modest men who came to the Post Office without much in the way of ideas but who recognised that the best way to get results was to allow an old and well-tried machine to function efficiently.

The Post Office had developed along two main lines. There was the traditional postal service; and the service of telecommunications which included telephones and telegrams of course but also broadcasting. When I went to the Post Office, and for some years afterwards, the postal and telephone services taken together paid their way; that is to say, taking one year with another and offsetting the eggs that the golden telephone goose had started to lay against the expensive labour-intensive postal machine. We vaguely hoped for a return to something like a standard twopenny post, a dream that evaporated with so many others in the nightmare inflation.

All these Ministers of mine were essentially juniors. Among those I got to know well there were none – even when they achieved some seniority – who were able to fight their corner in the Cabinet Room or with the Minister for Finance who controlled the supply of money. The Post Office always suffered from a shortage of capital for telephone development, and with Ministers allowing themselves to be treated as small boys there was never any real hope of catching up on the demand. The officials did the best they could with their opposite numbers in Finance but there was a limit to what they could do once the priorities had been fixed. The Post Office was always down towards the bottom of the list. We obviously did not count for much politically.

I had one Minister who was a sort of a throw back to 1932 when Fianna Fáil assumed office full of suspicion about a Civil Service that had been created by their predecessors in the atmosphere of a Civil War. That promised to be a difficult situation. He was pleasant enough to talk to, but he delayed so long over promotion proposals we put to him that he created an impression that they were being taken out and canvassed in political circles. I had to draw his attention to the fact that a ministerial colleague of his had sought to extract a subscription for the party from a man who had been promoted, the implication being that he or the party had something to say to the promotion which, of course, was not the case. Of the others, or most of them at any rate, I can sincerely say they were gentlemen with whom it was always a pleasure to work. The most popular of them, undoubtedly, were Michael Keyes and Michael Hilliard, and their political allegiances made no difference whatever.

Things usually ran very smoothly in the Post Office, but we had our moments of excitement. One, as I shall tell later in detail, was when Neil Blaney blew his top about Radio Éireann at a party Ard Fheis and drove the Radio Advisory Council of that time to the brink of resignation. Others occurred during James Everett's term of office. In the debate in the Dáil on our annual estimate Deputy Robert Briscoe, quite out of the blue, created a row about the entitlement of people to write to government departments without having to stamp their letters, a practice we proposed to end. Paddy Little, leading for the opposition, had not mentioned the subject at all but Briscoe, entering the chamber late and seeing an opportunity for political kudos, stirred up a majority against us. It was no pleasure to walk out that night behind a defeated Minister to meet the Taoiseach, Jack Costello, hurrying in to find out what on earth had happened. Deferring to the will of the House, the Taoiseach re-introduced the estimate next morning *minus* the offending proposal.

Everett was a simple man who concealed his inadequacies by putting officials in the front line. He took me to Leinster House to explain to a group of Senators where we stood in relation to the resignation of a Music Director and to Iveagh House to tell Mr MacBride, the Foreign Minister, why he, no more than Mr de Valera, could not have a short-wave station. But his big trouble arose over what became popularly known as the Battle of Baltinglass. Baltinglass was a surprising mistake. It arose out of Everett's decision to reject the advice of the Department that he should continue the local postmastership in a family that had given long and satisfactory service. This, naturally and rightly, gave rise to an enormous hullaballoo which was not by any means confined to the little West Wicklow town. It got into all the papers here and in Britain; a popular English periodical produced a special feature on it; and planes flew over the area to take pictures of the resistance on the ground; and there was plenty of that. Later still, there was a book on the subject, and talk of making a film. In the developing conflict there was on one side, the Minister and the forces of law and order imposing an unpopular decision; on the other side everybody else, apparently, including a British major-general and a cousin of the Queen. And the balladmakers got busy. One of their verses declared that the case had gone to the United Nations, leaving Ireland palpitating awaiting the result. But

> Get back behind your parallel, drop atom bombs and gas,
> And respect the boundaries and the laws of Sovereign
> Baltinglass.

Ultimately the battle ended rather abruptly. The Minister went sick, the man he had appointed resigned, and the person the people wanted was given the job. This followed a recommendation from a departmental committee which was set up to examine applications for sub-postmasterships, it being intended that in each case a single name should be given which the Minister would automatically approve. That decision was not adhered to when, shortly afterwards, a change of government occured. Everett's Fianna Fáil successor, Erskine Childers, said he would continue the departmental committee in being but, instead of a single name, three names should be put up to him, which was an obvious disimprovement. It always amazed me how politicians wanted to hold on to these jobs, feeling no doubt that the filling of them gave them some political power, whereas the probability was that in the process they made more enemies than friends.

Apart from postmasterships there was little or nothing in the way of patronage open to Ministers. And the occasional story I heard from earlier times did not convince me that it did Ministers any good to be able to make a minor appointment. Around the Corkman J. J. Walsh, the first Minister for Posts and Telegraphs or Postmaster-General there circulated stories of Corkmen flooding up to Dublin and into the public service. One of these was reportedly asked if he knew Irish, and he replied no, but he knew Walsh. Cáit told me of a Dublin man with what was called a national record who went to Walsh looking for a job in the Post Office. He was given one, but was speedily back in the Minister's office confronting J. J. himself. 'Do you know what they put me at?' he said. 'Cleaning lavatories'. 'Well,' said J. J. 'that's only a beginning. After all I had to start pretty low down myself.' 'If you did,' said my man, 'you jumped up bloody quick.'

Joe Cremins, with whom I spent a couple of happy years, was one of the jolliest men I ever met. He had a wonderful sense of humour, and a most infectious laugh. He took a delight in telling the story of his own beginning entering the postal service, not as a learner as so many of his contemporaries did, but as an *unpaid* learner, than which he would insist no more miserable worm existed. Interspersed with bursts of laughter he would tell of the Post Office strike of 1922 and of the Postmaster-General as he energetically set about breaking it, handing out instant promotions right, left, and centre to men he found at work. Walsh handed out more than promotions. He insisted upon Cremins taking a revolver on his way to meet an incoming mailboat. That was the way to deal with strikers!

O'Hegarty and Cremins were in the mould of the senior officials they had known in the British service. They were rigidly conservative men who believed in keeping the administration and the Post Office unions at a discreet distance from each other. They were strong disciplinarians. A phrase of Cremins I recall was 'Give me my pen till I cut the scut off him', this in reaction to misbehaviour he did not like on somebody's part. He was a trifle impetuous, and was disturbed, I think, when some postmen down the country spoke of taking him to court. Indeed it was just about this time that the Accountant, Joe Scannell, was beginning to pioneer an easier relationship with the staff, and Cremins and I began to accept invitations to functions connected with union conferences. Then the Ministers did the same. There were times, later on, when I felt that we had gone too far too fast with this fraternisation; on the whole, however, the change of direction was justified and left us psychologically better equipped to face the challenges of organised labour.

A man I now began to meet frequently was Bill Norton, the Secretary of the Post Office Workers Union. He had started at the bottom of the ladder, as a boy messenger, and ended a remarkable career as the leader of Labour's parliamentary party and as the Tanaiste of the Inter-Party government. He was an able fellow, and through skilful and reasonable negotiation achieved great things for his union and the working class in general. He was not unique in a world sense in climbing to the top as he did, of course. I remember being told by my Australian opposite number when he visited us that, at that time in his country, there were three former post office messengers, apart from himself, who had scaled the heights. They included a Prime Minister and a Cardinal. But Norton's achievement in Ireland was nevertheless very considerable.

In my very first conversation with Cremins he told me he was divesting himself of 'the mantle of culture', which he had worn for far too long, and was gladly passing it over to me. The mantle was, of course, broadcasting – that, and something more, as I was soon to see. The Post Office had never wanted to have anything to do with broadcasting but, having got it, it did its best with it, according to its lights. (It did even more than that so far as accommodation was concerned, yielding up to it, first, the premises in Little Denmark Street and, then, a floor of the G.P.O. building itself which was so badly needed for the Post Office's own expanding requirements.) But it meant that broadcasting had to live with a department that prided itself on paying its way and which, following the departure of the first Minister, J. J. Walsh, was controlled by a Minister, Ernest Blythe, who was also Minister for Finance, and by a Parliamentary Secretary, Michael J. Heffernan, who, with the Farmers' Party of which he was a leading light, was committed to a policy of rigid economy in public expenditure. So Irish broadcasting, which could do nothing without plenty of money, spent its early years under the worst possible auspices.

Like most of my contemporaries I had been mildly interested in the Irish broadcasting service since it began as 2 RN on New Year's night 1926. I had a cat's whisker, a fragile metal thread which, when guided to a fragment of crystal would, we were told, enable us to hear the first transmission. We heard a little of it. It came from that rather forbidding building in Denmark Street and was directed personally by the first Director, Seamus Clandillon, who himself sang that night as did his wife Mairéad. They were both well-known singers of folk songs, but already past their best. Indeed in less than two years their general competence in that field was to be questioned in the *Irish Statesman*. Donal O'Sullivan, then the clerk of the Senate, reviewing their book *Londubh an Chairn*, suggested that the Oxford University Press, and the Carnegie Trustees who had backed the venture, had been misled into publishing the book, believing that it consisted of substantially unpublished songs and airs and edited by competent people. The review also alleged 'ignorance and slovenliness' as well as 'a species of self-assurance and mutual adoration' that was fortunately rare in publications of that kind. Knowing the parties slightly, having done a little folklore collecting myself, I spent my holidays in the High Court when the charges and rebuttals inevitably arrived there. There was an extraordinary fascination about the efforts of counsel to promote the interests of their clients through 'experts' in such a way as to make their opinions comprehensible to the judge and jury, who in this matter were as the merest laymen. It was a confused and confusing case and after several days listening to the evidence the jury deliberated for seven and a half hours, and not surprisingly failed to come to a clear decision on the questions put to them by the judge. The plaintiffs' request for judgment was accordingly refused.

The case not only did the reputation of the Director of Broadcasting no good but must have cost him a fortune. The defendant's costs ran to £2,500 and were a factor in closing down the *Irish Statesman*, which was a national loss. Clandillon became a very unhappy man. On top of his failure to get satisfaction in the courts, he struggled without success to break away from the financial and staffing constraints to which 2 RN was subject, and he found the continuous parliamentary criticism of the station's standards irksome. The change of government in 1932 brought no improvement. The first two Ministers for Posts and Telegraphs in the new regime admitted they had no personal interest in broadcasting and could get on well without it, but one of them conceded that, in trying to satisfy so many divergent tastes, the unfortunate director was carrying a heavy burden. Sponsored programmes had become a feature of the daily schedules and a senior opposition deputy suggested in the Dáil, that, if the Director could not improve the programmes quickly, he should get out and let the sponsored programme people run the whole show. In 1934 Clandillon was returned to his original department and, when I last saw him, he was telling a porter at the Henry Street entrance to the G.P.O., in a voice loud enough to be overheard, how badly he had been treated.

With extra staff and greater consideration generally from on high, T. J. Kiernan, who took charge of the station after an interregnum, succeeded in raising the status of Irish broadcasting notably. He was an economist, specialising in State finance, and was a Civil Servant as was Seamus Brennan, basically an Education man, who took over in 1941 on the recall of Kiernan to External Affairs. 'Mac' Kiernan, whom I knew slightly, belonged to a different generation from Clandillon and moved in different circles but, like Clandillon, he had a singing wife who later acquired great popularity with ballads such as 'I'm a rambler, I'm a gambler, I'm a long way from home, and, if you don't like me, just leave me alone'. 'Mac' was particularly interested in serious straight talks as well as in unrehearsed discussion at the microphone and tried to widen the circle of individuals who were able and willing to contribute. I know that he got Gerard Murphy to debate something or other with me and encouraged us to be stimulating, which I don't think we were: we weren't asked a second time anyhow. Not that many people were anxious to broadcast for the fees then being paid. The university world generally, on which Kiernan would have liked to have been able to draw, kept its distance from Radio Eireann, and that remained the case until the Thomas Davis lectures at £30 a time in 1953 made it worth while for a scholar to produce an original script.

I had got to know Seamus Brennan very well when he was secretary of the Commission on Irish in the Civil Service of which I shared membership, with John Moynihan, Joe Walshe and John T. Lennon. His enthusiasm, energy and output in that job were quite prodigious. He must have seen every man and woman in the Service, encouraging them to use the language coversationally and in their everyday work, where that was possible, and appeared at the time to have had some success. I am afraid, however, that the promise of those days was not maintained. Seamus was Director of Broadcasting for about seven years, the last two of which overlapped with the beginning of my association with the service. He was the pleasantest of men to work with, a father and protector to all his staff, and his capacity in the Irish language helped to make of Radio Eireann internally a largely Irish-using unit.

The mantle of culture that Joe Cremins was so anxious to shed was, as I have said, no burden for Paddy Little, the Minister for Posts and Telegraphs when I entered the G.P.O. He was a cultivated man, perhaps the first Minister for Posts and Telegraphs of whom that really could be said. He had been in politics for a long time, coming to Sinn Féin through the Young Ireland Branch of the United Irish League, and had edited the political weekly, *New Ireland*. His father had sometime been Prime Minister of Newfoundland. Paddy's name first came to the fore in 1916 when the coterie inside the Supreme Council of the Irish Republican Brotherhood who planned to stage a Rising that Easter gave him, for publication, what was described as a decipher of a paper on the official files of Dublin Castle. This gave details of an order alleged to have been made for large-scale raids on buildings in Dublin, as part of a plan for disarming the Irish Volunteers. The censor prevented publication of the document, but Tom Kelly, a Sinn Féin Alderman, gave it wide publicity by reading it to the Dublin Corporation. It was officially denied that any such document ever existed; and it may be taken that that was the truth.

I heard it said – I can't vouch for it – that when de Valera, whose fortunes he shared before and after the formation of Fianna Fáil, made Paddy a minister he told him to concentrate on broadcasting, that the post office would look after itself. If that's true, it was an unnecessary direction, because that's what I think Paddy Little (everybody called him that) would have done anyhow. Certainly Paddy, who I am glad to think became a good friend of mine, devoted a lot of attention to broadcasting matters and it was during his time that the process of improvement began. His special interest was music: a piece well played or well sung was, in a word he frequently used, gorgeous. He attended the radio concerts for the real pleasure they gave him. He entertained visiting artists out of his own pocket. He directed and encouraged the efforts to expand the pool of orchestral players and to engage visiting foreign conductors, and he was the first to try to get a public concert hall. A Cabinet subcommittee in 1946 had examined and reported on the question, and government approval had been obtained to approach the Governors of the Rotunda Hospital for a lease of the buildings at that time occupied by the Rotunda Picture House, the Gate Theatre and a dance hall, and for an additional strip of ground in the Rotunda Gardens. The buildings were held under lease by the Capitol Theatre Company with whom an understanding had been reached that they would relinquish their interest in the lease which had only a few years to run and that the Post Office would negotiate with certain sub-lessees.

No definite agreement had been reached with the Capitol people when I came into the picture but I found the Rotunda Governors generally agreeable to what was envisaged. In anticipation of all the negotiations being successfully completed, Raymond McGrath, the Chief Architect of the Office of Public Works, then went abroad to look at concert halls and consult accousticians and on his return he prepared a sketch of a hall on the Rotunda site which, for the building only, was estimated to cost something over £500,000. It was to be erected on the virgin site, with the existing buildings to be used as a large foyer and as smaller halls for chamber concerts, lectures, and so forth. That was the position when the government changed in 1948. It was then decided to defer the erection of the hall, and the arrangements with the Governors of the Rotunda were cancelled. When Fianna Fáil returned to office three years later the matter was re-opened in the Department, but some thirty years further had passed before the utterly inadequate musical facilities of Dublin were substantially rectified.

The orchestral developments continued, however, and at first on the slenderest of shoe strings. Continental musicians after the war were to be had almost literally at two a penny; and some conductors who later achieved international fame, like Hans Schmidt-Isserstet and Jean Martinon, came to Dublin on salaries that in normal times would be regarded as peanuts, which was about as much as we were empowered to pay them. The visionary ideas that emerged from the G.P.O. were not always well received in Merrion Street. In Finance, where I had to go looking for money, I was once asked – I hope not too seriously – whether what an orchestra did for radio could not just as well be done with gramophone records.

I had often heard Finance, my old department, slated. It was said to be mean and miserable; so hard to get money, even small amounts, out of; it was antediluvian, and so forth. That was not my general experience, but occasionally I was tempted to regard 'the Boss Department' as it was called with dismay. I had to protest strongly to McElligott when one of his assistant secretaries alleged that Norton and the trade unions were being permitted to run a part of the Department of Posts and Telegraphs, this in the context of a 'go slow' by telephonists. That was in 1951, and a few years later I was rebuffed when I wanted to publish a history of Irish communications, including, of course, those for which the Post Office had been responsible. I had been given an undertaking by Howard Robinson, the author of the standard history of the British Post Office, that he would write it, without reward, and take under his wing a young clerk of ours whose articles on postal matters in the Post Office Workers' Union Journal showed considerable promise. Robinson knew his way through the muniment room at the British postal headquarters in London where most of the desired source material was likely to be found. All he asked was to be refunded the cost of an occasional visit to Dublin in connection with his work. I entertained him myself when he first came to Dublin and introduced him to historians who shared my interest in the project; but I could not move Finance, and the project fell through. I was annoyed. The young clerk I had in mind to be Robinson's amanuensis was naturally disappointed too, but he survived to become Chairman of the Labour Court; and recently I gathered there was a resident historian in the Post Office looking after matters such as these.

I backed, of course, all Paddy Little's and Radio Eireann's efforts to improve musical standards and shared the representation of broadcasting on a Department of Education committee that organised a summer school with master classes. While circumstances compelled us to look for artistes abroad we were anxious naturally that in the long term there should be a flow of professional Irish musicians, and we always kept the door wide open for native performers of moderate merit. Our purposes were sometimes misunderstood. I remember that, in response to an advertisement, an innocent girl from the country wrote to offer her services. She was, she said, a most respectable farmer's daughter of twenty-one years and had some experience of violin playing. 'First of all, I learned by rote', she told us. She had 'the accurate notes' of hornpipes and jigs she listed, among them the 'Blackbird', the 'Irish Washerwoman' and the 'Connaught Man's Rambles'. Modestly, in asking for particulars, she wondered if any special training would be given to improve candidates.

While he was in office up to 1948 Paddy Little presided regularly over the meetings of an advisory broadcasting committee and took me along with him. He displayed an eager interest in everything that came up for discussion, and did not by any means limit himself to musical topics. He was a deeply religious man, and some unusual meditations he wrote in a kind of free verse were published in the *Capuchin Annual.* He kept this activity to himself, hiding behind the pen name M. J. Labern. He did not like the appearance of so many of our towns – their dirty, run-down condition offended him – and with like-minded people he engaged in conversations, into which he drew me, with a view to a general brightening up. In this he anticipated the Tidy Towns movement which has done so much good. Again, though he never spoke to me about it, I believe he would have liked to have been a Minister for the Arts; at any rate he got me to draw up a sketch of what an Arts Department might encompass, which probably means that he was trying to get government support for the idea. There had been a Minister for the Arts in the first Dáil; indeed a Dante commemoration organised by his office in December 1921 coincided with the announcement that terms of a Treaty had been agreed upon in London between the representatives of Great Britain and Ireland. But if Paddy Little had a department of the arts in view, he failed to bring it off. He continued to be keen on greater State involvement in cultural matters however, and became the first Director of the Arts Council after his defeat in the 1951 General Election. This position was created as a result of legislation, introduced in consequence of a report written by Professor Thomas Bodkin.

With so little money available centrally we had to depend very much on local effort. We began to take the orchestra out to the country. We went first to Cork, the players travelling to and from that city in the one day to give a concert. It was a particularly fine concert as it happened, under Schmidt-Isserstet. The Lord Mayor graced us with his presence, but the Eroica was too much for him; he slept peacefully at my side all through it. Waterford had to extend itself mightily to prepare for a concert, but did so with enthusiasm – erecting a platform, collecting chairs and selling tickets – urged on by that fine musical personality Willie Watts. Galway came much later; on the night, the orchestra played in a ballroom that was literally beside the sea. We made opportunities for children to hear the orchestra, and I did some negotiating with Sir Robert Mayer whose British concerts had been so phenomenally successful.

The expansion of the orchestra made the top floor of the

G.P.O. unsuitable for rehearsals, while dependence on the church halls of Abbey Street nearby had sooner or later to end. We got the Board of Works to prepare the Phoenix Hall, which was where the Hospitals Trust had conducted their Sweepstake draws, and there for a considerable time the orchestra rehearsed in moderate comfort and gave concerts a couple of times a week to an expanding audience free of charge. That was an important period in Dublin's musical life.

Being given the mantle of culture did not, of course, mean that I was to work on broadcasting exclusively. I was essentially a Post Office man, and the first thing Cremins arranged for me was an educational tour of the head offices in the country in the company of a number of senior men. The actual itinerary was organised by the Chief Inspector of Services, Johnny MacDonnell, who had acted as Director of Broadcasting while arrangements for a definitive appointment were being made; but broadcasting was one subject we did not discuss. It may have been a sore subject for MacDonnell, who possibly felt entitled to be appointed substantively. Why he was selected to fill the post temporarily I don't know, unless it was because of his public relations talents. His claim to fame otherwise rested on his achievements in goal for Bohemians and the Irish international soccer side.

I soon learned, if I did not know it already, how the quality of postal services had deteriorated during the war due to the effect of fuel shortages on the railways, which had been the mainstay of the system for the carriage of mails. The mainline sorting carriages which greatly speeded the post had had to be discontinued. But immediately after the war, 'control' of key trains running to specific timetables was restored and the sorting carriage system re-established. New and more efficient rail and road services were introduced, so that it was again possible to provide that a letter posted up to 6 p.m. in the centre of Dublin would catch the first post next morning almost anywhere throughout the country. The rural postal services were also being reorganised, district by district; so that with motorisation, the conversion of foot posts to cycles, and improved layout of routes, a six-day instead of a three-day delivery was being achieved at much the same cost. Air transport, of course, was having a revolutionary effect on overseas mail services. Without surcharge, mails to and from Great Britain would soon be carried by air, and that method alone was adopted as the ordinary means of conveyance between Ireland and the European continent; indeed, we were to become a world leader in establishing a single rate of air-mail to extra-European destinations, regardless of distance.

We did not dare to talk yet about a comprehensive telecommunications service. Our telephone service was most inadequate. There were areas of the country, particularly in what were later to become tourist areas, where telephones were scarcely known. I saw the first line being laid, entirely for purposes of national defence, between Ballina and Belmullet, a matter of forty miles. In more populated areas, where there were some telephones, the service was frankly a bit of a joke. The problem was not of our making. There were no votes in telephones; hence little in the way of fresh capital. As for the telegraph service which at one time had been a valuable and relatively cheap means of communication, it was on the way out and had become expensive. However, as I have already said, we continued to make a profit on telephones and for a long time balanced out the losses elsewhere.

The change of government in 1948 surprised many people, I am sure, for those who had seen de Valera survive after the war when Churchill had been defeated in Britain thought that the Fianna Fáil grip on the electorate would never be loosened. However the desire to be rid of de Valera and put Fianna Fáil out was a sufficiently strong bond among a number of otherwise disparate groups to force them into an Inter-Party government. People rightly wondered how long MacBride's Clann na Poblachta could work with Mulcahy's Fine Gael and Blowick's Clann na Talmhan, and how the rival Labour elements led by Norton and Everett would get on together? Actually the deal – for surely there had been a deal of some sort – worked out pretty well, and ultimately broke down on an unexpected issue, a Mother and Child scheme in which the Minister for Health found himself at odds with the Catholic bishops. Jack Costello, a middle of the road senior barrister, who admitted that he was a Catholic before he was a politician, had been chosen as Taoiseach. That was a factor, I believe, that kept those unlikely bedfellows together for so long. Everett, who became Minister for Posts and Telegraphs – he had once been a postman – told me more than once, with obvious approval, that the Taoiseach was a saint. He was certainly a man of God; my last view of him, not long before his death, was as he came round the side of Donnybrook parish church on the way to Mass, holding on to the wall to support himself.

I knew him faintly to speak to before he entered government. In fact, he led in a libel suit in which W. T. Cosgrave, Tony O'Reilly's father who was the chief inspector of Customs, and I gave evidence for a friend who had been assailed as a hangman judge. On the way into court, Costello asked me if I remembered Hempenstall, a figure from the '98 period who had the ugly reputation of being judge, jury, hangman and all. I did, and when I was in the witness box Costello exploited that piece of Irish history to secure judgment and £3,000 for his client.

Other heads of government I knew were also men of God. What else can I say of W. T. Cosgrave, of whose support for Frank Duff's works of charity at a critical time I have written elsewhere? When Cáit and I turned into a parish church in Booterstown during a Sunday afternoon's walk we usually found Eamon de Valera and his wife Sinead already there at prayer. They were neighbours, and Sinead especially was an old friend. I served fairly closely under both de Valera and Costello and never for a moment had I reason to question their personal rectitude, whatever I might think of their policies. That undoubtedly gave me, as I am sure it gave other senior Civil Servants, a solid base for our consideration of problems.

Our first Inter-Party minister in 1948, James 'Jem' Everett, I had only seen before on the opposition benches in the Dáil. He at one time had a reputation of being a firebrand in local politics, and more recently had shown some antipathy to Paddy Little's ideas. But in office he revealed none of this to me; and he reversed nothing. When presenting his first broadcasting estimate, he said that, being a new boy, he wanted to give an adequate trial to the enlargement that had taken place as the result of the short-wave project, and while he would lay down policy as required, he promised to give the widest measure of freedom possible to the programme makers. He accepted the Post Office view that a Civil Service department was not a suitable medium for providing entertainment; and he made a strong case for the structural change that only occurred nine years later.

On the debate on his second estimate a year later he said that the programme officers had availed themselves of their new freedom, and that many matters of live interest had been discussed before the microphone which would have been frowned upon in the past. Controversial talks caused irritation, he said, but that was a risk that was worth taking; and he had not been perturbed when a Fianna Fáil deputy complained that Radio Eireann had recently 'honoured that play', *The Playboy of the Western World*. His attitude to the engagement of foreign musicians we found quite unexceptional. Being a union man I can well imagine his concern for Irish players but I am sure that he realised that the policy we were following was generally in the interest of these players, for many of whom the station's orchestras were now ensuring permanent employment. I can recall only one instance when he made a stand for a musician whom Radio Eireann wanted to displace. The doctor had said that his condition was so bad that he might drop dead in the middle of a concert, but Everett would not have him retired. He was a musician who had been in Ireland for some years and was a part-time coach and conductor of a union band, from whence the pressure on Everett to retain him no doubt came.

About this time a once internationally famous quartet offered their services, and we considered employing them, or some similar group, in Cork, which was pressing for a share of the development that was occurring in Dublin. Everett and I discussed this idea with the Lord Mayor when we were down there together on some departmental business or other. The Lord Mayor jumped at the idea of a Radio Eireann group being located in Cork to give concerts and teach, and at another idea of ours that we should add a broadcasting top to the city's new school of music. The Minister and I had seen the conditions under which Cork's contributions to the broadcasting schedules were being made. The studio, if you can call it that, was in a remote part of what had been the women's gaol, in a stone building at the end of a long exercise yard, and was reached by an iron stairway. There was a grand piano in the studio that had received a bullet in its innards in the Civil War which can't have done it any good. That apart, it was impossible to imagine a singer giving of his best, or a comic being particularly funny, in such surroundings.

After the June 1951 election which Fianna Fáil won Erskine Hamilton Childers became our Minister. He was three years younger than me, and like me knew nothing about the Post Office when he came to the G.P.O. But he was manifestly desperately keen to learn. His first contact with the work force came through a meeting in a pub the day he became Minister with the postman who had been delivering his letters. Having congratulated him and agreed to share a drink, the postman told him that he was the chairman of the Postman's Ball, which was about to take place, and would the Minister like to come to it. Childers was delighted to be asked, and certainly enjoyed himself immensely on the night, as he usually did on social occasions. Cáit and I were there among the guests, and with the Ball drawing to a close, the Minister invited us to his house on Bushy Park Road for a nightcap, and, whispering to me that we were getting very democratic, he agreed to give the postman and his wife a lift home. On the journey the conversation turned to the subject of spot prizes of which there had been many at the Ball, and the postman told of an occasion when he had won a prize through having a hole in his sock and a pawn ticket in his pocket. It was the funniest thing I had heard for a long time and I laughed outright. 'Yes,' said Childers, 'but do you mean to say that you actually had the pawn ticket at the same time as the hole in the sock.' 'Oh sure,' said the postman. 'But', said Childers, 'wasn't a pawn ticket a rather melancholy thing to bring to a dance?'

I got on well from the beginning with Childers and on my

fiftieth birthday which occurred shortly after our coming together he made me a present of his American mother's spiritual anthology. Later, when a new edition of his father's classical *Riddle of the Sands* was published he gave me a copy of it, too. I would have loved him to talk to me about the book or its tragic author, but he showed no inclination to do so, and I didn't press him. Father and son were both very English. Though young Erskine had spent most of his life in Ireland he was, I always thought, more English than Irish, and his speech betrayed this. People spoke about his Oxford accent, but 'you know,' he said to my wife one night at a dinner, 'it's not Oxford but Cambridge', as if that, in the circumstances, made any difference. We sometimes yarned a good deal, even about religion, and the problem of a mixed marriage he was about to make. But Dr McQuaid, the Catholic Archbishop of Dublin, was standing in the way of its taking place in the Pro-Cathedral; Childers had plans, however, to have it done in Paris, in Notre Dame. He was impetuous. His first thoughts about everything concerning the office went down on paper: he was endlessly writing memoranda; and when he heard that my son Eimear had taken first place and first prize in a class for foreign conductors in the Paris Conservatoire, he wanted to appoint him right away to direct the Radio Eireann Symphony Orchestra. I had to explain in detail to him why that could not be done.

It was Childers, when a couple of years in office, who approached the government about the future status of the broadcasting service. He told the Dáil of the government's decision. They had rejected, as too extreme a measure in a small country like Ireland, the idea of an independent corporation (he did not say, what some people might have surmised, that broadcasting was still considered to be too important a service to be withdrawn from State control) and had plumped for a degree of limited delegation of authority which was to be conferred without resort to legislation. A Comhairle of five persons was to be appointed and they would be responsible for the general control and supervision of the service. They were 'broadly speaking to take the place of the Department in assisting the Minister in the framing of policy and carrying on the administration of broadcasting'. Childers explained to some mystified deputies that the

Comhairle, despite the etymologically restrictive sense of the word, would be executive as well as advisory, but the Minister would remain in legal control of the service and would be legally responsible to the Oireachtas and the public for its activities.

The statement that the Comhairle was 'broadly speaking to take the place of the Department' went perhaps too far. The legal position was that the members of the Comhairle could only function as a broadcasting unit within the Department and to enable them to do even that much they had to be given temporary Civil Service appointments. And not merely were they responsible to the Minister but, like all other members of the staff, they were under the permanent head of the Department who, as Accounting Officer, had to account for all expenditure on broadcasting and everything else to the Minister for Finance and the Public Accounts Committee of the Dáil.

However, everybody worked hard to make the non-statutory Comhairle a success and to make it appear that they were more independent than they really were. The Department of Finance eased its rigid controls, the Post Office placed some of its best men, including the admirable Matt Doherty, at the disposal of the Comhairle, and a new professional Director, Maurice Gorham, went with the Secretary of the Department, and as his alternate, to the meetings of the European Broadcasting Union, the first time this had happened. The Dáil also responded to appeals from Childers and Michael Keyes, his successor in 1954, not to put down parliamentary questions on the ordinary day to day running of broadcasting, and when it came to Estimates time the Ministers continued an old practice of encouraging deputies to confine their remarks to the matters of general principle or policy for which the Minister retained responsibility. I remember Keyes saying that he did not want to be told that Dinjoe was better or worse than Joe Lynch, or that 'The Balladmakers' was the best or worst programme on Radio Eireann. It would be more effective to do that in a letter or on a postcard to the Director.

All of Gorham's predecessors, Seamus Clandillon, T. J. Kiernan, Seamus Brennan, Robert Brennan and Charlie Kelly, had been recruited from the Civil Service: Gorham's background was entirely different. A Stonyhurst and Oxford man, his career had begun in journalism but, before coming to *Radio Times*, had directed the B.B.C.'s wartime broadcasts to America, had founded the Allied Expeditionary Forces programme and the Light Programme, and had been the first post-war head of the B.B.C.'s television service. He was obviously a man not to be missed. My only worry, when I approached him, was that he would find the job too small for him and something of a backwater. However, I think he genuinely wanted to come and work in and for Ireland. He, and his sister Nora, were very Irish in their background and thinking, and Nora's husband, Kelly Bartels, a British Civil Servant, had helped me very considerably when I was looking in London for material for a biography of Madden, the historian. That was a link. Things were progressing very satisfactorily when Erskine Childers came on the scene in a flurry of enthusiasm and off his own bat proceeded to negotiate a salary with Maurice which he had to go back on, because MacEntee, again Minister for Finance, would not agree to it; he seemed to like putting Childers in his junior place.

But Childers's methods were at fault: he never really learned that there were some things he should leave to others. He wanted to be both company director and managing director. As Maurice Gorham said in his book Childers found it hard to let go his control of Radio Eireann, his interest in every detail of organisation and programmes so overflowing in constant telephone calls and copious minutes that it was sometimes tempting to ask him why he had taken the trouble to instal a new regime and a new director if he wished to run the service himself. And when he operated independently he was by no means as competent as he probably thought he was. Gorham was actually tempted to break off negotiations about coming to Dublin when the difficulty arose about the salary Childers had undertaken to pay him – he had other offers – but I asked him to hold his hand, and subsequently induced him to come. I sometimes regretted having done so, not I need hardly say because I ever had reason to question the value of his work, but because he was not treated with more consideration when television came along. Maurice had a strong feeling about the kind of people he had to work under. He felt very much at home with the members of the Comhairle, and I can't remember a solitary occasion when he seriously disagreed with me or my Post Office colleagues. He was none too happy, however, when he read of the persons likely to be given charge of television. He said publicly that he did not want to be committed to an Authority about which nothing was known.

When Childers left us in 1954 he was replaced by a Labour Minister, Michael Keyes of Limerick. Of him Maurice Gorham wrote something I willingly endorse. He was a man who did his job without ostentation and gave the Comhairle time to settle in. He saw the point when, following an intervention by Risteard Mulcahy when acting as Taoiseach, I told him of the danger that the liberty of expression we had given to Radio Eireann could be whittled down unless Ministers took a more liberal view of the problems of the day and also made sure of their facts before they criticised the station. It was Keyes who in October 1956 made the first cautious reference to Irish television but did so in terms that conformed fully to what he had heard and read in the department. He did not encourage the idea that it was likely to come soon: but when it did he said it would be publicly owned and managed. Keyes provided congenial company outside the office. I remember Maurice and I being entertained by him in a snug in Limerick during an interval in a symphony concert: we talked little if anything about music, but a lot about the game of rugby and the local club for which he had played. The conversation tended to be prolonged, and I had to remind Keyes that the second half of the concert could not proceed until he was seen to be in his seat. My personal relations with him were excellent; and I kept in touch with him in his retirement. I went to see him in his home during his terminal illness: I can see him laughing as he came down the stairs in his dressing gown to greet me, carrying a bottle of whiskey and two glasses.

He was with us from 1954 to 1957, and somewhere in that period I had a visit from an old friend from Land Settlement Commission days, Kevin O'Shiel, with an offer from his Minister, Joseph Blowick, to become the Secretary of the Department of Lands, which carried an Irish Land Commissionership. I was now entering my last decade in the Post

Office; but the Land Commissionership would enable me to stay on till I was 70. I was naturally very pleased to receive the offer, but the prospect of having to make a fresh start at my age in an area that would demand serious study of land law and practice was not attractive. I did not turn down the offer, but I asked for an increase in the salary which I assume could not be conceded. Anyhow I heard nothing further about it.

A man I got to know rather well through the Post Office and broadcasting was John Charles McQuaid, who, largely through the instrumentality of de Valera, it is believed, was the Catholic Archbishop of Dublin from 1940 till 1972. He had helped de Valera with the drafting of the Preamble to the Constitution of 1937 and the fundamental rights Articles, especially the much discussed Article 44 on religion. His opinions on the religious and social principles of the document were to a large extent influenced by the teaching of two priests who held extreme views on these topics. Father Denis Fahey, a priest of the Holy Ghost Congregation like McQuaid himself, and Father Edward Cahill, the Jesuit author of a book on the Christian State. It is believed that McQuaid, in the drafting of the Articles, pressed de Valera to go farther than he was prepared to do. He would probably have desired a statement to be inserted recognising the Catholic Church as the Church founded by Christ, whereas de Valera would only agree to recognise the special position of that church as the guardian of the Faith professed by the great majority of the citizens, and at the same time, recognise the existence in Ireland of other churches, congregations and denominations. Father Fahey was disappointed; he believed that what the Irish people had upheld over the centuries of persecution was being betrayed; that this was the first step in a process that would culminate in the full profession of the Catholic Faith being proscribed sooner or later by an Irish government. Other people about the same time were accusing de Valera of self-indulgence in the Constitution: that as Collins endeavoured in the 1922 Constitution to winkle more out of the Treaty than was in it, he was trying to placate left-wing republicans with *national* phrases and pious people with expressly Catholic bits.

Dr McQuaid was a native of Cootehill in Co. Cavan and carried to Dublin with him the antagonisms of that Border area. He certainly displayed them in his approach to anything in which he saw organised Protestant involvement. He got on extremely well with individual Protestants to whom he always showed the best side of him; but he liked all organisations with which he had relations to be under either Catholic leadership or primarily for Catholics. Hence he set up a Catholic Social Conference in opposition to Judge Wylie's idea of a Guild of Good Will; he frowned on the Civics Institute; and wouldn't allow Muintir na Tire, though founded by a Catholic priest, into his diocese. He didn't like Trinity College at all: he enforced the Hierarchy's ban on Catholics attending there and strove to prevent the Institute of Public Administration, whose President was John Leydon, from holding lectures within its walls. He may have had something to do with an attempt to wrest the Meath Hospital from Protestant control; and he so disliked the *Irish Times* that he never sent copies of his public statements to it. That Protestants recognised what he was up to there was no doubt, and this I saw particularly when, while working on my book, *Protestant Nationalists in Revolutionary Ireland*, I read the correspondence District Justice Liam Price received following his privately circulated biography of Dorothy Stopford, who had introduced the B.C.G. anti-tuberculosis drug to Ireland, one Dublin doctor going so far as to say that Dr McQuaid had nearly managed to stop all prevention work against tuberculosis. To Catholics and their associations he showed another, but no less autocratic side. I have written of his attitude to the Pillar of Fire and Mercier societies, but other organisations besides the Legion of Mary suffered from his manner of exercising authority over his flock. I remember being in Dr Theo Dillon's house in Killiney one night with Frank Duff and Jack Nagle, and being told by the leaders of the Society of St Vincent de Paul about the curt, hurtful messages they were receiving from the Archbishop in his own handwriting. And yet there was a nice side to the man, of which I was aware. He had a quiet sense of humour, too, which told in his favour. I remember hearing of a story from his Blackrock days concerning a boy who mimicked the President's manner of walking, with one shoulder slightly drooped, who was surprised to hear Dr McQuaid himself whispering in his ear, 'the other shoulder'.

Dr McQuaid was probably unhappy about the decisions that were taken at the Second Vatican Council on the subject of ecumenism; but, being an utterly loyal son of the Church, he found it necessary to respond to the Council's injunction about taking an active and intelligent interest in the matter. The first public sign that he was about to do so was when he agreed to sit on one side of President de Valera with the Church of Ireland Archbishop George Simms on the other at a lecture to be given in the Dublin Mansion House in January 1966 by Monsignor Arthur Ryan of Belfast. They were to be seated in the front row of the audience, facing a platform party consisting simply of the lecturer and the Papal Nuncio, with the organiser of the meeting, the Jesuit editor of *Studies*, Father Roland Burke Savage. I was there that night and noticed some seating confusion, but unknown to the crowded audience a little drama (or comedy) was being played out behind the scenes.

A couple of days before the meeting the *Irish Times* printed photographs on the front page of the two archbishops with a caption announcing that they would together recite the Our Father. We can only imagine what went through Dr McQuaid's mind when he saw that. To lead the prayer with a Protestant prelate was asking too much. It would make nonsense of the reassurance he had given his people on returning from Rome that no change had occurred at the Council to worry the tranquillity of their Christian lives. That reassurance did not fit in well with the ideas of the man outside Clarendon Street church who was heard telling an acquaintance that Vatican Two had knocked hell out of everything. However the announcement in the *Irish Times* drove Dr McQuaid into a fit of temper. He rang Father Burke Savage, clearly blaming him for the announcement, and told him that he would not say the Our Father with Dr Simms; he had given instructions that Father Burke Savage was not to be put through to him on the phone. He then went off to the Nunciature, where he spent two hours 'prancing about', and threatening to denounce Father Burke Savage to his Provincial. The Nuncio, who gave Father Burke Savage these details, did not share Dr McQuaid's concern. He had encouraged the holding of the meeting, was being urged to do so by members of the diplomatic corps, and said that he would suggest to the Jesuit Provincial to put any protest that came from the Archbishop into the wastepaper basket.

Next day there was a change of sorts. Dr McQuaid told the Nuncio that he would say the Our Father but from the platform, leaving Dr Simms with de Valera in the front of the audience. Father Burke Savage, therefore, saw to it on the afternoon of the day of the lecture that there were four seats on the platform, three as originally planned and one extra for Dr McQuaid. But that evening, when he went on the platform with the others there was a fifth seat; but by whom it had been placed there he did not nor does not know. It remained unoccupied for the duration of the meeting, a fact that gave the *Irish Times* the title for its editorial the following morning: *The Empty Chair*. That was not the whole story: for when President de Valera was brought to the front row of the general audience there was no seat for him; but, James Dillon, observing the dilemma, rose instantly and gave him his seat, making thereby, as a newsman reported, 'the most ecumenical gesture of the evening'.

As Secretary of the Post Office I met Dr McQuaid on a number of occasions, usually in the Palace in Drumcondra. He had the reputation of being shy, aloof, and hard to talk to, but that was not my experience. He was progressive too. I remember his anxiety to prepare for the television era, and he sent some young priests out of the country to learn the necessary craftsmanship. Over a cup of tea he would genially discuss the subjects that brought us together. I had no difficulty in reaching agreement with him, although I thought early on that there might be, when he raised the question of supplying him with advance copies of all the scripts of talks to be given by priests over the radio. I suggested he could get these scripts himself, without involving Radio Eireann in the process. He made the point that as the talks were broadcast from a studio in his diocese he was entitled to see the scripts, but he did not pursue the matter when I mentioned that whatever about the talks going out from a Dublin studio the transmitter was outside his diocese, in Athlone. We talked about broadcasting the Angelus Bell – an idea which originated, I think, in Radio Eaireann – and apart from its religious purpose, was to give the Irish programme a distinctive and attractive character. He was naturally delighted at the prospect, especially as the bell to be used was that in the Pro-Cathedral. We discussed the need for a regular Sunday broadcast of Mass for the sick and the infirm, to which he had at first objected, but he promptly gave in when I told him that my own mother, being confined to her room, had not heard Mass for years and was rarely visited by a priest. The Sunday Mass for the sick is now a revered institution, and I was recently delighted to read in the *Irish Times* a warm commendation by Archdeacon Cathal McCarthy of the men in Radio Eireann with whom, on behalf of the Archbishop, he discussed the affairs of religious broadcasting: Gorham, Ó Faracháin, Kelly and MacManus. 'It was natural for me,' he said, 'to admire especially the precision of their philosophical and theological insights and the consequent maturity of their judgment in matters of policy and practice.'

Though short on small talk, Dr McQuaid always enquired about individuals we both knew and for their welfare. 'How is Mrs So-and-So?' he asked me one day, referring to a neighbour of mine, and when I told him she was well but not very well off, he left the room and returned with fifty pounds in notes which he asked me to give her. He also used me in this way to bring assistance to the widow of a friend of mine, and saw to it subsequently that her children were educated in good schools. A cynic might say that this form of charity was easy for a person in his privileged position; but what does one say of the prelate who spent his Saturday afternoons with a former pupil who was enduring an acute form of mental disorder? There, I would think, was the genuine article. My daughter Blánaid, now a grandmother, still remembers his impressive words about Our Lady at her confirmation.

On the few occasions that I had to do business with other bishops I found the experience generally pleasant and productive. When, for example, an engineering workman started a hunger strike and picketed departmental premises, a word from his bishop made him change his mind. The bishop, when I spoke to him, saw immediately our predicament, recognising that a Christian, whatever his grievance about an organisational matter, should not put his life at risk. We were not so lucky in another case where, applying the Canon Law, a bishop wanted us to take action against an unmarried occupant of a sub-post office who was said to be causing scandal in a parish. Departmentally we had no reason to complain about the person named, and the manner in which the work of the sub-office was performed was beyond reproach. I found the parish priest and the bishop rather brusque when they discussed the matter with me, and my interview on a Saturday morning with the bishop ended with a statement by him that he proposed to denounce us publicly the following day. There was an election coming up and as soon as I could I gave the details of the situation to de Valera, who was then Taoiseach. He told me to leave the case in his hands. There was nothing from the bishop next day or any day. And the problem for bishop and priests that was said to have 'scandalised' parishioners was settled by the occupant of the sub-office getting married.

Dr McQuaid had been the president of Blackrock College before becoming a bishop and was the contemporary of other distinguished men who had been students of that college, notably Eamon de Valera, Alfred O'Rahilly and Frank Duff. O'Rahilly, even more than McQuaid, was a complicated character. When I first made the acquaintance of this stocky sharp-featured Kerryman it was in University College, Cork where he was registrar. I had travelled down one morning in the late 1920s in the hope that he would let me see the papers in his custody of Pierce McCann, a gentleman-farmer and Irish Volunteer who had died in an English prison during the influenza epidemic of 1919. In a very brief interview, however, he gruffly refused me. That he was right in doing so I discovered almost a half-century later. My interest in the papers had been awakened by a lady friend of mine, who may have had a romantic interest in McCann, and it was just as well that O'Rahilly did not at that time give them to me for, when he did so, I found that they were essentially a collection of love letters involving another lady who was to occupy a high place in public life. O'Rahilly, during his long life, had been a Jesuit student, a member of the Dáil, a writer of a book on money, a married man and father of children, as well as president of a University College. In the election to that position he was opposed by a professor of Irish, and his own notoriety as a lay theologian was signalled in a telegram announcing the result. It read: Thomas Aquinas 20, Finn MacCool 5. (The figures are imaginary.) At the time he parted with the McCann letters all those things were behind him. He was a priest, living in Blackrock College, and acting as a spiritual guide to a Patrician group that met once a month in Frank Flanagan's house on Mount Merrion Avenue and over which I sometimes presided. The Patricians were another of Frank Duff's societies; its aim was to stimulate adult Catholics to know their faith better, and members of this particular group included Paddy Little, W. T. Cosgrave, and Sean MacEoin.

In this context I got to know O'Rahilly well. He was a sprightly and humorous conversationalist, a man with a point of view on every subject, but an egoist to his fingertips. He was critical of us laymen. We had no guts, as he had had when one of us. He would have exempted Frank Duff from that criticism, for he saw Frank's Legion of Mary as a rare example of what earlier was called Catholic Action. Which reminds me that one night, years before, when lecturing to the debating society in the Morning Star Hostel in Dublin, O'Rahilly was asked what Catholic Action was. He replied by asking the questioner if he knew what Catholic inaction was, and being assured he did, O'Rahilly said, 'Well, that's Catholic Action.'

Cáit and I were invited to O'Rahilly's ordination and to breakfast afterwards with a large company that included de Valera. The relationship of those two men had been lifelong and close, though at times de Valera had no sterner critic than O'Rahilly. After the meal, in a scintillating speech, O'Rahilly brought down the house by saying that that morning he had had de Valera where he had wanted to have him for years, on his knees before him, and his hand near his throat, and had surprised himself by giving him his blessing. The ordination card I have treasured. It includes from scripture the words: 'About the eleventh hour He went out. . . . He said: Go you also into My Vineyard.'

SEVEN

THE BIG decisions affecting broadcasting were not taken in the G.P.O. We did not originate the short-wave project for which money from the Exchequer was freely made available; and we had little to say to the decisions about television. As a forward-looking organisation we watched television developments generally, of course, and realised that television would somehow sooner or later come to Ireland, but the actual determination as to when we were to have it and in what form was reached by a Cabinet committee in which, I believe, the views of the Taoiseach at that time, the strong-willed Sean Lemass, prevailed. The short-wave project arose out of de Valera's anxiety to avoid a recurrence of the isolation imposed upon us in the war as a consequence of the neutral line we had followed. In pursuing that line we were, as I have already suggested, more than fair to the British. We made adjustments at the outbreak of the war to suit them, and during the war, to avoid leaks of information or criticism we cut unscripted programmes to a minimum, compelled correspondents using the Radio Eireann studio facilities to submit their scripts for examination, and eliminated all weather forecasting; even sports commentators were not allowed to tell what the weather was like. There was one unexpected breach of neutrality, however, that caused more amusement than embarrassment. The popular Joe Linnane asked a 'Question Time' competitor in Belfast who was the best-known teller of fairy tales, expecting to be told Hans Christian Andersen: what he got was Winston Churchill. A formal protest came from BBC Belfast; and it was a long time before a Radio Eireann team crossed the Border again. At the end of the war in 1945 Churchill assailed Irish neutrality in a victory broadcast and de Valera's speech in reply went out in French as well as English on a 1½ kilowatt transmitter. This was little more than a gesture as Radio Eireann had no effective coverage in France.

Radio between 1939 and 1945 had assumed an importance it never had when the world was at peace; and, with the British naturally suspicious of the operations of the German and Japanese diplomatic missions in Dublin, Ireland felt itself almost entirely cut off from the outisde world. If the American networks wanted broadcasts from Ireland they could get them by means of the radio-telephone but this was routed through London, which meant that the British Post Office had control over what went through. The 1½ kilowatt transmitter at Athlone through which an attempt was made to establish direct communication with the United States had proved ineffectual; and the Emergency Scientific Bureau reported that the power could not be increased to 20 kilowatts in the absence of certain parts which could not be obtained. That was in September 1941; for the rest of the war we were dependent on Britain for communication by speech with America; but, fortunately, we had a wireless telegraph circuit through which diplomatic despatches could go. The opposition, at the time I came into the picture, were less concerned about the need to obtain wavelengths than the use the government was likely to make of them. They feared that the political image of the government only was to be projected, and for that reason alone the shortwave project should be rejected.

A secondary criticism, but not a very serious one, was that a station that had not yet learned what to call itself – was it Raydio or Raddio Eireann? The announcers used both forms – could not be trusted to speak always with an Irish voice. General Mulcahy, the leading opposition figure, romanced about the beauty of the Irish voice and implied that it was not what was usually heard from the Irish transmitters. 'If we're going to be heard more widely throughout the world,' he said, 'I think that we ought to be heard by the kind of voice that we have so common in Ireland, and that is so pleasant to hear. It may be on the street, in the country, going up an Irish hill or along a river that voices are heard that are delightful to the ear and that refresh the spirit.' He made no claim for the voices heard in Dáil Éireann, but a deputy on the same side was later to claim that the best English was spoken in that House, 'though I would except myself from that' he humbly added. In the same debate the Labour man Brendan Corish, who always had a kind word for Radio Eireann, said that it was one of the few broadcasting stations in the world which made a real effort to disseminate culture. This, however, was a view not generally shared. Paddy McGilligan, for instance, considered the national station 'stereotyped and unimaginative'. James Dillon, when he took up the attack on the short-wave proposals, said that their whole purpose was 'cod', and he ventured to swear that within five years when the rabbits started playing leap-frog in Rineanna, the short-wave masts would be converted into knitting machines to knit the rabbits' wool. The hyperbole apart, something like that did happen, without a single programme being sent overseas. The 100 kw transmitter that had been installed at Athlone was scrapped. Nevertheless the preparations for a short-wave service did broadcasting for home consumption a world of good. They gave Radio Eireann, for the first time, a proper news service, script writers, outside broadcast officers and a professional repertory group of actors.

An area of considerable development was that of music, and I was happy to be able to share in it, though I did my damndest to turn my son Eimear away from it. Practically since childhood I had been a witness of the plight of serious musicians. Most of them could not get a job, while the few who seemed to corner whatever was available were objects of criticism and jealousies. A composer-organist I knew went about looking as abjectly miserable as the poet Mangan must have done in the previous century; and it was sad to see good players, if they were employed professionally at all, reduced to playing in cafés for a pittance. The arrival of broadcasting improved the situation considerably, and it became possible for an enlarged station orchestra to give a series of successful public concerts. A normal progression from that, with Paddy Little urging on gently from the rear, was our present symphony orchestra and it became my job to look for support for that idea in quarters where symphony orchestras seemed uncalled for. This body of players, many of them foreigners, had to be helped to *unionise* themselves and, though it was an unusual role for a departmental official, I did precisely that.

An old school butty of mine, C. E. Kelly – everyone called him Charlie Kelly – became the Director of the projected Overseas Service. Like me he had not gone to the university from Senior Grade, but had entered the British Civil Service at the very bottom. He was in 1919 an Acting Assistant Clerk but, under the Free State administration, he moved upwards in a variety of positions until in 1941 he entered the Post Office as Deputy Director of Broadcasting. He was clever and adaptable, and since the early 1920s he had shared with Tom Collins the ownership and direction of the humorous monthly, *Dublin Opinion*, and over the initials of C. E. K. provided the principal cartoons. These were widely admired as witty, and sometimes irreverent, commentaries on the passing scene. In March 1947, however, while Joe Cremins and I worked together, our Minister, Paddy Little, drew attention to some of these cartoons and said that in his opinion they constituted active participation in politics which, of course, was taboo for a civil servant. I doubt if Paddy had made his move off his own bat; the intervention would more likely have been prompted by his ministerial colleague, Frank Aiken, who did not like the way he and his pipe figured in the cartoons. Aiken had also a very sensitive wife, a violinist, who around this time complained of the way she had been treated in Radio Eireann and I had to draft several letters to Aiken in an effort to mollify her.

Joe Cremins and I interviewed Charlie Kelly, went over the offending cartoons with him, and told him what the Minister, ours and his, had said about them. He professed to be greatly surprised that any of his work should be considered remotely political. He said he had never had any connection with politics, and had always been most careful to avoid any association or activity which could be considered to be actively political, and had refused an invitation from the *Irish Press*, the Fianna Fáil paper, to do a cartoon for use in a general election campaign. He made the point that, taken out of their context in a purely humorous journal, some cartoons might assume a somewhat more serious and tendentious character than they were intended to have, but he thought that the well established character of *Dublin Opinion* would save his cartoons from an over-serious or actively political interpretation. However, he was prepared to defer to the view of the Minister and the government. He felt that it would be quite simple for him to avoid the type of cartoon which, in the light of that view, might be capable of being regarded as an active participation in politics; and he undertook to consult Joe Cremins or me in regard to any future cartoon concerning which he had the slightest doubt. We thought that, in all the circumstances, this might be regarded as an adequate safeguard, and recommended to the Minister that it should be accepted. The Minister agreed but made it clear that the responsibility would remain entirely with Charlie no matter whom he might consult. The matter appeared to end there, but when the first Inter-Party government took office, Paddy Little mentioned in the Dáil on an estimate introduced by his successor, Jem Everett, that he had tried to control *Dublin Opinion* from taking sides in politics, and Sean MacEntee described the paper as a party partisan journal which was consistently anti-Fianna Fáil. These criticisms did Charlie no harm. In fact he became Director of Broadcasting as soon as the post became vacant.

I have good reason to remember the short-wave project. Our Engineer in Chief, T. J. Monaghan – he whom a French journal described as *long comme un jour sans pain* – and Matt Doherty of the Post Office secretariat went with me to the first post-war assembly of the International Telecommunication Union at Atlantic City, New Jersey, in search of the frequencies without which Ireland's voice, pleasant or unpleasant, representative or unrepresentative, could not be heard at all in foreign parts. We crossed the Atlantic on the *Queen Elizabeth* and I would have wallowed in all the luxury were it not that my injections which had had to be repeated left me frightfully sick. I finally called in the ship's doctor who gave me a strong dose of quinine which cured my trouble. As I left the liner at New York I noticed that a book I had brought out with me was missing. I could understand why. Its title was *The Tremendous Lover*; but the thief was likely to be disappointed when he opened it. I need only say that the author was the prior of a Cistercian Abbey.

Anybody who was at the Conference is not likely to have forgotten it. It ran through the whole hot summer of 1947, in that crowded, third-rate imitation of Blackpool where, outside the Conference, there was nothing to do but exercise on the kind of railway platform alongside the sea they call the boardwalk. The Russians and their satellites were there with all their new-won authority, and everything the conference touched turned into an East-West political debate in the course of which the division of the radio spectrum which we were so anxious to see expedited seemed to get farther and farther out of sight. All the delegates wanted to talk about were the amazing developments that were already taking place in the field of television. I squeezed one morning into a crowded basement room in a hotel on the boardwalk to see simultaneous transmission in colour of an operation being conducted in a hospital in New York. It was an extraordinary spectacle and made me wonder even more whether our priorities at home did not require readjustment. We could not avoid some involvement in the political issues: for example, those that arose in the negotiation of an agreement with the United Nations for the recognition of the ITU as a specialised agency, and which committed it and its individual members to all-out action in certain circumstances. Ireland had not yet become a member of the United Nations. She had been politically neutral in the last war and might be so again. So we went to Lake Success on the Union's negotiating team and saw to it that the position of countries like Ireland was provided for.

Knowing that we would have a lot of lobbying to do to win support for what we were looking for, we had brought out a fair quantity of Irish liquid refreshment which was mainly stored in my quarters in the Ritz-Carlton hotel; and, after a discreet interval, we invited some heads of delegations and others to come and sample it. Before any of these people arrived I discovered that all three Irish representatives including myself were 'pioneers', non-drinkers of alcohol. Something had to be done about this. I said to my colleagues: 'Look here, fellows, from this moment, we are all drinking whiskey', and we did, or pretended to. We did something else: I asked the Irish ambassador in Washington to lend us somebody who could both drink and look after our public relations, and we started to give influential people at the conference an occasional bottle. It helped.

I got some short breaks during that tedious conference and took full advantage of them. I saw some family in-laws in New York city, visited friends in Baltimore and Scranton, did a week-end retreat in Philadelphia and attended a Marian Celebration in Ottawa. Paddy O'Keeffe, the Secretary of the G.A.A., sent me tickets for an All-Ireland football final that was to be played in New York's Polo Grounds, and Cáit, obviously excited, asked me in a cable to represent her family at the match. There were three O'Reillys on the Cavan team that were to play Kerry. I did more than that. I brought a party of Irish-Americans to the game wearing Cavan favours and they shouted lustily for a team and a county they may not have heard of before. We went by underground to the venue and I was delighted to hear a number of Irish-speaking Kerry supporters who had come to New York from I think the direction of Boston. The match was played on a pitch that was too small and on which the players tried to keep themselves cool by dipping into barrels of water; and, afterwards, when I had bid good-bye to my Cavan relations for the day, Paddy O'Keeffe brought me to the celebration dinner. It started hours late, why I don't know, but, as we waited for something to eat we were 'entertained' by a choir of policemen to 'Irish' songs like 'Who put the overalls in Mrs Murphy's chowder?' and 'When Irish Eyes are Smiling', that would never have been tolerated at a G.A.A. function in Ireland.

Of the retreat in a suburb of Philadelphia, I remember a number of things. On the train going there I met a fine young fellow who had just been demobilised after the War in the Phillipines, and he was making the retreat in order to ensure God's guidance on his future. The retreat itself followed a format I knew so well from Milltown Park and based on the Spiritual Exercises of Saint Ignatius. An unusual feature, however, was a service of prayer with hymns and a procession to the American flag, conducted by the lay organisers of the retreat. The procession should not have surprised me but it did. I had got used to seeing the national flag on the altar in other churches; but I did not expect that the retreatants would have been asked to march to it as part of the retreat programme. I must have been seen to be an outsider among the retreatants because, after the first lecture, when I was walking alone, a man beckoned to me and asked me if I was Irish? I said I was. He smiled. 'Do you by any chance come from Dublin?' I said I did. Then the smile became a grin as he said, 'Do you happen to have any Hospital Sweepstake tickets?'

Five months is a long time to be away from home and I suppose I felt it, despite all the novelty and attraction of what I saw, heard and read while I was in the United States. Cáit also felt the length of the separation. The result was to prove the truth of the old saying that absence makes the heart grow fonder. The letters we exchanged during that period, which I have recently re-read, leave me with the conviction that in them we opened our hearts to each other in a new way. The family was growing up, the boys already at the university and she, on her own, was now doing everything that before we had done together. She looked to the choice of nursing home for my father who had had a stroke, and brought my mother to 'holiday' with her. 'I worried a lot at first about your father' she told me, 'and it interfered with my sleep at night; but one night it occurred to me that this was getting us nowhere so I just handed over all responsibility to Our Blessed Lady and ceased to worry. Since that everything has gone swimmingly. Your father is much better. Your mother is in spendid form, and they are both looking forward to being home together at the end of the month D.V. So why worry?' In an incidental note, towards the end of my American sojourn, she revealed how she was praying that 'we two always with God's grace, would help each other and ours and influence those in contact with us so that our little world may be more pleasing, and make up for others who have not the same chances.' She was greatly influenced by Frank Duff, shared his spiritual ambition, and never missed the Legionary prayers he had composed. She would tell me of his visits to the house, and those she paid to him and his little mother. Frank had promised to look in on the family occasionally, and his letters told me what he had found. 'You need have no sort of misgivings in regard to them,' he wrote. 'All without exception are in the very best of form. Your letters are looked forward to and read with incredible eagerness. Therefore the time you spend on them is not wasted.' He naturally mentioned the contacts I was able to make with the Legion of Mary: and was enthusiastic about the attention I had given to the Negroes in a talk I had given in New York. 'Just to the extent that we win the coloured people,' he said, 'will we win the whole situation. The coloured people are the majority of the world's population; the Legion fully asserts the idea of equality.'

I was delighted that Frank was 'looking in on the family', for he was a joy to meet socially. He had a wonderful sense of humour, and an endless stack of stories from real life. Many of them were downright funny, sometimes about oddly innocent characters. One of these was a pious young man who told Frank during the 1920-21 troubles that he had been up to Mountjoy Prison and had offered himself to be executed for Ireland. The warder on the gate, a bit of a wag, dealt with the eccentric offer by saying, 'Thanks very much, but we're not hanging anybody just at the moment. I'll take your name and address, though, and we'll send you a card when you are wanted.' Cáit would have loved that. She had overheard two Dublin 'wans' talking about a film: 'It's all about the life of Bernadette,' one of them said. 'Oh is it?' said the other. 'That's strange. I heard she had no life at all. Didn't she spend all her time in a convent?'

During those months away from home, Cáit was my *alter ego*, my 'secretary', and the channel of information to me about everything of importance that was happening in the world of the theatre and music. She kept closely in touch with the office, of course, and would relay what Joe Cremins talked about over the phone and in his visits to Booterstown Avenue. He had seen a photograph of me, with Monaghan and Doherty in our summer suits on the boardwalk in Atlantic City and thought we looked like 'three spivs out for the day'. In the month of September, as the Conference moved towards a conclusion, I was finding it difficult to sleep and from my bedroom in the Ritz-Carlton, I told Cáit why. 'It is hot', I said, 'but that is by now quite endurable: what gets us all down is the appalling humidity. We are wet all the time, and changing clothes and taking douches and showers is no good. We go to bed wet, we are wet all night and get up in that condition. How the Americans stick it year in year out I don't know. At the present time I am wet, I have hardly anything on, or covering me, and yet the damp, wet clamminess persists! To make matters worse we are now most of the time indoors and have cut out the 'free' Mondays. We worked twice last week from 10 a.m. until the early hours of the next day, and I only got back a little time ago from conferences that lasted all day. Two of these were small meetings of working and drafting groups where the work is close and detailed. You have to keep your eyes and ears open all the time. . . .'

The marathon had to end. I came home on the *Mauretania* and arrived at Cobh to be greeted aboard by Cáit who had been taken out by the local postmaster. We had a few days together in Tramore, before facing home.

I was plunged into the politics of European as distinct from worldwide broadcasting almost on the day I arrived in the G.P.O. Broadcasting of necessity requires to be regulated internationally, if only to control transmissions and regulate the division of the available frequencies. Ireland had been a member pre-war of the *Union Internationale de Rediffusion* which sought to fulfil that purpose in Europe, and had benefited from the various plans that had been worked out at Lucerne, Montreux and other places. We naturally had had no contacts with this body during the war, but when the war was over, an invitation was received to attend a meeting in Brussels, and to this meeting in the rich subterranean rooms of the Hotel Metropole I went with Leo McCauley of the Department of External Affairs and our own T. J. Monaghan. We were confronted there with proposals to wind up the U.I.R., whose headquarters had been in Geneva with a technical centre in Brussels, and to replace it with another body to be based entirely in Brussels. We began to hear allegations in the corridors of the hotel, which nobody ventured to substantiate, that the Secretary-General of the U.I.R. had not acted as independently vis-à-vis the Germans as he should have done during the war, so that the Brussels centre had been used by the Germans for their own purposes.

There appeared to be little truth in this, although one wonders how the Germans could have been kept out of the centre if they insisted on making improper use of it. Two Belgian technicians had since the war been punished by their government for collaboration: their names might have been on one of the sensational posters I saw stuck up all over Brussels at that time.

The meeting had been in progress for some days before the Russians arrived. They had never been a member of the U.I.R., were averse to having anything to do with it but soon made it known that too little time had passed since the end of the war for enemy and neutral nations to be treated as equals. They were privy to the proposal that the U.I.R. should be dissolved, and in its place that there should be a new body, *Organisation Internationale de Radiodiffusion* (O.I.R.) with new statutes and a new central location. The proposal involved giving full representation to seven federated republics of the U.S.S.R. (Carelia, Moldavia, Byleorussia, Ukraine, Estonia, Lithuania and Latvia) which were said to have absolute radio independence. That block of votes, with those of their European satellites (Poland, Czechoslovakia, Bulgaria and Yugoslavia) if conceded would have constituted a block of votes sufficient to influence every serious issue. France, similarly, appeared to be ranging support from countries that fell within their sphere of influence (Morocco, Algeria, Tunisia and Monte Carlo) so that the U.S.S.R. and France if they combined could have had an absolute majority.

When things had reached the point when it looked certain that the U.I.R. was about to disappear, a powerful Douglas aircraft was engaged to bring to Geneva almost 40 individuals representing member countries, including us three, to do what was needed. I remember being impressed by the contrast between that richly upholstered and spacious plane and the converted bomber that had carried us to Brussels from London. In Geneva, things did not go according to plan. There were days of debate, lunches by the lakeside, and all kinds of backstage manoeuvring before a motion to wind up the U.I.R. was voted upon – and defeated. Two negative votes – Switzerland, of course, and Franco Spain who had not been invited to the Conference in Brussels – in addition to a number of abstentions turned the tables. We were among the abstentionists, and had to accept vice-presidential office to maintain the U.I.R. in being. That involved me personally in many meetings abroad, in the company of Georges Conus, an indomitable little fellow from Swiss Radio, and representatives of Denmark, Italy and Turkey. There were protracted discussions with the B.B.C., who had left the U.I.R. in 1940 but were opposed to the O.I.R. plan. All the Scandinavian countries took the same line as we did and we worked closely with them.

At what was perhaps the first meeting of the Bureau of the U.I.R. which I attended at Ouchy-Lausanne some of the questions we had heard about in Brussels came up for consideration. One concerned the position of Mr de Reding, the Secretary-General of the organisation at the time it was said to have fallen under German influence. The allegations against him had not, of course, been made openly and were anything but specific. The most that the outgoing President of U.I.R., M. Glogg, could tell us was that in the course of his visits to London and Brussels he had encountered a certain reserve so far as the activities of de Reding during the war were concerned. In a Commission of Conciliation I had attended at the June Assembly in Geneva, the need for a purge had been mentioned but was not pressed when it was intimated that de Reding intended to tender his resignation. When I met my vice-presidential colleagues at the Ouchy Bureau meeting, I found them anxious that the removal of de Reding should not be overlooked, as the future of the Union depended on his ceasing to be connected with it. The issue was to be settled on consideration of a document purporting to be a report on the activities of the Union over seven years but which was in effect the apologia of an accused person, de Reding, and which, while conceivably well founded, contained statements which we were not in a position to verify. De Reding had also asked for a Commission of Enquiry. As a representative of a neutral country I had no intention of doing anything which would look like taking sides. At the same time I did not see any point in conceding a Commission of Enquiry which might well exculpate de Reding for lack of evidence, but would not satisfy those who were suspicious of him. I, therefore, at an early stage made it clear to the Bureau that it was not, in my opinion, its business to express views one way or the other on the tenor of the Report. I said that so far as I was aware no allegations had been formulated and that there could be no question of an enquiry in the absence of specific charges. This view was supported by the other members and, after considerable discussion, a resolution was adopted appreciating de Reding's desire to see his behaviour justified but rejecting the notion of an enquiry so long as precise facts were not forthcoming. We thereupon gave de Reding a discharge for the good government of his office in Geneva during 1944 and 1945, and we gave him an opportunity of saying a few words for incorporation in the minutes on the subject of rumour mongers.

In the course of time, and incidental to the hardening of East-West relations, the French and Belgians left the O.I.R., and accepted a B.B.C. initiative which led to the formation of what is to-day the very successful and harmonious European Broadcasting Union (E.B.U.). The original U.I.R. was absorbed in this body, the headquarters remained in Geneva and the technical centre in Brussels. Officerships and appointments were satisfactorily shared out and faces saved in a splendid compromise. Sir Ian Jacob, the Director General of the B.B.C., chaired the reconciling gathering at Torquay in February 1950, and European broadcasting owes a great deal to his ability and charm. I saw a good deal of him during that time and have a pleasant recollection of conversation that ranged far beyond our official preoccupations. He had been Churchill's military secretary in the war and he told me once, as we flew pleasantly across Europe to a meeting somewhere, of hazardous sea journeys, and of the untiring Churchill rousing the sickly Roosevelt in the middle of the night to put some brainwave to him. Jacob, of course, did not call them brainwaves. He found Churchill a great man to work for. He could be trying at times, of course, in forcing his point of view but yielded ultimately to his experts if they resisted strongly enough. He was a tough drinker, but Jacob believed he had some rare physical gift of being able to get rid of brandy, or whatever he drank, without doing damage to himself. He never wore pyjamas, and insisted on wearing a silken night shirt or vest which it was hard to get during the war. He had to have a clean one every time he went to bed, which he did twice a day. His staff resorted to ironing the used shirts, but Churchill raised Cain when he saw through their game.

As I said earlier, we had for some years given thought to the general question of an Irish television service, without any prompting from government or individual ministers. We could not possibly avoid the subject. It recurred in communications circles everywhere we went in Europe and America, and at home many thousands of people put up aerials to get the spill-over programmes from Britain. I remember that, when driving Jacob through a Dublin suburb, he pointed to the aerials and asked jokingly if we were thinking of paying something for the programmes. Sooner or later we were going to have television, that was evident, and as to the form in which it should come, we in the Post Office would be expected to have some ideas cut and dry for consideration by the government. In 1953, therefore, I set up a little committee in the department to consider the possibilities. Maurice Gorham was on it with me, as well as T. J. Monaghan, and Matt Doherty. We produced a couple of reports and these I showed to whoever at the time happened to be the Minister.

The abdication of Edward VIII in December 1936 had appeared to be a strictly English affair, but the Dominions, now sovereign states, had to pass their own legislation to regulate the situation insofar as it concerned them. In the Irish case de Valera moved to amend the existing Free State constitution by removing the remaining reference to the King and Governor-General, and simultaneously introduced an External Relations Bill which, when enacted, made the continuance of the King's Commonwealth powers dependent on the *ipse dixit* of the Irish government. That, with the Constitution of 1937, was the position when the first inter-party government with John A. Costello as Taoiseach took office in February 1948. One of its earliest acts was to fill the vacancy in the secretaryship of the Department of Posts and Telegraphs – the Post Office, as we liked to call it – caused by Joe Cremin's retirement. They appointed me, as

I must assume the outgoing government would have done.

De Valera would have preferred to have let the Anglo-Irish position rest as it then was but, among the constituent parties of the new government, there was a desire to clarify the situation. Were they essentially a republic, as Fianna Fáil claimed, or not? MacBride of Clann na Poblachta spoke of irritations that had survived in the External Relations Act, while Norton of official Labour regarded that Act as a fraud on the public. Costello for Fine Gael, in an address in Ottawa, referred to the inaccuracies and infirmities of the Act, and, later introduced a measure to repeal it altogether, stressing that the government's aim was to remove ambiguities and put Anglo-Irish relations on a better basis. The repeal measure was a Republic of Ireland Bill. The name of the country was to remain as it was set out in de Valera's 1937 constitution, Eire or Ireland, but the description of the state was to be as the title of the Bill indicated, the Republic of Ireland. The British reacted by passing into legislation a guarantee that there would be no question of ending partition without the consent of the Northern parliament; and thereafter used the word Eire when referring to the territory formerly of the Irish Free State, leaving the rest of the country as the territory of the Northern State. Whenever we could we tried to insist on the word Ireland; *Eire*, though it appeared on our stamps, being an embarrassment, Similarly the British seized on the appelation Irish Republic in preference to the Republic of Ireland, emphasising their strict view that the country was constitutionally and geographically divided.

The Republic of Ireland Act became operative on Easter Monday, the 18 April 1949, and the public celebrations, from which Mr de Valera and Fianna Fáil abstained, focused on the General Post Office building where my office was situated, because of its 1916 associations. We also had accommodation across the road from which the military parade could be viewed in comfort. There, with Cáit, I entertained the Taoiseach's and Tanaiste's wives, Mrs Costello and Mrs Norton. I suppose, looking around me I wondered what the future had in store for Ireland, for the Post Office and myself. I was never happy personally with our national preoccupation with status, and I would have preferred if the G.P.O. was allowed to get on with its job and not be so often a venue for public meetings and military parades. However, the future was to be kind and my own career as head of a department largely uneventful though on two occasions I had to take legal advice as to whether I should sue newspapers about references that I considered libellous. I followed the advice that was given to me in both instances: in one a newspaper corrected what they had said and paid a sum in damages; in the other, counsel advised me not to press the case. These were relatively small matters and I would not mention them except that they bring to mind an occasion when the French conductor Jean Martinon, obviously very hurt, asked me whether he should proceed against a newspaper critic of his performances. His lawyers had advised him not to. I agreed: though I entirely disliked the form of the comment from which he was suffering. I doubted whether in a matter of opinion he, a foreigner, with limited competence in the English language, was certain to win with an Irish jury.

My family underwent a transformation in the fifties. Both my parents were dead, four of my children were married, and we had gone to live on the Stillorgan Road. The new house was not as big as No. 3 Booterstown Avenue, and it lacked anything like the old-fashioned kitchen which in Booterstown had enabled the girls who worked for us to enjoy with their friends a form of Gaeltacht life, but it was big enough to entertain my colleagues on the Council of the European Broadcasting Union when they came to Dublin for the first time. A common practice at these international meetings is for the host country to set a day aside to take the guests on a tour of the surrounding countryside. Dublin was well placed to do this, the only problem, and it was a serious problem thirty years ago, was to find a hotel which could be relied on to serve a good meal attractively. Maurice Gorham and I thought we had better look around ourselves before settling the itinerary. We had lunch in a place in Co Wicklow that would today be entirely suitable, I am sure, but that day as we finished our meal we were witnesses of an extraordinary sight. A bloated tom-cat jumped up on a side-table near us where the waitress had left a jug of the cream we had been having with our sweet and coffee, stuck his paw down deep into it, pulled out the paw, and before our eyes, licked the cream off it! We did not bring the European broadcasters to that hotel! I could hear some of them saying, 'how Irish'!

On the way back to town that night, having looked at other possibilities, we went into a pub near Brittas for a night cap. As we sat there, a local came up to share with us his knowledge of the countryside. 'Did you ever hear tell of Robert Emmet?' he enquired. We confessed that we did, but I said nothing of what I had written about the man. 'Well, I'll tell you', he said, 'who gave him away'. He gave us the name of a family and went into details about 'their seed, breed and generation'. The information may not have been accurate – and I am not saying that it was not – but I remembered from that occasion how much could still be recalled of an event that occurred a full century and a half earlier and wondered how long it would be, with radio and television, till this sort of folk memory disappeared.

I continued to travel, and in 1953 paid my first visit behind the Iron Curtain to Warsaw. That Poland was almost hermetically sealed became apparent as soon as I went looking for an air ticket; only one airway – through Amsterdam – was open from the West which meant a full plane of western administrators from Schipol. Travelling into Warsaw by bus we had our first look at what the city had gone through in the war and the efforts that were being made to restore it. There were ruins on all sides, and the new buildings were nothing more than ugly blocks of concrete. In the area where we were to live considerable progress towards normality had been made, however; 'the old city' had largely been restored and most of the conferenciers were deposited in a new skyscraper hotel. Not far away the Church of the Holy Cross was in fair condition and was endlessly crowded whenever I was there, but dominating the scene from every direction was the vast Palace of Culture which Stalin had conferred on the Poles and a perpetual reminder to them of their enslavement. The organisation of the conference being in the hands of an international union was as efficient as any I had attended, and the Polish administration, it must be said, made a brave attempt to entertain us. When by the end of a fortnight the major appointments in the Union which had brought me out had been made I was able to go home via East Berlin.

Frank Duff had asked me to make enquiries about the

mysterious disappearance of a pioneering Polish legionary, a man who had spent some time in Ireland after the war and with whom Frank had travelled to Cork by bicycle. He lived down towards the Czechoslovakian frontier and my official commitments prevented me from going to see him. I therefore wrote to him and asked him to come to Warsaw, but he did not turn up and, having no other means of looking for him, I went to the British Embassy, the secretary of which I had discovered was married to a Barry Egan from Cork city, and he very generously took up the quest, though without success. Frank's friend appeared to have vanished into thin air.

In the second half of the fifties there was a second interparty government, followed by a period when for the last time de Valera functioned as Taoiseach, and appointed Neil Blaney to be our Minister. He came in March 1957 and was gone by Christmas. He had promised well, I thought. I remember going with him to Sligo to open something or other and was pleased with the use he made of a draft speech we had given him, adding to it advantageously as he thought the circumstances demanded. He might be good, I thought, on the Post Office side. But he got off on the wrong foot as regards broadcasting. He, or the government of which he was spokesman, delayed about endorsing the powers of Comhairle Radio Eireann; he told the Dáil that the government had neither made up its mind about a statutory corporation or the introduction of television. That was in May. It was six months later, in response to a request from the Department for decisions to enable us to deal with applications that had begun to come in from British programme contractors and others, that he announced that Ireland, without cost to the State, was to have a television service. It would be largely commercial in character, and proposals from private interests for the concession would be welcomed. The popular discussion of this prospect had hardly begun, however, when a newspaper report of a speech by Mr Blaney at the party's Ard-Fheis put the cat among the pigeons. On the subject of a greater independence for Radio Eireann he was reported as saying that the very arguments in favour of this were the strongest arguments against it, that since Radio Eireann had got some freedom with its own Director and Comhairle, the programmes had disimproved. That was not how the Director and his staff saw it. They were in fact quite outraged; and so worked up was a member of the repertory company that he openly insulted the Minister at a public dinner and had to be suspended. We could not have an employee behaving like that to our Minister, whatever the provocation.

I myself, as soon as I read the newspaper report, made enquiries and understood that the offending passage in the report of the Minister's speech was a quotation from something that had been said on the floor of the Ard-Fheis, and a statement to that effect was put out by the Government Information Bureau some days later. That it was not issued immediately made my position vis-à-vis the Comhairle very difficult. They were demanding an apology, and threatening to resign. However, the situation ended with the transfer of Blaney to another department, a step which Mr de Valera told me he had planned for some time and which had nothing at all to do with Blaney's speech. For their part the Comhairle were happy to forget the prospect of having to resign; they looked to a happier time under the new Minister, Sean Ormonde.

A lot of proposals came in as a result of the announcement welcoming applications for the television concession. Some promoters came to the Department for interview. Those from across the channel, had one of them been acceptable, might have given us something like the service Ulster Television now puts out. An exotic submission came from a continental group in which a stateless individual was the outstanding figure. This gentleman was first made known to me by the Foreign Manager of one of our banks. He had been introduced to them by a Swiss Bank and had deposited a substantial sum of money as an indication that there was plenty more where that came from. He knew nothing whatever about Ireland but, hiring a car, he made a rapid tour, spoke to some people and then formulated his proposals. These essentially asked for a licence to broadcast commercial radio programmes on short, medium and long waves to Britain, Europe and the eastern seaboard of the United States, in return for television stations he would build in Ireland. When he discovered on his tour that we had a language problem, he promptly said that all Gaeltacht families would be given a free television set. What he was after was permission to set up a sort of Radio Luxembourg, which had started business as a pirate station and was still under something of a cloud in international broadcasting circles. I didn't think that was the sort of reputation we would have wanted to acquire. There was other obvious, and to us, seemingly overwhelming, legal and technical difficulties, but the foreign gentleman produced a body of experts from abroad to argue how these could be overcome. He found plenty of support in Ireland, too, for his ideas. Directors of a number of semi-state bodies, led by an Irish industrialist, came to see me and urged that this particular application should be accepted. The industrialist went out of his way to tell me ever so bluntly that I, a Civil Servant, had nothing to lose unlike this promoter who was risking his own good money!

That case apart, we knew that a good deal of lobbying was going on for the television concession. But the government left us very much in the dark and we naturally feared that an unhappy choice could well be made if an individual group was put into a monopoly position. However, in March 1958, the government handed over all the applications to a Commission of twenty persons presided over by a High Court judge, with terms of reference that aimed at ensuring that no charge should fall on the Exchequer and that the control of programmes would rest with a public authority. We were not consulted about the Commission, its terms of reference or its personnel, among whom there was a fair amount of dead wood, and nobody was appointed to the Commission from either the Department or Radio Eireann. We had, of course, to provide the secretariat and any technical assistance that was required.

The Commission concluded its work in May 1959 and presented a majority report, a minority report, and a number of separate reservations. These were published, but the recommendations on the various applications were not. Then an extraordinary *volte face* occurred. The government, again without consultation with us, but obviously returning to our television committee's reports, rejected the views of the Commission and proceeded to set up a statutory authority to run both television and radio without any commercial promoters whatever. This authority was to receive a repayable capital sum to get it under way, and would finance its activities by licence fees to be collected through the Post Office, and by advertisements. The announcement to this effect was made by Michael Hilliard who had taken over from Sean Ormonde, and it was he who was to steer the necessary legislation, the Broadcasting Authority Bill, through the Oireachtas. My official connexion with broadcasting more or less ended at that point. The mantle of culture left the G.P.O. for good, and I believe it was for good in both meanings of the word.

Maurice Gorham in his book on Irish broadcasting's forty years suggests that the government's change of policy might have been influenced by what I had said when giving evidence at the Commission. I had got Ormonde's permission to express my personal views and I remember saying that I would prefer that Ireland should have no television at all if the alternative was to allow private commercial interests to take over. But I can only surmise as to how the government's final decision was arrived at. Sean Lemass, who a couple of months before had taken over as Taoiseach from de Valera, had no doubt a lot to do with it. He asked me to go and see him. The interview was brief. I was concerned, I told him, about the quality of programmes. We were fortunately placed in close proximity to what was probably the best service in the world, the BBC, an entirely public service organisation, and I suggested that we might explore the possibility of a special arrangement for an extension of their service as a back-up to such programmes of quality as we could produce at home on a similar public service basis. He made no comment, but as I spoke of the BBC I felt that the chauvinists among us would not take too well to any arrangement with the *British* Broadcasting Corporation. Lemass was said to be 'looking for things to do'. Here was something that had been a long time coming; now it was to be pushed at all speed. And, indeed, the television service was got under way in a remarkably short time; only nineteen months elapsed from the appointment of the Broadcasting Authority for Radio Eireann and Telefís Eireann and the commencement of regular transmissions. We in the Post Office were able to give the Authority the 24-acre site at Montrose, and had already identified the most suitable sites for VHF sound and television transmitters.

Lemass was a pragmatist. At the outset of his period in Industry and Commerce he had put Ireland behind a high tariff wall, but later reversed this policy to suit early joint entry with Britain into the Common Market. He had also seized an opportunity which my colleague Ken Whitaker recommended to him to meet the Northern Premier in Belfast, which seemed to indicate his belief that the two governmental entities in the small island of Ireland should work together for their mutual and common good. One immediate benefit of this meeting was that we, civil servants, could call the Northern state and government by the name they recognised and cease hiding behind allusions to the 'six counties'. With such a practical mind it was not at all surprising that Lemass would change his mind about television and that some of the people who had been identified with commercial submissions to the Commission and were active in his party had to reconcile themselves to the change. I may have been blamed for this. If so it would explain why, when on the last day of 1961, the world and his wife were invited to the opening blow-out in the Gresham Hotel, Cáit and I were not. Somebody or bodies who had been elected to the Authority did not like us. They did not like Maurice Gorham either. Otherwise they would have appointed this most cultivated Irishman who had unequalled experience of all forms of broadcasting to be their Director-General instead of an unknown and relatively inexperienced American.

Lemass threatened to be critical of Telefís Eireann from the start, not of the programmes which might have been more to the point but of the Authority's attitude to public policy. He made this clear to Hilliard who seemed frightened whenever the Taoiseach called him on the phone and I happened to be in the room. I suspect Lemass 'bossed' some of his colleagues, and left a quiet man like Hilliard without words when, for example, he was told that the Authority's concept of being free and independent was being pushed to an intolerable extent. The government, Lemass insisted, had not set up the television service for the purpose of publicising criticisms of national policy or arousing opposition to it and it would have to be understood that national policy was what the government of the day decided it to be. Telefís Eireann would have to be wholly supportive of that line and he would not hesitate to change the legislation or the composition of the Authority in order to ensure that they did so. It was like as if we were back to the days when the Department of Education laid it down that Irish history was to be employed as an instrument of national edification. The issue was not pursued, however, when Lemass retired in poor health. He died in 1971.

By the end of that year death had also taken the last of Cáit's immediate relatives, her sister Eileen. Harry had preceded Eileen by a number of years as had Cáit's parents and mine. My three brothers, Paddy, Séamus and Tommy, remained, two of them younger than I, but when all three died I was left like Oisín after the Fianna, as the Gaels used to say.

However, I must not anticipate. Ten years earlier – in 1961 to be precise, Cáit and I had the holiday of a lifetime. We flew to Paris and on by train to Rome via the Italian Riviera. In Rome an old Finance friend, Leo McCauley, who was now our ambassador to the Holy See, arranged a private papal audience and entertained us to lunch in the Villa Spada. Cáit, whose knee had been giving her some trouble, asked me to ensure that, having knelt to Pope John as she intended to do, she would be able to get up again. In fact any intervention on my part was unnecessary. The much-loved Holy Father would not allow her to kneel! When she moved to do so he put an arm around her and drew her towards him and blessed her. We went straight from the audience to St Peter's and Cáit was enthralled when we received Holy Communion almost immediately in the Blessed Sacrament chapel. She saw Providence at work in a wonderful sequence in which she was being allowed to participate. Woman-like, she had gone to great trouble to prepare for the meeting with the Pope, and had kissed and hugged the lady who told her in the pensione that in her all-black outfit she looked perfect.

From Rome we went to Salerno and up into the mountains to a villa above Ravello. The climb by stone steps from the village distressed Cáit so much that I thought we would never get to the top; but when we reached the villa, she recovered immediately, and lost herself in the beauty that surrounded her, especially the view of the islands of Majora and Minora down below in the Mediterranean. There was an ugly side to the idyllic life of Ravello, however. 'The morning we were leaving', she told our daughter Nóirín in a letter, 'we saw two men hoist a basket of sand on to the back of an oldish woman, and it was so heavy it took the two of them all their time to lift it. She bent like a beast of burden and took it on the back of her neck, and off with her struggling up the sixty and more steps to where our villa was situated. I shivered to look at her. . . . How little we know how the other half lives.'

From Ravello we went to Capri, and from there to Montreux. Cáit found it strange arriving at Geneva on the way 'after all the years since our honeymoon there'. For one thing we now came by air; and the place, with all its modern blocks of flats, looked more prosperous than as she remembered it. She started a letter home as soon as she settled into a bedroom which had three windows and a small balcony overlooking the blue of the lake of Geneva. She was resting, she told them, before going out to a *diner aux chandelles*, in the hall of the Knights of the *Chateau de Chillon* which was being given as part of a Television Exhibition in which the International Telecommunication Union was involved. The occasion was so marvellous as to be beyond imagining: yet Cáit, I believe, enjoyed it even more than anyone else among the guests. I had known almost from the day I first met her of her love for Byron's poetry. She knew *The Prisoner of Chillon*, the story of the national martyr Francois de Bonnivard, largely off by heart, and understood its historical significance. In the chateau that night I could read in her eyes how she was reacting to the words:

Chillon! thy prison is a holy place
And thy sad floor an altar – for 't was trod,
Until his very steps have left a trace
Worn, as if thy cold pavement were a sod,
By Bonnivard! May now these marks efface!
For they appeal from tyranny to God.

Looking back on that Paris – Rome – Ravello – Montreux holiday, our second honeymoon she called it, Cáit said she had something to think of for the rest of her life even if she never went away again. She did go away again, on other honeymoons. We had wonderful holidays in Vienna, Munich and the Bavarian Alps in 1964, and in Portugal. Labour troubles in the Department forced me to cut short my stay there, but Cáit's sister replaced me, and together they had a fortnight in Cascais to which in recollection they often returned. It is strange how amid beauty on the grand scale the memory of small things remains fixed in one's mind. One morning, on the way to Innsbruck and Salzburg, our bus stopped at a small town on the German border. We went into the parish church to say a prayer. It was full of soldiers at a requiem for a comrade: that was impressive, but what held our attention and stirred us so that as I write I can hear it was Bach's double violin concerto being played in the organ loft!

In August 1966 Cáit received a letter which amused her, and me when she showed it to me. It came from Archie Potter, a friend of ours from the world of music who heard when on holidays in Paris that I had died and he wrote to offer sympathy. It was a charming letter but its object was misplaced and should have gone to the relatives of a namesake of mine. It was, however, refreshing to read into Archie's obituary that some people, at least, approved of things I had been trying to do.

I was in my last civil service year, 1966-67, when Jack Lynch replaced Lemass as Taoiseach and unwittingly created a problem for me and my staff by appointing Erskine Childers to take charge of both Transport and Power and Posts and Telegraphs. Childers was to have a Parliamentary Secretary, Paddy Lalor, with special responsibility for the latter department. That seemed to be all right, the amalgamation being justified by the diminution of the Post Office as a result of the broadcasting developments; and the appointment of a parliamentary secretary looked like a return to the Blythe/Heffernan situation in the days of the first government. But we reckoned without Childers. Lalor was the first to arrive in the G.P.O. and we immediately installed him in what had for years been the Minister's room. But then Childers came along and made it known that he had not come on a passing visit! As Minister for Transport and Power he had an office in Kildare Street but he also intended to function fully as Minister for Posts and Telegraphs from the G.P.O. and would oversee from there the duties he proposed to assign to his parliamentary secretary. Accommodation was always tight in the G.P.O. but we fixed Lalor up with an office in our solitary small waiting room. In these circumstances, the general staff naturally looked to me for a direction as to whether their submissions should go to Childers or to Lalor, and Lalor, greatly distressed, began to wonder about his political position once his 'small boy' status became known. My personal relations with Childers began to disimprove. We had worked well together in the forties: now, a senior man, he was much more assertive and from the moment of his arrival started to send minutes to me in a flood. Civil servants in other departments he had been in told me about this practice of his and had indeed asked for advice as to how to deal with it; writing minutes to the Minister could deflect senior officials unduly from their proper duties. I must say I did not like the prospect one bit, but with my retirement coming up I kept going.

By now, I was involved in the development of communication satellites both on a global and European basis, had entered into an arrangement to take a modest share in the British station at Goonhilly Down, and had signed for Ireland the documents that emerged from a plenipotentiary conference in Washington. I flew to the United States for that purpose but came home by boat. There were few travellers aboard for some reason and I found myself many times alone on deck in mid-Atlantic. One day, straying into a saloon where a dancing class was being taken through the cha-cha, I was grabbed and made to partner a lady who stood forlorn on the wide, scantily occupied floor. I was never much of a dancer, but here was a case of *toujours la politesse*. I don't think she was sorry when at the first opportunity I left her.

It was on an August afternoon in 1967 that, after roughly twenty years occupancy of the Secretary's job I left the G.P.O. and never once went back to it. While I was putting a few personal things together to take away with me, Childers rang to thank me for my services and to wish me well. That was nice; though with our rooms beside each other, it would have been nicer still if he had come to my room to say his good-bye or made an opportunity to say it in his. Maybe he had sensed my uneasiness about the parliamentary secretary situation. In any event I left the building quietly and went home by bus. The official entertainment came later, from my Post Office colleagues and the heads of the other government departments. All of these were, and remain, my friends. I had no feeling of regret at leaving the communications field, however, though I remember with satisfaction that when a vacancy had arisen some years earlier for a Secretary-General in the International Telecommunication Union, the State Department in Washington made it known that they would like to see my name among the applicants.

EIGHT

ANOTHER career, aspects of which I had already savoured and liked, was now beckoning to me. It was to devote all my time to research and writing. Ever since my old landlady in Booterstown had told me about Madden the man and the writer I had been working on a biography of him, pursuing him everywhere he had travelled, collecting what I could about him and digesting his many books. That biography was one I had to finish in my retirement, and as I could not discern much interest among publishers for an English language life of him, I turned to producing one in Irish.

There were many other subjects involving research that attracted me. Before I left the Civil Service I had done an article for *Studies* that caused me to look at the sequence of priests who from the earliest days had taught Irish in the National Seminary in Maynooth – Paul O'Brien, Martin Loftus, James Tully (for 48 years), Michael Logue, Eugene O'Growney – and then Michael O'Hickey who in the eyes of Irish language enthusiasts became something of a national martyr. He is regarded in that sense still by some people; and it was to enable me to make up my mind as to whether he is entitled to be so regarded that I paid particular attention to him. He had occupied the chair of Irish from 1896 till 1908, though his knowledge of Irish, especially of the vernacular, was never profound, and he was a poor teacher. He was, however, an outstanding propagandist for the revival of Irish both inside and outside the College, was at one time a Vice-President of the Gaelic League, and had engaged in various controversies with government departments and boards of education. It was in this capacity, as a defender of Irish as a bulwark against a national disintegration he saw threatening, that he confronted the Standing Committee of the bishops over the question of Irish as a compulsory subject for admittance to Birrell's new National University. That was an issue on which the bishops insisted there was room for a point of view other than that being strenuously advocated by the Gaelic League. Their own opinion was that Irish should not be a compulsory subject; in that they agreed with Dr William Delaney, the Jesuit head of the Catholic University College, who argued that neither the students nor the Irish language were ready for such a regulation.

It was something other than the issue of Irish for matriculation which really landed O'Hickey in trouble, namely his use of intemperate language and his obstinacy. Things were not being made easy for the College authorities at that time by the existence among the students for the priesthood of an ultra-patriotic group known as the Sheikhs, one of whom was a pugnacious young Northener who declared that what the College needed was a proper spirit of insubordination. He had to be expelled, naturally, and went to America to find a bishop who was prepared to ordain him. O'Hickey, egged on to a degree by these students, wrote a paper that was published in *Sinn Féin* in which, speaking of the members of the University Senate, which included two archbishops and Dr Delaney, he declared that he could entertain no hope that they would acquit themselves in a manner befitting Irishmen and were more likely to identify themselves with the enemies of Ireland. In such circumstances he told the students that he could do nothing but recommend the Senators to their prayers. There was no reason to think that these remarks had been made in a jocular spirit: so he was rebuked by the bishops, yet given a chance to mend his ways. He did not take the chance. Instead he expressed his profound conviction that by the part he had taken in the public controversy that had ensued he had done the College and the interests of religion a service. He was then dismissed, and all efforts on his part to get Rome to reverse the decision came to nought. In the prolonged and bitter debate about how he had been treated most of the pro-Gaelic League journals supported him, but D. P. Moran, the editor of the *Leader*, appeared to me to have spoken wisely when he wondered whether the authorities of Maynooth had in anything they had done exceeded their rights in regard to a man whom they had charged with the education of the students. After all one expects discipline in a seminary, and concentration on institutional priorities. O'Hickey was obviously leading in the opposite direction.

The year before I left the government service, the fiftieth anniversary of the Easter Rising was being commemorated and I had done a book on that subject which the reviewer in *Irish Historical Studies* perceived as the most original contribution that had been made to the study of that event. As the Civil Service head of the Post Office for twenty years and working in the G.P.O. I was uniquely placed to say something fresh about what had happened at the very centre of the Rising, and particularly about Arthur Hamilton Norway, my predecessor who had been in the building on the morning of Easter Monday.

Like myself, Norway had interests outside the job. He had written travel books and a commentary on Dante's *Divine Comedy*. His wife had written a little book of reminiscences of Easter Week, and one of their sons, the novelist Nevil Shute, had in his autobiography touched on his experiences. So it was unlikely, I felt, that Norway would have allowed what happened to him to pass without written comment. I determined to explore this possibility. I was aware somehow that Nevil's widow was still alive, and one night from a West End hotel in London I rang her, told her who I was, and what I was looking for. She was most kind. The family papers, she told me, were at that moment on the high seas on their way back from South Africa where Nevil had died. She would go through them as soon as they reached her and if she found anything like what I was looking for she would send it to me. Within weeks I had in my possession a typescript giving what a sports writer might call a blow by blow account of everything that happened to Norway that Easter. He had been in his room on the Monday when the Under Secretary, Sir Mathew Nathan, called him on the phone and asked him to come at once to Dublin Castle. A plan was being prepared to make large-scale arrests of Sinn Féiners and it was necessary to deny them access to all telephone and telegraph facilities. In the Castle, Nathan was telling Norway of the arrival of Sir Roger Casement by submarine from Germany and of a German arms ship that had been captured when they heard the shots being fired that killed the policeman on duty at the Castle Gate. From that point, Norway's story developed to its inevitable end, a feature of which was that he had to protest personally in London against the indiscriminate dismissal of members of his staff accused of participating in the Rising, and was instrumental in having a committee of enquiry set up which acted as a brake on the military. At his instance, also, the Postmaster-General, Persse, told the Prime Minister that the allegation that the postal service was honeycombed with Sinn Féiners would not on investigation prove to be accurate.

It was this account that sent me looking at Nathan's beautifully bound papers in the Bodleian Library in Oxford and those of Asquith that are deposited in the same place. Going through the Asquith papers I experienced the thrill of finding Patrick Pearse's letter to his mother, and the poems he wrote on the eve of his execution and, what was more important historically, the summary prepared for the Prime Minister which revealed that the Director of Military Intelligence had a full month's warning of the Rising; a piece of entirely accurate information that had not been acted on. One of Pearse's poems was to his mother, the other to his brother Willie, whose life Patrick believed would be spared but who in fact had to face the firing squad. The letter and the poems, written in Arbour Hill Barracks, had been withheld from the Pearse family by the British Commander-in-Chief, General Sir John Maxwell, because of what he considered to be their triumphalist character. He sent them to Asquith instead. Their appearance in print gave my book an extra dimension.

The search through Nathan's papers disclosed many things, including his fondness for female company. One of his lady friends was Dorothy Stopford, the historian Alice Stopford Green's niece, about whom I have written recently in my book on Protestant Nationalists, and whom I had met as the wife of Liam Price, the antiquarian who was a colleague of mine on the Irish Folklore Commission. She had done tremendous work for tubercular children and saved a family Cáit and I were interested in. Amber Blanco White, another lady friend of Nathan's, intrigued me a lot, and I went to see her in her Hampstead home when I was working on the 1916 book. A rather scruffy-looking maid led me to a room that had a number of good pictures on the walls. Amber arrived almost immediately, shook hands, and stretched herself out on a chaise longue. Her looks belied her years. She was still a beautiful woman and promised at first to be communicative. But when we had talked a little about her immediately personal problems – her husband was lying ill upstairs and the maids from Ireland were troublesome – she turned to the subject of Nathan but deliberately avoided any reference to her intimate correspondence with him that I had already seen. She spoke of their association with cold detachment. She had met him, she said, on some committee or other when she was in the Ministry of Labour and he in Pensions after his removal from his post in Ireland. He was a dear, charming, impressive-looking man, but a philanderer, a man who thought women existed to serve him; a bit of a humbug too, she thought, and not very sincere. She could have told me more about her own past, her affair with H. G. Wells, by whom she had a child, her role in at least one of his novels. But that, as the lawyers might say, was not *ad rem*. I thanked her, bid her good-bye, and sometimes wondered in later years whether she read the chapter in my 1916 book in which I said some of these things about her.

A third lady I encountered in Nathan's correspondence was Constance Fletcher who, as Constance Heppel-Marr or Constance Spry, made a niche for herself in contemporary society. Her father George Fletcher, shared the secretaryship of the old Department of Agriculture and Technical Instruction in Dublin with T. P. Gill, formerly an Irish parliamentarian. I knew both of them slightly. I had consulted Gill when writing my Parnell book. He and Fletcher were adepts at passing the buck. Fletcher once wrote on a paper, 'Yours I think' and sent it to Gill. Gill sent it back in a hurry with the words, 'Thoughtful but inaccurate'. Constance emerged from the Rising with distinction. She was awarded a medal by the order of St John of Jerusalem for organising a hospital and attending to casualties under fire. English like her father, she did not like Ireland. After 1916 and Nathan's dethronement 'all was dust and ashes'; she would prefer to wash dishes in England than remain in so benighted a country, but as Constance Spry, the floral decorator, she did rather better than that for herself.

To Nathan's female acquaintances I should add two of his relatives who, having learned of my book which I had subtitled *The Story of Mathew Nathan*, came from London to see me. They knew absolutely nothing about Ireland, understandably, but Cáit and I were delighted to entertain them, and our daughter Nóirín drove them to see Nathan's lodge in the Phoenix Park, by then for many years the residence of the Papal Nuncio. The evening they left Dublin they were asking questions. 'Mr Ó Broin', one of them said, 'do you have any colonies?'

In 1967, the year I retired, a biographical essay of mine on *Charles Gavan Duffy* was published. I had written it at intervals during a boring conference. The suggestion that I should write it came from the firm which had published so much of the literary by-products of the Young Ireland movement of which Charles Gavan Duffy had been a co-founder, but this had also been the wish of Louise, Duffy's youngest daughter, who was a friend of mine. She collaborated closely with me, supplied background family information, and read my script. She was a remarkable woman. Having spent her youth in the south of France, she came to Ireland, became an educationalist of distinction, and an Irish language pioneer. She was one of the first graduates of Birrell's University, taught in Pearse's school for girls, Scoil Ide, and afterwards at the Dominican Training College in Eccles Street. Later, in partnership with Annie McHugh who married Ernest Blythe, she opened Scoil Bhríde, a school in which Irish predominated, and was its principal until 1940. This was a strange development in Louise's life, for she was a grown girl before she became aware that there was such a thing as an Irish language. Her father had kept this fact from her.

Louise was also a founder member of Cumann na mBan,

the women's auxiliary of the Irish Volunteers, and served on its executive until 1922. During Easter Week she was in the G.P.O. under her former headmaster, but made it clear to him from the outset that she disagreed with what he and his colleagues were doing and did not wish to have anything to do with the actual fighting. She was utterly upright, frank and fearless. She told me that when her father died, the Irish nationalists of the day insisted that he should be brought from Nice to be laid before the high altar in Dublin's Pro-Cathedral and given a public funeral. This entailed considerable expense which the family naturally assumed the Irish people would meet, but that was not done, and the Duffys were left with a burden they were ill-fitted to carry. I wanted to tell that story in the biography, but Louise would not allow me. But why should it go unrecorded? It surely has a moral for us all.

When Louise felt that her own call to glory was not to be long deferred, she disposed of her keepsakes. To Frank Duff, in whose Legion of Mary she had worked, she gave the gold insignia of her father's knighthood, expecting perhaps that it would be incorporated in a chalice or monstrance. But Frank had a sense of history and handed them over to me to ensure they were returned to Australia. There they really belonged, he said; it was for Australians to say what should be done with them. What Louise gave me for myself I have retained, a drawing of her father when he was the young editor of *The Nation*, a photograph of him, who had been the Prime Minister of Victoria, old and bearded, and a scrapbook entitled *Ars Vitae*.

I suppose the fact that I was working on the Gavan Duffy book was one of the reasons why in that year 1967, Cáit and I had a holiday in Cannes, not, I hasten to say, in one of those luxurious hotels on the sea front which you see on the postcards, but in the upper town in a villa rented to us by a community of nuns who fed us, allowed us to go to Mass in their convent, and were generally charming. We went over a couple of times to Nice where the Duffys had lived and were shown around by friends of Louise. It was a lovely inexpensive holiday. The provision the municipality made for visitors enabled us to go bathing every day as splendidly as if from any one of the privately-owned strips of beach. We were in and out of Monaco and St Tropez, went to see Matisse's chapel at Vence and visited St Raphael which was the honeymoon address the first owners had given to our house on Stillorgan Road. We spent a day, too, on Lerins, the little island standing off the coast where St Patrick may once have studied in a colony of ascetics. The ascetic life is still practised in an abbey on the island but how it is done among crowds of flimsily-attired trippers is a cause for wonder.

My reading in Oxford had convinced me that a necessary complement to a book on Nathan was one on Augustine Birrell whose Irish career had begun on the night a crowd of Gaelic Leaguers and Sinn Féiners rioted in the Abbey Theatre against Synge's *Playboy* and ended in the ruins of a rebellion he had failed to prevent. I had looked elsewhere for his papers with little success. But before going down to Southampton to embark on a three weeks cruise with which we had planned to start our retirement, Cáit and I worked for some days side by side in the Bodleian Library exploring what I could find about him there. This was exceedingly profitable.

The cruise went extraordinarily well. The weather was splendid, the sea undisturbed and on the days we went ashore there was always something special to see. We visited the shrine of St James the Apostle at Compostela, looked at Mount Etna, had a day in Malta, listened to a fine talk in the blazing sun at Corinth – I remember de Valera's enquiry as to whether Paul ever got a reply to his long letters to his friends there – all of that and more in Mediterranean waters before we came back to Gibraltar and down by the coast of Africa to Madeira where Cáit and I surprised ourselves by doing a mad toboganning ride over the cobblestones.

In a diary that Cáit kept during the cruise she hints that I was tired, and spent a lot of time either sleeping on deck or lazing in the swimming pool. She enjoyed herself strenuously, dressing up in what for her were unusual togs, sampling various foods at *al fresco* lunches, improvising for fancy dress balls with costumes made of coloured papers, going to the miniature race meetings, trying her luck at bingo, and, of course, meeting people. At table we had an English couple who could have come straight out of 'The Archers', a radio serial Cáit had followed for years.

In Piraeus where our ship, the *Andes*, had docked we received an invitation to lunch with the PTT people, and that meant, first and foremost, for Cáit as it would for any woman, a hair-do. Having no Greek was a problem but as Cáit said in a diary she kept for consumption at home, 'We used our brains. Daddy first saw a barber's and from the lettering outside we deduced the whereabouts of a ladies hairdresser. A man sitting outside the barber's showed us across the street and into a building where he rang for a lift. He said nothing at all so we thought he was a deaf mute. I got panicky then and made Daddy come with me. It was up a couple of floors and we emerged into a lovely modern salon. Immediately they took me on. A beautiful young Greek girl, a real artist, had the whole thing done in no time. We could not speak to each other, but with hand signs and smiles we succeeded, and I don't think I've ever had as nice a set. Daddy meantime went across again to the man who took him inside and gave him an old-fashioned scissors hair cut, but a really good one. We came back to the ship and got togged up in our best. I wore my pink Moygashel. Then our hosts arrived and took us to the most exclusive place in Athens, the Royal Yacht Club. What a setting, what colour, the Club itself dazzling white with creeping flowers of red and yellow and blue, and on the balcony on both sides glass cages full of birds of every conceivable hue chattering and whistling as they hopped about. We had lunch in the open just above the King's yacht. . . .'

I was glad to get back to Birrell when the cruise was over. I had come to have some kind of fellow-feeling for the poor old fellow. Up to the last minute he had appeared to be a successful Minister. He had been the political head of the British government in Ireland for nine years, much longer than any predecessor. The Chief Secretaryship was recognised to be a difficult post, one that politicians did not seek – indeed they tried hard sometimes to avoid being given it, although it carried a normal ministerial salary and the house in the Phoenix Park that is now the residence of the American Ambassador. Birrell held the job because that was what his leader Asquith wished. Between those two men there was an unusual bond of affection which showed up at its most painful best when Birrell resigned in 1916. Birrell was so upset that he could not remember what words were spoken when he took leave of the Prime Minister in his room in the House of Commons; and Asquith, jingling some coins in his pocket, just stood at the window and wept.

Birrell likewise was liked by the leaders of the Irish Parliamentary Party, with whom he worked in an easy relationship. They had no doubts about his love for Ireland, and his desire to see her prosper. He was 'sold' on home rule though he confessed to Lloyd George that it was the most unlucky cause a mortal man was ever associated with, its path being strewn with ghosts and skeletons. One of the things I was able to establish was that, with Birrell's approval, Nathan conducted detailed consultations with the Irish Party leaders for the takeover of Irish government as soon as the war was over. Birrell, and no doubt Nathan also, avoided the Kildare Street Club, ate in pubs and small restaurants, went regularly to the Abbey Theatre, and devoured the output of the Irish literary figures of the day. His ex-officio position on the Local Government and Congested District Boards enabled him to see a great deal of the Irish countryside and especially the West where he placed a mentally handicapped son in lodgings. His wife was also an invalid, and for a politician seeking during the war to maximise the recruiting figures for the armed forces, he had the misfortune to have an artistic son who was a conscientious objector. A revealing passage in his autobiography that I return to often describes a recruiting meeting in Galway which he attended with the Lord Lieutenant and John Redmond, the leader of the Irish Party. 'It was a really huge assemblage,' it runs, 'and had the cause been really popular, and had Redmond been a Dan O'Connell, they should have sworn in lusty recruits by the thousand . . . but the soul was not there and how should it be? The folk who love fighting were gone or going, for the love of fighting and the lure of pay, and as for the rest, they looked on, half amused. . . .' Birrell admitted that the West of Ireland tugged at his heart louder than the war, and as soon as he discreetly could, he abandoned the orators and went off into the countryside to enjoy the vision of hills glistening with snow and bogs that were a glorious red.

He was certainly an exceptional person to be in charge of British relations with Ireland. He tried to understand the Irish mind and encouraged Nathan to do the same. Being a writer himself – an essayist and critic of distinction – he had a feeling for the aims and activities of the Irish literary and dramatic movement and recognised the value of the language restoration policy, although he considered it would be a mistake to displace English by Irish altogether. He was unusual in another important respect; he thoroughly despised the Dublin Castle tradition. He saw it as cut off from Irish life; his idea was to bring Irish life and government together in a natural way.

What destroyed him politically was the inability of the British Intelligence Services to make full use of the information they possessed about the oncoming Rising; that and the delay of twenty-four hours in deciding to arrest the Sinn Féiner leaders. Birrell, of course, had to accept responsibility for all of this and for not taking more repressive measures earlier as the Southern Unionists had advised him to do. To have acted in that fashion however, would have offended the Irish Party who kept on telling him not to pay too much attention to the Sinn Féiners, an unimportant minority in the country. That advice fitted in with his own inclinations. He did not want to disturb the country at a time when recruits were increasingly needed for the armed forces. When out of the blue the Rising occurred he was desperately upset and, somewhat out of character, called for immediate salutary punishment. A short shrift should be given to the Sinn Féin leaders, both the fighting men and the stump orators. The others might be sent to the trenches!

In the search for Birrell papers I had the good fortune to meet Sir Charles Tennyson whose *Stars and Markets* added considerably to my knowledge of Birrell's domestic circumstances. Sir Charles, who was a grandson of the poet laureate and Birrell's stepson, was most helpful, as indeed was another relative and Birrell's executor, Christopher Medley, who had Birrell papers in his solicitor's office in London. I first met Medley over lunch in Birr as he was on his way to a fishing holiday in Connemara. Conscious of the fact that the papers were those of a former Cabinet minister he wanted to make sure that, because of my odd name and my association with a book about an Irish rebellion, I was a proper person to entrust the papers to. The highly successful lunch led quickly to an inspection of the papers in his London office, to a solid friendship and to an introduction to the old Liberal publishing firm of Chatto and Windus who produced my Birrell volume and whose chairman came to the launching in the Abbey Theatre.

The book which I called *The Chief Secretary* was well received. It was gratifying to open the *Sunday Times* and see that a reviewer of the eminence of Raymond Mortimer thought that the biography was scholarly, objective and uncommonly well written. The Anglo-American historian George Dangerfield spoke of my distinguished writing on the period, while among Irish critics Terence de Vere White spoke of it as a quite perfect book. That might have given me a swelled head; but the modest sales enabled me to keep my balance. Chatto's were pleased nevertheless and made no difficulty whatever in accepting the manuscript of my next book, *Fenian Fever*. By then I had lectured on Birrell in University College Galway, on Fenians and Ribbonmen in University College Cork, had finished the Madden biography, and spent months treading the stone steps of the Tower building in Dublin Castle to look at the State papers.

Cáit and I went to Scotland in 1969 on a sentimental journey. I had not been there for forty-eight years. On the first occasion I had enjoyed the beauty of the bens, the long lazy hours on Loch Linne, the effort to write poetry for the girl I had just met in Ireland. Now, she and I were back together traversing similar ground and water, and writing postcards for our children and grandchildren. We did most of this when the mist came down, as it inevitably did.

We had another reason for coming to Scotland. We wanted to hear Scots Gaelic and to try to speak a few words of it. We stayed in Arisaig, a place that was fairly typical, I imagine, of the Gaeltacht in decline everywhere. The priest could speak Gaelic; so could the postmaster and the postman; one of the waiters in the hotel knew some; the older men in the bar also; but English had already triumphed. All these people preferred to speak English; perhaps, like myself, it was more convenient to use English with people who had more enthusiasm for Gaelic than ability to speak it. Their conversation, therefore, turned rapidly from a *cé mar thá thú*? or *Thá é frasach* to 'How's the holiday going'? But unlike Ireland, where the decline is equally rapid, nothing in the way of literature in Gaelic was on view, nothing but a phrase book, *Gaelic without Groans*, for which, at twelve shillings in the money of that time I could not imagine many buyers. Apart from place names and a large-scale Ordnance Survey map in the hotel the only other Gaelic I saw during our stay was contained in the British Railways notice which said, for no apparent reason, *Leanaigh go dlúth ri cliú bhur sinnsir* – and another on the back of a motor-car which said *Thá [picture of a tiger] agam na ma thanc*. No marks for getting that one; and not many for recognising the meaning of *Fáilte don Eilean Sciathánach* at The Kyle of Lochailsh as we boarded the ferry for Skye.

But if Gaelic was on the way out in the Western Highlands, many people assured me that it was a pity, and that the general attachment to clan history, tartans, kilts and the pipes was no substitute, though those things might continue to mark Scotland off as a different country from England. In that respect the Scots behave exactly as the Irish do. To lose Gaelic is a tragedy, but as individuals they are not going to do anything about it. We met no Nationalists in the hotel nor did we expect to; and the people who gave us an account of Scotland's politics saw Scottish Nationalists as a divided lot. The memory of Bonnie Prince Charlie was as strong as ever in those parts, however; I don't know how many times the historic landmarks were pointed out to us. We had no car, but we got out in the interplay of mist and sunshine, saw some stretches of the most delightful countryside, bought a few things, sampled various malt whiskies, and loved the company. I also did a broadcast from the Glasgow B.B.C.

That August a priest cousin of Cáit's died in Cushendall

and I travelled with relatives to the funeral. The train was delayed in Portadown and searched by B Specials. August 1969 was, of course, the month in which the North really blew up, with Nationalist-Unionist strife getting so out of control that the British army had to be deployed in the streets. That was new, but the rest was not. From a distance I had been aware of the Northern bitterness since my earliest days. My mother had told me of an occasion when she had been brought on a visit to Belfast as a child and passed a night with Protestant relations. She was put to bed with a girl of about her own age and when the light went out, she was pinched under the clothes and a voice said 'that's for you, you Fenian bitch.' It was just the same almost a century later. In Cushendall, when we got there, sorrow for the passing of an esteemed pastor was forgotten in the problem of finding accommodation for the crowds that had run for safety out of Belfast, many of whom slept on the floor in private houses. After the funeral we crossed the Border by car and saw a platoon of medicos from the Irish army. What were they doing? Were they there to help refugees that were streaming southwards, or was there a more sinister meaning to the statement of a mild-mannered Taoiseach that we could not stand idly by?

Whatever about the politicians, I, in my new career, was certainly not idle. In 1970 I lectured on Birrell, Russell, Yeats and Joyce in Sussex University for Hugh Kearney; in 1972 Leland Lyons, who considered me to be 'a serious historian,' invited me to speak in Canterbury where in the University of Kent he was then the Professor of Modern History; my subject was 1916 and its consequences. Lyons was a delightful host; he put me up in his rooms in Eliot College and entertained me liberally. That year, also, I talked in Scariff, Co. Clare, to the Merriman Summer School on the trial and imprisonment of O'Connell, and in Benburb to a religiously mixed audience on the history of home rule. With the situation in the North of Ireland worsening, the Buckinghamshire Education Committee organised a weekend course in Missenden Abbey which was intended to give people who were not Irish an impartial survey of Irish history up to Partition. Lecturers in modern history from Corpus Christi and Balliol in Oxford gave the first lectures, taking their listeners as far as the Act of Union. I had been invited to take over at that point and gave three talks: on the period from the Union to the aftermath of the Famine; on Fenians and home rulers; and a survey of the subsequent years down to the entry of Fianna Fáil to the Dáil in 1927. On the final afternoon I led a discussion in which Sir Charles Tennyson, who had recommended me to the Education Committee, participated. He loved Ireland, its literature and art, knew the country well, and had met some of its leading literary figures. That was a heart-warming occasion; and the Warden of the school wrote later to assure me that from the viewpoint of the promoters the whole course had been a most satisfying experience.

The following year, 1973, with Cearbhall Ó Dalaigh, soon to be the President of Ireland, in the chair, I gave a Blythe lecture in the Peacock Theatre. Blythe himself was present. I spoke about Yeats's revolutionary background, a subject prompted by my researching of the division in the I.R.B. that led to the emergence of a rival I.N.B., an Irish Nationalist Brotherhood. This thesis I developed later in a paper I read in University College Galway which was published in *Galvia*. Yeats had said that he was an I.R.B. man, a claim that was supported much later by Dr Paddy McCartan, but I established, to my own satisfaction at least, that he was more likely to have been a member of the breakaway organisation.

Some of the scholars were evidently taking note of what I had been doing in my new career and were good enough to appoint me to the presidency of the Irish Historical Society. I was elected a member of the Royal Irish Academy, became its senior vice-president, and chaired a group whose recommendations enabled the Academy to establish a National Committee on Foreign Affairs. I also became a member of the Irish Manuscripts Commission.

In 1971 *An Maidineach*, the biography of Madden that had been so long gestating, saw the light. I had been greatly helped when searching for confidential material for it by the Bishop of Clonfert, Dr Duignan. I had been staying with him in Loughrea during the Emergency when at supper one night he asked me what in the literary or historical field I was interested in at the moment. I told him about Madden and the gaps in my knowledge that were delaying a book. He said nothing as if he had not heard me but, as soon as we had finished eating, he took me to the house, not far away, of one of his parish priests, another Madden. He had a large collection of Madden's papers, beautifully bound, and I was allowed to take all of them away on what proved to be a very long loan. That night I whiled myself to sleep reading the telegrams about Madden's final illness that passed between his wife Harriet in Booterstown and their gynaecologist son on Merrion Square. A few things connected with *An Maidineach* stick in my mind; Barney Stafford Johnson's detective work leading to the discovery of the Madden grave in the old cemetery in Donnybrook, Maurice McGonagle's work on a faded photograph of Harriet so that we now have a good idea of what she looked like; and, of course, P. S. O'Hegarty's son's cordial acceptance of the book for publication. Sean thought these *Wanderings of an Irish Gentleman*, as he called the book, made a better book even than my Parnell, and he commended its style and readability.

The material I found in the Irish State Paper Office led to the production of *Fenian Fever, Revolutionary Underground*, and *The Prime Informer*, as well as the paper on *Revolutionary Nationalism in Ireland* I read to the Trinity College conference of historians in July 1975. I used complementary sources also, of course, those in our own National Library, the British Museum, and the Public Record Office in London; while in my frequent visits to Oxford I read in the Clarendon papers in the Bodleian and the Earl of Derby papers which were then with Lord Blake in Queen's College. I also browsed among Disraeli's papers in his house in Buckinghamshire; and through my work on the papers of Lord Naas in the Irish National Library I was able to give the journal of the Military History Society the detailed story of the Phoenix Society which, beginning in 1856, predated by a couple of years the Fenian brotherhood.

Theo Moody had become a rather intimate friend of mine since the 1950s when he was on Comhairle Radio Eireann, the Broadcasting Advisory Council, and had brought me to post-graduate students of his in the areas in which I had been acquiring some competence. He had found my *Prime Informer* book helpful when preparing his 1965 Conference of Historians lecture on '*The Times* versus Parnell & Co.', and joined me in the preparation of a joint article on the I.R.B. Supreme Council from 1868 to 1878 that appeared in *Irish Historical Studies* in March 1975. That was a collaboration I enjoyed immensely. The subject was an exciting one and involved an examination of documents pertaining to the period after 1867 when the Fenian movement was rehabilitating itself. The Supreme Council was understood to have shown countenance to the home rule movement under Isaac Butt, and it was important to confirm that this was the case, which we did. We were also able to establish an I.R.B. constitution of 1869 whereas formerly the earliest known one was dated 1873. The fact that we were looking at I.R.B. papers other than constitutions and addresses to the Irish nation with which historians were familiar, was in itself an original situation. It is of the nature of a revolutionary conspiracy that it tends to leave as little trace as possible of its internal workings; but here we had shorthand notes of the proceedings of the Supreme Council for the period between 1874 and 1879. The problem was to decipher them. We had first to find out what particular shorthand system the author of the notes had used, and a person who could read them for us. A long pursuit ensued, ranging from consultations with skilled stenographers in Radio Telefís Eireann and Leinster House to the Pitman Institute in London, the University of Bath, to an authority on the history of British shorthand and ultimately to a former city librarian of Canterbury. He identified the shorthand as one first published in 1786, and in large measure succeeded in deciphering what was hidden from us.

My *Revolutionary Underground* is the story of the Irish Republican Brotherhood from its beginning as the Irish Revolutionary Brotherhood in 1858 to its end in 1924. It could equally have been called the history of Fenianism or the history of Fenian disasters; because, though noble and able as many of these Fenians were, they were hopeless at planning revolution, and worse at keeping their plans to themselves. The Young Ireland affair of 1848 had been notoriously brief and ridiculous; but the Fenian rising of 1867, into which much preparation had gone on both sides of the Atlantic and on which vast sums of money had been expended, was a demonstration of the utter inability of Irish and Irish-American rebels to make a plan, to adhere to it, and to keep it secret from the enemy. They failed utterly to do this, with the result that six days before the Fenians were to rise, the British government were in possession of the full details of their plans.

That the 1916 Rising was allowed to take place was a different matter. The information available to the government in London would have enabled them to forestall it; but rather than disclose the source of their knowledge to the Germans they inadequately informed the Irish authorities who were desperately short of information of their own, though many tongues seemed to be blabbing. That there was to be a Rising was known to many people outside Irish Volunteer and Irish Citizen Army circles. John Dillon found Dublin full of the most disquieting rumours the Wednesday before Easter, and told John Redmond he was sure the Clan na Gael men, the American counterparts of the I.R.B., were planning some devilish business.

In the prison camps later, the strategy of the Rising was deplored by men like Michael Collins. If intelligence had been better, Dublin Castle could have been taken; and anyway what was the point of locking up the insurgents in isolated buildings, to be, as it were, cockshots for the British? If the fight was to be continued, it would have to be planned on a different basis, by the revivification of the I.R.B. certainly, and by an assault on the British intelligence service. In retrospect what Collins did in this regard seems so simple. He got members of the Dublin police force to work for him; and he organised a full-time 'Squad' to neutralise the detective division of the Dublin Metropolitan police by shooting the most active of its political members and creating a condition of near panic among the remainder. He dealt in a similar fashion with British Secret Service personnel when they came to Dublin.

In later years I got to know some of Collins's men personally: Liam Tobin who was his Deputy Director of Intelligence and leader of the Squad; Ned Broy and Dave Nelligan, of the group that Collins had working for him inside the G (Detective) Division; Charlie Dalton and Joe Guilfoyle of Tobin's intelligence staff; and in the Squad itself Vinny Byrne, whom I knew best of all since our days with the nuns. I saw him on the morning of Easter Sunday 1916 lined up on Stephen's Green before moving into action, and I have been meeting him on and off ever since, usually nowadays after the 11 o'clock Mass in the Pro-Cathedral. He is such a fine fellow that when I hear Collins's men described as thugs and murderers, I know how that sort of language misconceives the situation in which Collins and his men operated.

Vinny told me about the Squad and how from the house in Upper Abbey Street they called 'the dump' they were sent out on various 'jobs'. They might be out all day, and for a number of days, looking for their quarry. They would go out, six or eight of them at a time – two here, two some paces behind, two on the other side of the street and two behind them. If they saw 'their man', they would follow him until they reached a quiet spot, and then dispose of him. If on a day nothing was stirring they would leave 'the dump' about one o'clock and go home; but they were always available whenever they were wanted.

Vinny was recruited into the Squad in 46 Parnell Square, which was the headquarters of the Keating Branch of the Gaelic League, and he was introduced to Collins. He met him afterwards twelve or fourteen times in all. 'Collins knew me so well that he always called me Vincey,' Vinny told me. 'During the Provisional Government period I was on duty one day in Government Buildings when Collins, in uniform, arrived with Andy Cope, the Assistant Under-Secretary in Dublin Castle. Andy wasn't a bad sort. I turned out the guard. Collins said: "How are you, Vincey?" and, turning to Cope, he said: "Meet Vincent Byrne, one of the men who bet you out of the country". Collins drew you like a magnet.'

I personally saw Collins twice only, at one of the public meetings of Dáil Eireann in 1919, and in 1921 when he was signing autographs at a gathering in the Gaelic League Hall at 25 Parnell Square. I never spoke to him; but it was my good fortune to become a close friend of his family, and I have written a fair amount about him: a long chapter in *Revolutionary Underground*, a 'life' in the Gill and Macmillan series, and an edition of the letters that passed between him and the woman he intended to marry. That correspondence came to me out of the blue. Like so many people, I had always believed that there were Collins' letters somewhere but very few had surfaced, until one day, almost by accident, I met the sons of Felix Cronin by Kitty Kiernan, who had kept these letters after Collins's death. Some critics saw in the correspondence when it was published, as I hoped they would, more than simply an exchange between lovers, but a picture of the appalling life Collins lived from the decision to meet the British across the table in London to the ambush at Béal na mBláth. Since the book appeared two further letters of Collins to Kitty Kiernan were sold in London to an American buyer. Written from London in March and June 1922, they speak of the very bad news from Ireland which was alarming 'the powers' with whom he was negotiating. It would be so pleasant to be relieved of all responsibility, he says, but not to stand up to that responsibility would be cowardly. He could not help thinking that the Irish as a people were destined to go on dreaming, vainly hoping, striving to no purpose. They would have cause to remember their extremists. How prophetic!

In August 1975 Cáit and I reached the Golden Jubilee of our marriage; and our extended family of sons, daughters and grandchildren, not to mention other relatives and friends, pulled out all the stops to ensure that it was celebrated worthily. There was so much to be thankful for. Naturally a Mass was said in the house presided over by our friend since Mercier Society days, Joe Carroll, now a bishop of the diocese. The celebrants were two very dear friends: Michael O'Carroll whom I had first met on one of these occasions for 'interested enquirers' at Blackrock College, and the intrepid Frank (F. X.) Martin who was perhaps the first of the scholars to recognise something of merit in my efforts to write history.

And Frank Duff was there, of course, looking a trifle pinched. The lessons were read by our sons, and the mass-server was a grandson. It was a wonderful day altogether and Cáit, in a flowing frock, and belying that she had been my wife for half a century, lived every minute of it to the full. It was a joy to see her thus. The children laid on many surprises for us, particularly the presence of the O'Brien sisters. They had reared our family, given Cáit close companionship when I was away from home, and had made of the old house in Booterstown a Gaeltacht in miniature. Letters were read to us from former colleagues wishing us well. One was from Cearbhall Ó Dalaigh, now the President of Ireland: he was younger than both of us but we had been close friends for a long time.

For some years in early autumn Cáit and I had been going on holidays to the Spanish coast outside Barcelona, spending a few days on the way there in Lourdes. This particular year we did the same, and as if the hotel on the Gave and near the Poor Clare Convent where we always stayed had been alerted – perhaps it was – we were given a bedroom in which gold colouring predominated. How that thrilled Cáit. Somehow, too, we seemed to benefit more than before from the company of the Immaculate One, when we went to visit her at the Grotto. One thing Cáit was thankful for, and which she continually mentioned in her prayers, was the relief she had been given from the pain she had suffered in recent years and which had forced her to sleep always on a narrow plank bed. Ironically, she had first felt it as we left the Cinerama at the bottom of Talbot Street having greatly enjoyed *The Sound of Music*. The trouble arose from a 'wedged disc' like what happens when a drawer gets jammed and can't be moved one way or the other. To diagnose the source of the pain, however, was one thing: to cure it was another. Certainly Cáit felt she was not benefitting from what was prescribed in the nursing home and was glad to leave it. We then went with her down into the heart of the country to be examined by a bone-setter whose reputation had reached us, but he promptly confessed he could do nothing for her but warned us against a surgical operation. Cáit began to fear she would not walk again, when, on the way out of a symphony concert in the Gaiety, she had to sit down on the stairway in the Gaiety to ease the pain. Then Nóirín heard of Barry Dunham, a young osteopath with a medical degree who had opened in Dublin. He did the trick. At the second manipulative session he said, 'Did you hear that? That was the crack I'd been waiting for', the sound of the disc returning to its normal position. The splendid career, that Cáit's and other cases we knew of betokened, came to a sudden end when Barry, speeding back to Dublin from a fishing holiday, ran into a wall and was killed outright. His death dimmed a vision I had formed of trained doctors with acquired manipulative skills dispensing with the tearful paraphernalia of traction which Cáit had rejected.

Roughly about this time I, too, had begun to receive medical attention. I was suffering from what appeared in the documents as O.R. or osteo-arthritis. A dull pain in my arm threatened to affect my writing capacity, so I did not delay in going to the Dublin Rheumatism Clinic which was directed by Dr Tommy O'Reilly, a man I had got to know as a member of the Television Commission of Enquiry. From him I got speedy and entirely effective treatment. He relied mainly on a Swedish drug which he injected right into the points of pain. We became good friends; and from our conversations in his consulting room high up among the chimney pots, or in Baggot Street where I often met him on his way to or from the supermarkets, or in my house to which he sometimes came, I learned a great deal about his Wexford background, his days at Clongowes, his involvement in the I.R.A. as an intelligence officer on the anti-Treaty side during the Civil War, his experience as a doctor in England, his days on the National Council of Fianna Fáil, and the eccentricities of some of his political friends. He was refreshingly frank, and when he told me he was thinking of writing his memoirs I encouraged him to do so. I thought if he could write as well as he talked he could produce a stimulating book. However like other people who had sought my advice about writing something, Dr O'Reilly's intention exceeded his capability, I fear. He died with nothing done; but for enabling me to continue writing I had dedicated my I.R.B. book, *Revolutionary Underground*, to him.

Early in our Jubilee year Ernest Blythe died. I had seen him in his house not very long before, and found him mentally alert and well able to answer questions I put to him which had a bearing on *Revolutionary Underground*, but so physically feeble that to get to a dining room table on which his papers were piled up in seeming disarray he had literally to crawl from his place by the fire. I was rather depressed by this, and by the appearance of the house. Such a change from the days when as his secretary I used visit him and Annie. He was buried in St Patrick's Cathedral. I was at the funeral, of course, and wondered what Annie, who had predeceased him by many years, would have thought of the obsequies. It was not what she would have desired, but she would have recognised how typical it was of Ernest that at the end of his days he was still a Protestant. The service was delightful; though Ernest would not have appreciated the musical side of it. I don't think he had a note in his head.

Apart from the Irish language and the political scene, especially that of Northern Ireland, his abiding interest was the theatre. He had subsidised the Abbey when Minister for Finance, had been its managing director for a quarter of a century, maintaining a company in the Queen's during the difficult years after a fire had destroyed the old theatre, and directing the re-building with money for which he had turned to Sean MacEntee and Frank Aiken. One happy feature of that period of his life was how well he got on with people with whom he had fallen out in the twenties. Year after year at pantomine time into which Blythe threw so much of himself, I joined him to welcome the de Valeras to the show. These were occasions that gave him great personal pleasure. He loved to meet Sinéad particularly – in one of his autobiographical volumes he has described her as a miraculously good teacher as well as being an exceedingly attractive girl – and I have a feeling that 'the long fellow' won her from Blythe and Sean O'Casey and possibly others who competed to walk home with her at night time from the Gaelic League.

Before 1975 was out both Sinéad and Eamon de Valera were also dead, Eamon in his 92nd year, a few months after his wife. He had been the dominant political figure all through my life; and indeed had only let go of the presidency, which he had held since 1959 in succession to Sean T. O'Kelly, a couple of years before his end. He was almost totally blind and had to be led everywhere; yet in March 1965 when Roger Casement was being re-interred in Glasnevin I saw him standing erect, seemingly for hours, in the bitter snow at the graveside. How he did it I don't know; though I can appreciate that his strong frame, his abstemious life, and those morning walks to the office along the Strand Road where I often saw him had something to do with it.

The Irish language was undoubtedly the biggest cultural factor in his life. He and Sinéad had taught it in the early days of their marriage in a summer school at Tawin in South Galway which Casement financed; and when he came on a visit to my region during the Emergency he brought me and Todd Andrews down there one day in his car. Irish was no longer spoken in Tawin I believe; at any rate Irish was not the object of our visit but to look at a fast-moving stream which from memory he thought might be an electrification prospect. From his early days in the Central Branch he had devoted time and thought to the revival and, when he was in a position to do so, made Irish the first national language in the Constitution. At the formation of Fianna Fáil a decade earlier it might have appeared to occupy a secondary position in his mind to the attainment of a united republican Ireland, but in time he was to say that if he could have a united Ireland by giving up the restoration of Irish as the spoken language of the majority of the people he would say 'no'. He was to discover, however, that the vast majority of the people were not going to put themselves to the trouble of learning a second language. That was assuredly a cause of great disappointment to him, as was no doubt a growing realisation that the achievement of a united Ireland was as far from realisation as it ever had been. We were destined, he feared, to sink into an amorphous cosmopolitanism, with neither a past nor a distinguishable future. Over a hundred years earlier Thomas Davis more succintly had said that to lose the national language was death. De Valera might have seen other things in our national behaviour that also spelt death. The utter rejection of his ideas about frugal living, for example; or, what was worse, the emergence of 'the shabby sordid republic ruled by knavish corrupt politicians and the ignoble rich' that Standish O'Grady had prophesied.

Civil servants are no less mortal than politicians; and, about this time, two of the most distinguished of them died, Jimmy McElligott in 1974 and Joe Brennan in 1976. Since the earliest days of the State these two men had been inseparable, and had followed each other into the highest positions in the land. Their close friendship ended, however, in 1953 over an underwriting matter, Brennan disapproving of McElligott acting on behalf of his Minister, without consultation with him, the Governor of the Central Bank of whose board McElligott was a member. They may never have spoken to each other after that, but of such matters I knew nothing whatever and would have assumed that they had continued to meet day after day as they had done for years for a bit of lunch. McElligott I knew better than Brennan. I had worked under and with him for as long as he was Secretary of the Department of Finance, and always harmoniously. He went into retirement before me as a matter of course, and when my time came to follow him he sent me a note offering me the best wishes of a large circle of friends, among whom he reckoned to be included. Thereafter I met him occasionally, and I was delighted when he came to a couple of meetings of the Patrician Group which met near his house, on Mount Merrion Avenue, and read a paper which Frank Duff described as 'unorthodox but thoughtful'.

My friendship with Brennan only really began at McElligott's funeral. He saw me there and asked me to come to his house: he had, he said, something to show me. He knew of my interest in his period, though he had been anything but helpful when I approached him about his 1916 experiences as Nathan's private secretary. When my book on that subject appeared all he would say about it to me was that it was 'interesting'. What he was now willing and anxious to show me were eight papers that he had surreptitiously prepared for Michael Collins while still a British Civil Servant in charge of the Finance Division of the Chief Secretary's Office in Dublin Castle. Collins had undertaken to submit something to the Committee on Financial Relations of the London Conference in response to a paper from the British side and was looking for somebody capable of writing it. Paddy McGilligan, who had been in Clongowes with Brennan, believed that he was the one man capable of doing what was required, sought him out, and introduced him in a highly nervous condition to Collins, a man with a price on his head. It is not quite clear to me what use was made of the papers, but Brennan claimed that one of them 'broke a deadlock in the Committee'.

After his death I wrote a piece on Brennan as a public servant extraordinary for *Studies* and, when his diaries and the friendship of his family became available, I composed the book about him that the Institute of Public Administration published under the title of *No Man's Man.* It was a tribute to an independent-minded man of outstanding integrity. Brennan's sister Margaret Elizabeth, an Ursuline nun, with her recollections, was a considerable help to me in the writing of it. I went to see her several times in that vast community house in Cork's Blackrock suburb, and our relationship was enlivened by her enjoyment of the biography. The last time I saw her, she was confined to bed, but I was allowed to see her. She was as bright as a new pin. She took my hand and, noticing how cold it was, she said: 'Don't let them put you off here with a cup of coffee. Insist upon a glass of whiskey. You need it.'

When we returned from Spain in the autumn of 1975 our daughter Nóirín met us at the airport in her new car. She was in sparkling form. When we got home, she took Cáit down to the kitchen and told her that she was thinking of having a go at becoming a Carmelite. She had been to Paris at a psychology conference and on her way back had dropped into the Lisieux Carmelite Convent for Mass. Something in the singing of the nuns immediately spoke to her of how distant their love of Our Lord was from her respect for Him, even her admiration of Him. At Holy Communion, on impulse, she gave herself completely to Him, and was filled with a 'peace beyond understanding'. As time passed at home she moved to asking Him what she should do, and gradually recognised that she was being called to the Carmelite way of life. Excited and happy, Cáit hurried into the drawing room where I was reading to tell me all this. Then Nóirín herself joined us and I told her she was doing the right thing, and,

I hope, communicated a little of my pleasure at her decision. The call to her was in a sense a call to her family. We were to facilitate it, certainly not to put obstacles in its way as I am afraid sometimes happens. The call to a life of closer union with God through prayer was to be fulfilled in a convent which was enclosed, cut off if you like, in order to safeguard the praying soul against the grosser distractions of the world, to make it easier to contemplate God's revelation of Himself. I think I faintly knew something of what was involved in Nóirín's decision, but – and this was a big but – she would first have to finish a job she was doing for the Department of the Public Service. Of course, she said, of course. Having worked in a couple of commercial concerns after leaving the university she was now with the Economic and Social Research Institute, and had recently been enquiring into the employment and living conditions of government typists. She had reached the point of reflecting on her findings and of framing a report. This, in the upshot, took her two years, a lengthy period undoubtedly which enabled her and the Carmelites to test her vocation. She had always had a hankering after the contemplative life, and now, with half a life in the world behind her, much reading of the classical spiritual literature, and that rich personal Lisieux experience, she knew in her bones that her early instincts had been sound. After a motoring holiday in England with Cáit and me, she 'entered'.

The holiday *à trois* was unusual. We went across Wales to Shrewsbury and after a night there went on to Cambridge where we dallied for days and then travelled down to London and Brighton where we dallied more. Then I went to Oxford to visit old haunts and they went to Stratford-on-Avon where they had tickets for a Shakespeare play. But wherever Cáit and I together dallied, Nóirín ran off to visit a community of contemplatives somewhere. She gave other indications, too, of the direction of her mind; and quite suddenly the full realisation of what she was about to do dawned on me. I had been aware that a process of stripping herself of her worldy goods had to be gone through. She had to resign her pensionable post, to dispose of her library, to sell her car, to close her bank account and to make all the consequential dispositions. Seeing it all occurring, stage by stage, I suppose it should have impacted on me sooner that we were going to lose her, but it was only when she threw her handbag on the dining room table the day she was 'entering' and said to her mother 'that's about all' that I realised what the break that was being made meant. The other children though married and settled comfortably could still come to see us. Nóirín could not. She was to live for the rest of her life an absentee. We would have to go to see her in future, and then not every day but on certain days, and behind a grille. We could not hug or kiss her again, not that I had ever done much of this with any of my children, but as soon as I thought of it I wanted to do it.

When Cáit and I returned to the empty house that Sunday evening we saw the bag on the table but didn't touch it. It was still there next morning when we came down. The flood gates opened. I, who had not cried since I was a child, started to bawl. I could not control myself, and the sounds I made were ugly. Cáit checked me. 'They'll think we're fighting', she said, referring to the men who were installing central heating. She went out into the hall and spoke to the overseer. 'We're feeling a bit down this morning,' she said, 'Our daughter has left us to become a Carmelite.' He started to cry. Through the croaks she heard him say 'And my son has joined the British Army.'

On a November day in 1980 Frank Duff, my oldest and dearest friend, died. I had not been seeing much of him of late, but I knew that he had continued to work himself to the bone, and for recreation still cycled over long tracts of the Irish countryside. Whenever he came to our house he had always come on his bicycle, but when he came to a Mass for Nóirín, before she left us, I noticed he had not his bicycle with him for once and Nóirín, at the end of a long day of celebration, drove him home in my company. He was in complete agreement with what she had decided to do; he told us she would be an honourable member of her religious community and would do an infinite good in a world that needed so much the presence of the contemplative life.

He had continued to live on his own, though twice assaulted by raiders and his head smashed with an iron bar. His death came as might have been expected, suddenly, and after the Requiem Mass which Cáit and I attended with Eithne, Frank's godchild, I started to write his 'life'. I felt I should do this without delay, knowing him so well and in order to balance the hagiographical stuff I feared would be written about him. That was one thing I knew he would hate; so my book was a 'life with warts and all', not that there were many warts really. I assumed the 'top brass' of the Legion would like it: none of them I knew well would, I thought, have expected me to write anything other than an account of the realist, the fighter, that the Frank Duff we had lived and worked with essentially was. I was wrong. They did not like the book, and I fear did what they could to ensure that the rank and file members would not read it, or even hear of its existence. It was never mentioned in *Maria Legionis*. So it was remaindered. However, I am vain enough to think that, if there is ever a question of Frank being considered for canonisation what it tells about him cannot be overlooked.

After what I may call the handbag episode Cáit and I soon recovered our composure, as we hoped the overseer did his. In our case we had only to see the radiance in Nóirín's face behind the grille to recognise that in Carmel she had found her heart's desire in a varied but like-minded company of sisters. We went to visit her once a month, and in between times Cáit and she wrote to each other. I saw all those letters. I would see Nóirín's because she always addressed them to both of us, and I would see Cáit's because she insisted I should always see what she had written to make sure that it was 'all right'. Her letters were budgets of news that did ample justice to what was happening in our expanding family. And, dear oh dear, how a family expands when the grandchildren, and we had eight of them, begin to procreate! The first greatgrandchild, which made our own youngest child a grandmother, came in May 1983 and Cáit hastened to break the news to her daughter in the monastery in Kilmacud. 'My darling Nóirín [she wrote], we have just heard from Blánaid (breakfast time) that Vivienne has a son, 9½ lbs, and I am going to give Blánaid for her your lovely pram cover. Thank God everything has gone so well. He is to be called Mark. . . . Isn't it wonderful to have lived for the day. May God bless them all. . . .'

Time passed more quickly now, or so it seemed. Before we realised it, Nóirín had made her first profession in a quiet ceremony, and three years later the date was fixed in January 1984 for the great day of her final profession. Cáit immediately wrote to her 'darling'. 'What can I say?. . . I bow my head in humility and thanksgiving to Our Lord for having chosen you, and trusted us to prepare you for the time He was ready to take you to Himself for His very own. Thank God a thousand times for choosing you to join His community at Kilmacud, and may your prayers bring many good souls to Him in your life. May you by your prayers bring many sinners back to Him too, and many vocations. We look forward with great joy to your profession. . . .' She added that another greatgrandchild who had arrived, Stephen, would be baptised the following Sunday and she begged prayers for him also. At the end of her letter she mentioned that a Sister of St Clare was coming to give her Holy Communion that morning. She was going to work in the parish which meant that Cáit would receive more often. She rarely left the house now, and in the house she had a number of distressing falls which betokened that there was something seriously wrong with her. However, sitting in the sanctuary near the altar in the Convent Chapel in Kilmacud, she came through the profession ceremony extraordinarily well and later enjoyed a meal in the parlour with the family, some Carmelite fathers, a priest from the parish, and the trio of clerics who had graced our Golden Jubilee celebrations. Afterwards, all the sisters came with Nóirín to the grille to join us. Later Cáit wrote to tell Nóirín how happy she was. She had learned so much from Nóirín's religious experience, so much she had not realised before. 'May God be thanked', she said, 'and may I never forget all I owe to Him in seeing you so happy. Another thing: it has brought the family together round you which is wonderful. . . .'

She fell again one morning and cut herself badly. The

ambulance came but made difficulties about taking her to the hospital just around the corner from us. The crew would not take us to a hospital which wasn't on call. I argued: wasn't it absurd to refuse to take a patient the few yards to St Vincent's which they had told us would be 'on call' anyhow within half an hour, but would take her to another hospital far from us who had no transport of our own to facilitate visiting her, *et cetera.* While this was going on Cáit sat there in the hall, utterly quiet, with blood oozing through the cloths I had put on her head, making them redder and redder. One of the ambulance men, probably as much affected as I was, came up with a suggestion. 'Maybe if you went by taxi, they would deal with you?' he said. I let them go, got a taxi whose driver, though concerned about what the bleeding might do to the inside of his car, brought us to the hospital. There, as before, Cáit was treated quickly and efficiently.

Writing to Nóirín subsequently, she said: 'I have only learned that you were told about my accident. We were not going to bother you about it. Anyway I'm great now, the stitches are out, and I'll be sore for a while, but the good God is leaving me a little longer with you all. . . . Everyone has been and is being so kind to me. . . . God bless you, my darling, and don't worry any more about me. I'm taking life easy till the scar wears away. . . . Kay [our housekeeper] is touching up my hair, and I think I now don't look too bad.'

At the end of April she confessed to having had another couple of falls 'which gave me a few more bumps on the back of my skull. I didn't bleed though, thank God, and I suppose the Lord will look after me.' Nóirín assured her that the Lord was doing just that. She sent her a picture of the Good Shepherd she had been keeping beside her. He had brought herself safely through everything, and as she looked at it now before parting with it, she said: 'I see you, darling mammy, as the lamb in His arms, whom He is taking special care of, so that you won't have to worry about whether you fall or not.'

The terror of falling had, however, become an obsession with Cáit, and her general condition worsened. She was so weak that we had to abandon the idea of going to an ecumenical society dinner in Blackrock College for which places had been reserved for us. She wrote what was to be her last letter to Nóirín early in May. She was suffering from what she called rheumatics but which was manifestly something much worse. To go to bed she had literally to crawl up the stairs. She asked Nóirín to pray for patience for her. With that request she sent her love to all the Carmelite sisters, and wrote of her hope that vocations to their little convent would multiply. She was more distressed daily and I, never good in such situations, strained her patience. She said something she thought had hurt me and wanted to go to confession to tell God what she had done and to ask for pardon. I could not restrain her; and went with her in a friend's car to the parish church where a priest who didn't know her had arranged to meet her. She refused absolutely to go to one who did know her. The priest was all kindness and wanted to save her trouble by sitting down beside her in the seat outside his confessional. But no, she had to go into the box, and there standing, as she always now had to, because of the pain in her knees, she closed her eyes, and confessed her mighty sin. She went through that ordeal for me: pent up within her was an extravagant love that her daughters recognised better than I did, and left them assuming too readily that my love for her wholly corresponded. I now deeply wish that it had been so.

One afternoon towards the end of May when I came into the bedroom I found her up, sitting in her night things on the edge of the bed, a picture of misery. She had told me more than once that she was dying, and now it was starkly obvious that she had come to the end of her tether and realised her need of immediate specialist treatment. She made no objection as she would have done earlier when I said I would set about getting her into hospital. I was, to be frank, relieved to have her acquiesence, because I had long ago promised her never to *put* her anywhere. So, of her own accord, and a very sick woman, she became a patient in Our Lady's Ward in St Vincent's Hospital, where she was so sweetly looked after. I can't say that too often.

Word went speedily through the family of what had happened. My eldest daughter, Eithne, arrived from Donegal to take her mother's place beside me. My youngest girl Blánaid – she whom my father endearingly called a holy terror – was endlessly attentive. My sons, Eimear and Cóilín, gave close support; and from the little Carmelite in Kilmacud there came a flurry of deeply concerned messages. Cáit's condition continued to worsen, however, despite all the skill and care. As she began to lose consciousness, I read to her what was to be Nóirín's last letter. 'You know how much I love you', she had written, 'and I love you even more now these days when you need so much care.' She enclosed with her letter a picture of a chick in a man's hand with a caption, in French, which said, 'every creature, even the smallest, is in the hand of God as if it were His only care.' And that's how Cáit died: as a chick in the hand of a caring God. We miss her greatly.

It's a little over a year since the pain of being without Cáit began. In an empty house I sought distraction from thinking of her by going back to the job I had in hands at the time of her death, a book I wanted to call *No Petty People*, the phrase Yeats invoked in his passionate protest on behalf of the small Protestant band which had proved itself, as he said, the chivalry of Ireland. My American co-publishers, however, did not like this title, so the book appeared under what had been an explanatory sub-title of mine, *Protestant Nationalists in Revolutionary Ireland*. In it you will read as much as is relevant to the nationalist theme in the lives of Hyde, Yeats, Plunkett, Russell, Hobson, Blythe, Moore, Markievicz, and others, all surrounding or dovetailed into the history of the Stopford family. That hitherto had been reflected through the pen and personality of Alice Stopford Green. In *Protestant Nationalists*, however, the outstanding Stopford is Alice's niece Dorothy who, having been a guest in the Under Secretary's Lodge during Easter Week 1916, became so much more Irish than the Irish themselves that she joined Cumann na mBan, the I.R.A.'s women's auxiliary, and functioned as a medical officer to the West Cork Brigade in the early twenties. It is at times an incredible story, but always fascinating.

When that book was put to bed, to use a newspaper editor's phrase, and the pain of loss persisting, I allowed myself to be induced to write my memoirs, my autobiography – what a frighteningly big word! I had been asked to do this many times by many people but had always rejected the idea. Perhaps Michael Gill caught me at a disadvantage. Anyhow when he asked me I thought I should do it, and started right away. In the hotel bedroom in Lahinch that Cáit and I had shared the previous year it occurred to me to write, first, an account of the circumstances of our first meeting on that mountain road and the race she said I allowed her to win, and all that was to follow of love and affection. It was the easiest thing I ever wrote. I then went backwards and forwards until I had written all you have found in my first chapter. Other chapters were not so easy to put together, but I surprised myself by quickly finishing the whole book. I fear there is little in it of the mysterious and partly subconscious process from which books are said to be made, and little philosophising. You may have liked it that way. If you didn't, if the memoirs lack grace or have bored you in any way, as they may well have done, blame me of course, as well as the unwise publisher who pressed me to write them.

Dublin
September 1985